The Scar

The Scar

A PERSONAL HISTORY OF DEPRESSION AND RECOVERY

Mary Cregan

W. W. NORTON & COMPANY
Independent Publishers Since 1923
New York | London

Grateful acknowledgment to the following for permission to quote:

Excerpt from "After great pain a formal feeling comes" from *The Poems of Emily Dickinson*, edited by Thomas H. Johnson, Cambridge, Mass.: The Belknap Press of Harvard University Press, Copyright © 1951, 1955 by The President and Fellows of Harvard College. Copyright © renewed 1979, 1983 by the President and Fellows of Harvard College. Copyright © 1914, 1918, 1919, 1924, 1929, 1930, 1932, 1935, 1937, 1942, by Martha Dickinson Bianchi. Copyright © 1952, 1957, 1958, 1963, 1965, by Mary L. Hampson. • Excerpt from "Not Waving but Drowning" by Stevie Smith, from *Collected Poems of Stevie Smith*, copyright © 1957 by Stevie Smith. Reprinted by permission of New Directions Publishing Corp. • Excerpts from *Laments* by Jan Kochanowski, translated by Stanislaw Baranczak and Seamus Heaney. Translation copyright © 1996 by Stanislaw Baranczak and Seamus Heaney. Reprinted by permission of Farrar, Straus & Giroux and by permission of Faber and Faber Ltd. • Excerpt from "Marina" from *Collected Poems* 1909–1962 by T.S. Eliot. Copyright 1936 by Houghton Mifflin Harcourt Publishing Company. Copyright © renewed 1964 by Thomas Stearns Eliot. Reprinted by permission of Houghton Mifflin Harcourt Publishing Company and by permission of Faber and Faber Ltd. All rights reserved. • "Anthem." Words and music by Leonard Cohen. Copyright © 1992 Sony/ATV Music Publishing LLC and Stranger Music Inc. All rights administered by Sony/ATV Music Publishing LLC, 434 Church Street, Suite 1200, Nashville, TN 37219. International copyright secured. All rights reserved. Reprinted by permission of Hal Leonard LLC.

For information about permission to reproduce selections from this book, write to Permissions, W. W. Norton & Company, Inc., 500 Fifth Avenue, New York, NY 10110

For information about special discounts for bulk purchases, please contact W. W. Norton Special Sales at specialsales@wwnorton.com or 800-233-4830

Manufacturing by LSC Communications, Harrisonburg
Book design by JAM Design
Production manager: Lauren Abbate

Library of Congress Cataloging-in-Publication Data

Names: Cregan, Mary, author.
Title: The scar : a personal history of depression and recovery / Mary Cregan.
Description: First edition. | New York : W.W. Norton & Company, [2019] | Includes bibliographical references.
Identifiers: LCCN 2018050858 | ISBN 9781324001720 (hardcover)
Subjects: LCSH: Cregan, Mary,—Mental health. | Depression in women—Patients—New York (State)—New York—Biography. | Depression, Mental—Treatment.
Classification: LCC RC537 .C748 2019 | DDC 616.85/270082—dc23
LC record available at https://lccn.loc.gov/2018050858

W. W. Norton & Company, Inc., 500 Fifth Avenue, New York, N.Y. 10110
www.wwnorton.com

W. W. Norton & Company Ltd., 15 Carlisle Street, London W1D 3BS

1 2 3 4 5 6 7 8 9 0

FOR JAMIE AND LUKE

"Yet why not say what happened?"

—ROBERT LOWELL, "Epilogue"

Contents

Preface

Going through a box of old photographs recently, I came upon one taken long ago at a baby shower in a friend's New York apartment. I'm seated at the center of the photograph, wearing a gray winter dress, my eight-month pregnancy mostly hidden behind the gift-box on my lap. I'm twenty-seven. A small stuffed bear sits at my feet beside its crumpled wrapping paper. My husband is to my left, looking relaxed, holding a beer, and several of our college friends are in the photo as well, drinking, eating, watching me open their presents. I'm holding up another gift I've just unwrapped: a newborn's onesie in white, sprinkled with tiny bears outlined in pink and blue. Looking at this young woman many years later, I feel a rush of fear and pity for her, unprepared as she is for what will unfold a few weeks later when her baby dies.

Another photograph sits on the desk where I write. It was taken thirteen years later, after a divorce and remarriage, on a visit to Arizona in the springtime. In the background, out of focus, is a blur of mountain, aspen trees, and blue sky. In the foreground, in close-up, I'm hugging my rosy-cheeked nine-month-old son, his broad forehead and dark hair much like my own, his eyes lit up in a smile as his father snaps the picture. On a hike that day, I had let the baby down from his carrier to test his legs and watched him grasp the big round boulders along the side of the trail. The photograph was taken a moment later, just as I've lifted him up, and our faces reflect the pleasure of being outdoors in the sunshine. I keep this photograph on my desk because it radiates happiness and comfort: it reminds me of what I've been given, and how love for my husband and son continues to anchor and sustain me.

This book is about the difficult path I traveled between the moments captured in these two photographs. After the death of my infant daughter, I fell into a depression so severe and unrelenting that I was admitted to a psychiatric hospital where I nearly succeeded in taking my own life. Since then, I have never taken the fact of my existence for granted. Instead of living as I do now—teaching, writing, spending time with friends and family, taking pleasure in watching my son grow up—I might be nothing more than a fading memory in the minds of those who knew me as a woman who died young, in sad and desperate circumstances. I'm aware, as I remember that long-ago day of gift-giving, that my own life has been another kind of gift: a second chance. Even so, the depression that emerged so clearly at that time has never entirely left me. It is the trace of bad luck that lingers, amid so much good fortune that has come to me since.

Depression is far more widely acknowledged today than it was back then. The word "depression" is ubiquitous, and the disorder is too—though depression takes a variety of forms and diagnostic labels. In 2016, nearly 11 percent of Americans from eighteen to twenty-five experienced a major depressive episode (as did 9 percent of adolescents from twelve to seventeen and 6.7 percent of the general adult population). The correlation between depression and suicide is striking: the risk is significantly higher for people with mood disorders, and highest among those who have been hospitalized.

When I was diagnosed with a major depressive episode in the wake of my first child's death, I had no idea what the long-term implications of that diagnosis would be. I didn't even grasp that I was facing a long-term situation. Nobody could tell me whether my depression was the result of an inherited vulnerability, or whether it was rooted in my temperament, or my life experience, or to what extent it was a combination of all of these. Nor could even the most dedicated and sympathetic doctors provide clear answers to what seemed the simplest and most urgent questions: What exactly *was* depression? Why did some medications work, while others didn't? Would I ever be able to put it behind me?

Five years ago, I began trying to answer these questions, initially in an effort to understand competing claims in an ongoing debate about whether the antidepressants I'd been taking for many years were merely expensive placebos. I had already read a number of memoirs and other popular books on depression, but I began to investigate the subject more widely and intensively. I had earned a doctorate in English literature and was comfortable doing research outside of the discipline in which I had been trained. And as someone who had lived with depression—and experienced the worst of it—I approached medical, social, and cultural questions about the disorder and its treatment from an insider's perspective that few of the historians and scientists who have written on the subject can provide.

Once I decided to include my own history in this investigation, I worried about the exposure that would come with publishing what I was writing. In my large Irish Catholic family, the tacit understanding was that it was best not to draw attention to oneself. A couple of decades leading discussions and lecturing in college literature classrooms had brought me a greater ease with the self-exposure necessary for teaching. Yet in all professional settings and most social ones, this particular story—my past, my diagnosis, the vulnerability to recurrence, the ongoing, quiet necessity of dealing with being depressed for months at a time—has remained deeply private.

A couple of years into the project, a close friend asked me why on earth I would want to revisit the worst days of my life. The simplest answer is that after decades of trying to keep it hidden and behind me, I wanted to turn to the past and face it squarely. Those who have lived through a traumatic experience will know what I mean. I wanted to understand what had happened. Having survived to tell this story, I've long known that I have something to say about what happened back then.

The first two chapters were the hardest to write (and because of the sadness they contain, may be the hardest to read). But once I had written them and better understood the gravity of my subject, I realized that telling this story—and sharing it through publication—was a way of refusing the shame and stigma that still cling to the subjects of mental illness and suicide. I often think about what might have been different for that young woman at the baby shower, who didn't know that help existed for the inchoate feelings she had long had about herself, and who didn't realize that while feeling devastated was a normal response to the loss of an infant, feeling suicidal was not. This book is written for her, and for the young women in my family who have inherited the same vulnerability. It is also for the countless people who find themselves struggling to cope with internal forces that feel overwhelming but—as I try to show in these pages—are survivable.

This book is more than a memoir. It seeks to build a bridge from my individual narrative to the broader landscapes of literature, cultural history, and science, where the questions I've been asking have been addressed by many who came before me—writers, poets, psychiatrists, historians, chemists, and neuroscientists. I've found a deep satisfaction and a sense of fellowship in reading writers of the past, who did not have the benefit of even the partial scientific explanations we now have. Centuries-old accounts provided accurate descriptions of the harrowing state of mind that leads to suicide and a confirmation that the illness that beset me has been described with great consistency across time. When we lose sight of the long history of the illness formerly called melancholia, we lose this sense of continuity. While the experience of depression is intensely solitary, reading has been a way of binding myself to the larger effort at understanding and to the community of sufferers. Recognizing my own experience in that of others—those who endured the peculiar madness of melancholia, those who laid themselves down the first time for shock treatment, those who fell again and again into the void and had to make their hesitating way back—has been a means of finding a history into which I could insert myself, one in which my experience makes some sense.

In the chapters that follow, my accounts of loss and mourning, melancholia, shock treatment, the asylum, and the development of antidepressant drugs situate my personal experience within the long, hopeful, and as yet incomplete movement toward effective treatment and cure. I've been able to return to the person I was in my twenties and thirties aided by hospital records, notebook entries, and the memories of people who were close to me at the time, even as I'm also present in these pages as a much older self, reflecting on the repercussions of these events and the continuing presence of depressive episodes over the past three decades. Sometimes memoir and context are interwoven; sometimes they are juxtaposed. In both cases, it is my hope that those who are not experts—those afflicted with depression as well as their loved ones—will have a better understanding of the past and of the road ahead, and at the same time, I hope to allow those whose lives are committed to treating depression to see one patient's experience from the inside.

I

What Happened

For no reason that I could identify, my right shoulder began to ache. Within a few months it became so stiff that I could barely move my arm and so painful that I couldn't sleep at night. A bright ring of inflammation on a scan revealed a frozen shoulder—something I'd never heard of, but apparently a not uncommon ailment in middle-aged women. Lots of physical therapy was in store. An odd thing about that, I found, is that you have to spend a lot of time with someone who at the outset is a complete stranger, while this person manipulates your body at very close range. Twice a week I would lie on a table in a sleeveless shirt while Frank, my physical therapist, dug his fingers into my shoulder joint, trying to coax my arm back into arcs of motion it used to move through easily. He was in his twenties and single, and I was old enough to be his mother. We shared the kind of conversation that arises between two people whose lives don't overlap much. We talked about our weekends, about places we'd traveled to, about our families, about our work. We tried to make each other comfortable. So things became awkward when, facing me and pulling on my arm as pain shot through my shoulder, Frank asked, "How'd you get that scar on your neck?" I hesitated for a second and then said lightly, "Um, I'd rather not talk about it." Our eyes met, registering the gap, and then we stepped over it and talked of something else.

After six weeks the shoulder was no better, so I tried a new doctor who injected a steroid into the joint and sent me to a different physical therapist. Jessie was a former ballerina; she and her partner did much of their work with dancers in the city's ballet companies. On our first day together, I was lying on the table and she said, "How'd you get that scar on your neck?" We were alone in a small room and I simply answered her. "I gave birth to a child who died, and I got very depressed. The scar is from a suicide attempt." She flushed. "I'm so sorry for asking." "Oh, it's okay," I replied, "It was a long time ago." I felt bad for her, and wished I had lied about it. The next time, we had to work a little harder at making each other comfortable again.

Over the years on the occasions when I've been asked this question, I'm always surprised that I don't have a convincing lie ready. What kind of injury would produce a noticeable diagonal scar over the left carotid artery? A mugging at knife point, maybe? A car crash? It should be easy enough to make something up, but I've never been good at that. If a doctor is asking, I tell the truth because I assume the doctor is reading my body for a medical history. But physical therapists are experts in anatomy too, and maybe both of mine were asking because they knew it was a dangerous injury. Still, it was intrusive, and unrelated to the shoulder problem. I could have said to Jessie what I had said to Frank: "I'd rather not say." But that hadn't gone so well either. I've gone through life wanting people to assume that I'm a rational, dependable, normal person, and the best and easiest way to do that is not to talk of it at all.

It *was* a long time ago, and I'm old enough to wonder why I haven't been able to reduce the impact of that event in my history. I want it to be safely and firmly in the past. I badly want, even, to be able to forget about it. Instead, the scar is there in the bathroom mirror each morning when I brush my teeth, a daily reminder of my surreal descent into mental illness. Three months after my daughter died, I was so depressed that I had to be hospitalized. On my second morning in a locked ward, I stepped into the shower with a glass jar of moisturizer and dropped it on the floor. Then I felt along the left side of my neck for the strong pulse of the artery and pulled a large piece of broken glass firmly across it. It was a determined and, in the words of the hospital report, a "highly lethal" effort to end my life. I had no intention of living on into a future where any telltale mark would survive the moment, no thought of vanity, no thought of anything but making my exit.

Life as I knew it had ended with a shattering loss, a wholehearted effort at self-destruction, a long stay in a psychiatric ward, and many weeks of shock treatment. And then it began again, in partnership with a psychiatrist, and with a long-term, shaky effort to regain my equilibrium and to convince myself that I was not hopelessly defective. But the scar is there, as is the daily medication. All that must really have happened, that awful series of events I would undo if I could. And a part of my mind—a sort of inner monitor—has remained on guard, making sure any downward fluctuations in my mood stay within the range necessary to get on with life.

It was unsettling to be asked about the scar twice in such a short period, because at the time I was already thinking about those events in the past. My daughter, had she lived, would have been the same age I was when I lost her. I had begun to think seriously about writing this book, prompted by events in my family and in the news. That same year, a niece was diagnosed at seventeen with major depression (her diagnosis was later changed to bipolar type II).

Both of my grandfathers experienced periods of severe depression, and so did my father. A few other members of my parents' and my own generation have had what looked to me like depressive episodes. (Only two in this group, so far as I know, consulted a psychiatrist, and I hesitate to guess whether the others met the criteria for an official diagnosis.) Most recently, another person in our youngest generation received a diagnosis of major depression, at nineteen. My own diagnosis came when I was twenty-seven, although I later recognized that episodes began when I was in high school and continued through college and right up to the catastrophic postpartum episode I was hospitalized for. To me, all this looks like evidence for genetic vulnerability, but it's a subject that, until recently, my family has rarely talked about. In 2013, a genome-wide association study revealed that five disorders—major depression, bipolar disorder, autism, ADHD, and schizophrenia—share genetic roots. All but the last of these are present in the three living generations of my family.

I wondered what my young relatives' diagnoses would mean for them in the long term. What, if anything, is known that might make living with a mood disorder less burdensome than it has been for me? Are most people more familiar with the signs of a life-threatening case of depression than they were thirty years ago? In many ways, things seem not to have changed all that much. While successive editions of psychiatry's official diagnostic manual reflect the profession's effort to improve the classification and description of the mood disorders, treatment has remained pretty much the same: either a combination of psychotherapy and psychotropic drugs or drugs alone. For more severe and dangerous cases, there is still hospitalization, and there is still shock treatment. The most significant change is that the research and development pipeline for mainstream psychiatric medications has run dry. Most medications have passed out of patent and are available in generic form, and not enough information about these illnesses has been discovered to convince big pharmaceutical companies to invest in developing new drugs. Researchers are conducting small-scale trials with party drugs and psychedelics—ketamine, MDMA, psilocybin mushrooms, LSD, ayahuasca, and cannabis—because the change in consciousness they induce may prove useful for breaking the hold of depression as well as addiction, PTSD, and the psychological distress of cancer treatment. Ketamine has been shown to reduce the symptoms of treatment-resistant depression, including suicidal thinking, within hours. But it has to be given by injection or intravenous infusion, is very short-acting, and comes with troubling side effects. More technologically complex innovations, like transcranial magnetic stimulation and deep brain stimulation, are available to people whom standard antidepressants haven't helped. The effectiveness of these new techniques is a matter of controversy, and many insurance companies won't pay for them. Joshua Gordon, the current director of the National Institute of Mental Health, recently said that we don't know enough about the brain "to even begin to imagine what the transformative treatments of tomorrow will be like."

As a long-term user of antidepressants, I was troubled by a growing debate about whether these drugs were effective, or whether perhaps they were doing more harm than good. At least 10 percent of Americans over the age of six were taking antidepressants, yet in 2008, an apparently authoritative study reported that in 75 percent of people the positive response was caused by the placebo effect. I read about this in an article called "The Epidemic of Mental Illness," which also questioned what appeared to be an alarming rise in the number of the mentally ill in America. Its author was Marcia Angell, former head of the *New England Journal of Medicine* and long-time scourge of the drug industry. Could this apparent epidemic be caused, she asked, by the proliferation of people taking psychiatric drugs for relatively minor ills, and by the growing tendency to assign a psychiatric diagnosis to just about anyone? Angell addressed a number of disturbing trends in public health, including the extent to which the profession of psychiatry has, over the last twenty-five years, been influenced by marketing forces in the drug industry. She also cited Robert Whitaker, who in his book, *Anatomy of an Epidemic*, argues that psychiatric drugs like antidepressants, taken over the long term, cause a negative feedback cycle in people's brains. The body gets used to the presence of extra neurotransmitters and scales back its own production so that when the drug is no longer present, people become depressed and start taking the drug again. Antidepressants, he says, actually cause chronic depression by interfering with the body's homeostasis. According to Whitaker's unsettling argument, by taking these medications you may be causing harm to yourself. I began to wonder whether I was a fool for taking my medication so faithfully. Other experts responded that antidepressants *were* effective for the majority of people with serious depression. I didn't know what to think.

When I arrived at this dilemma I had been enjoying an unaccustomed state of wellbeing, feeling confident and at peace for long stretches of time. I thought with amazement that maybe I was feeling how "normal" people feel. Maybe the illness, having held me in its grip for so long, was letting go at last. I wondered if I might be able to stop taking my daily antidepressant or whether that would be needlessly risky, given my long history of frequent recurrence. David Foster Wallace came to mind. He had stopped taking Nardil, the medication he had been on for years, in the hope that one of the newer medications would relieve him of Nardil's side effects. Nardil is an MAOI, an older class of antidepressant drugs that can cause serious hypertensive reactions if the person taking it eats certain foods. Wallace did have, on occasion, these dangerous reactions. But he had been managing well enough on his long-term drug, and when he tried several of the newer antidepressants they just didn't work for him. When he tried to go back on Nardil again, that didn't work either—at least not quickly enough to save him. He hanged himself in September of 2008. His wife, the artist Karen Green, found his body and has made works of art that express her sadness and anger. One was a forgiveness machine, "seven feet long, with lots of weird plastic bits and pieces." You wrote down on a piece of paper the thing you wanted to forgive, it was sucked into the machine and shredded at the other end. In a California gallery, the machine was overwhelmed by users, but Green herself did not use it. "Forgiving is never as easy as we would like," she said. "Apparently quite a lot of people cried." His close friend Jonathan

Franzen wrote about what Wallace's suicide meant for him and the lingering anger he felt about it—even as he traveled to the far edge of South America carrying his friend's ashes.

A year after Wallace died, the German goalkeeper Robert Enke stepped in front of an oncoming express train near his home. His wife said he'd been in treatment with a psychiatrist and had been suffering from serious depression for the past six years. The goalkeeper's position as his team's last defense, and the fact that goalkeepers often take the blame for lost matches, led to unbearable anxiety and pressure for Enke, who did not admit to his coach or the team's sports psychologist that he was depressed. In 2006 his daughter died at age two of complications from a congenital heart defect, after a series of surgeries had given them hope of her survival. In 2009 he and his wife adopted a second daughter, and Enke feared that the child would be taken from them if he admitted to his depression.

The deaths of Wallace and Enke bear witness to the worst that depressive illness can do. Despite the scale of their accomplishments, they remained vulnerable to the slow disintegration of mind and self, to despair and self-loathing, and to the compulsion to die. Having gone through that uniquely horrible experience and having worried for a long time that I wouldn't live to grow old, I'm troubled when I read about high-profile suicides like these. It's as though I've lost a comrade in a shared struggle. But most deaths from depression are the ones we never hear about: those of people who went undiagnosed, or who didn't have insurance, or succumbed to drug addiction or alcoholism, or whose families didn't notice what was happening, or who got away despite the best efforts of their doctors and loved ones to help them. The profoundly depressed person can't see that her thinking is distorted and, after a certain point in the downward spiral, can't hear or comprehend the people who argue that she has a life ahead if she can just hold on.

THE STEEP DECLINE in my state of mind began after the death of my first child. Anna was born just before dawn on a Sunday morning, after an easy, trouble-free pregnancy. My husband Jake and I loved her immediately, surprised at the power of our attachment to our fair and fragile-looking daughter. We took a couple of photographs and marveled at her until the nurse took her away for bathing. Relief soon turned to anxiety when we learned that Anna's Apgar score was low and her body temperature didn't return to normal after her bath. They wanted to keep her in the nursery on a warming table. We were disappointed, but assumed everything would be okay. That afternoon, my parents drove up from Pennsylvania to see their first grandchild. My mother recalls something that I didn't know at the time: when the nurse held Anna up for them to see her through the nursery window, her legs dangled limply. I do remember that she was lethargic and had difficulty nursing. Because she was kept in the special care nursery for observation, I didn't have much time with her at all. In the evening various updates arrived, none of them good. Her blood sugar was low, her breathing was too fast, she might have an infection. We signed a consent for a spinal tap, which was terrifying enough in itself, and they found no infection.

The next day there was no denying that something awful was happening. Anna's skin was bluish—this was cyanosis, caused by a lack of oxygen in her blood. A cardiologist came into my room to talk with us. Through the window behind him I saw the tarred roofs and water towers of a stepped array of apartment blocks, all looking entirely normal under a bank of low-hanging clouds. He said he feared a heart problem, and his cautious manner of speaking made it clear that whatever was wrong was very, very bad. He delivered the news and left the room as quickly as he could, but grief broke from us in strange animal sounds before he could close the door. Everything went sliding sideways in that moment, as if reality were breaking up, splitting into dangerous, unrecognizable shards.

This was 1983, and I hadn't had an ultrasound during the pregnancy. Many hospitals didn't have ultrasound machines until a few years later. Beth Israel, the New York City hospital where I gave birth, didn't have any way of looking at Anna's heart, so they had to transport her uptown to Mount Sinai for an echocardiogram. Jake went along with her in the ambulance. I was still a patient of the obstetrics ward, so I waited alone in my room for what seemed hours, until Jake came in again out of the rainy night, sobbing and soaking wet. Anna's echocardiogram had revealed a condition called hypoplastic left heart syndrome; the left side of her heart was underdeveloped and unable to pump oxygenated blood through her body. "She's going to die," he said. "We need to get you discharged and get back to Mount Sinai." A nurse checked the episiotomy stitches, then said I could get dressed and go. Out on the street it was evening, and dark. I was confused about what day it was. It was pouring now, and we passed the iron railings along Stuyvesant Square that I had gripped during contractions as I made my way into the hospital, fully in labor, with the baby coming very quickly. It had been dark then too, before sunrise the previous day. Now we rushed uptown in the rain, the red and green blur of Christmas lights streaming down the car windows. The doctor who gave Jake the diagnosis had told him that Chil-

dren's Hospital in Boston could try to treat Anna for this condition, but that she wouldn't live long enough to get there. He was pretty brutal about it.

When we arrived at the neonatal intensive care unit a nurse, very gentle and kind, took us to the incubator where Anna lay splayed in her diaper, her body pale, her limbs blue. Her eyes were closed and she was very still, delicate, beautiful. The doctor removed the ventilator; it was only making her a little more comfortable and it didn't matter now, he said. The nurse swaddled her in a blanket and carefully transferred her to my arms. We held her and gazed at her face as she faded out of life. At a certain moment—Jake was holding her—it was apparent that she had died. Her stillness slackened, her barely perceptible breathing ceased. We stood for a while longer, holding her, then handed her back to the nurse. There was nothing to do but sign the papers, receive her death certificate, and go home.

Before the 1980s, all children born with Anna's heart defect died within a week. Less than a year after her death, an infant known as Baby Fae was born with hypoplastic left heart; she received a baboon's heart in the world's first interspecies transplant operation on an infant. Her body rejected the transplant and she died three weeks later. Today the best chance for survival is a prenatal diagnosis and a staged series of three complex and high-risk surgeries to reroute blood flow, the first taking place within days of the child's birth. It can be difficult for survivors to lead fully normal lives, and some children later require heart transplants.

We hadn't ever given a thought to death, but now we would have to decide quickly about burial. Jake's father felt strongly that in accordance with Jewish law Anna should be buried by sundown of the following day, and offered us a place in the

New Jersey cemetery where his parents had bought a family plot through a burial society. But the cemetery asked the inevitable question: is this a Jewish child? No: since I was a Roman Catholic, the cemetery could not accept her. So we found ourselves that same day among the green mounds of a cemetery in Westchester County with our parents, standing under striped golf umbrellas in teeming rain, while a small bald man in a red bow tie did everything but stand on his head to try and sell us a half-dozen burial plots. His enthusiasm was unchecked by his knowledge of what had just happened to us. We should decide, *right now*, that Anna should be buried here, in a large family plot where we all could join her when we died. I walked away and watched the hard sell at a distance from under my umbrella. I couldn't help finding a savage humor in the scene. Minutes later Jake and I came to an agreement: it would be cremation, of course.

The next day we were solemnly dressed, being driven up the West Side Highway in the backseat of a black hearse. Jake's father had generously taken charge of all these decisions and arrangements. Our driver was a silent man in a navy suit, and the back of his head made us self-conscious about talking, even though there wasn't much to say. Our parents followed in the other two cars of our abbreviated cortège. The weather was warm for December, and the deluge continued. Through the foggy air the Hudson was brimming, looking as though it might tilt and flow right onto the highway. As the windshield wipers slapped furiously back and forth, I felt a powerful sense of dread about what would come after this day. I had given the funeral home that sweet little onesie, in white with tiny bears, to dress Anna in—the one I was holding in the picture taken at the baby shower. She was there, our own delicate corpse-child,

in a small white casket on the seat behind us. I had a strong urge to touch her again, reached back to touch the coffin, and recoiled to find it had an embossed, Styrofoamy texture. I wondered whether this model was what the funeral home suggested for baby-coffins-intended-for-cremation. Probably there was such a category. A whole bitter world of death, with services and products to meet it, was opening before my inexperienced eyes.

We soon arrived at yet another cemetery where, after the rabbi from my in-laws' synagogue recited the beautiful mourner's Kaddish, we stood with our parents and watched the little coffin advance on a conveyor belt through a metal curtain, into the door of the furnace that opened to reveal, for a few seconds, a square of vivid orange flames. Then the door slid shut, and we all went home.

A few hours later, Jake wanted to go back to pick up the ashes. I was in a daze. I didn't understand why the hurry, given that it was all over. Ashes could wait. But Jake was feeling, and rightly so, that what was left of our child belonged with us and not in a strange place. Back we went. The people there insisted on referring to "the cremains," and handed us what looked like a plain coffee can labeled on the top with Anna's name. We drove home again and now, alone for the first time since her birth, we had no idea what to do with ourselves. I suggested that we write down what we wanted to remember of her brief life, and Jake sat down and wrote several pages that are now a detailed record of those two days. I wrote a couple of sentences and couldn't go on. The hours since I had pushed her out of my body, which was keeping her alive, had hardened into something unspeakable. Emily Dickinson did have the words for such a state:

This is the Hour of Lead—
Remembered, if outlived,
As Freezing persons, recollect the Snow—
First—Chill—then Stupor—then the letting go—

Women who have gone through a similar experience—a stillbirth, a late miscarriage, an infant's death during labor, the instances are many and varied—live through an abrupt shift in their physical and emotional reality. The body and mind have prepared for childbearing in ways more primal than we even comprehend, and suddenly there is no child. The night Anna died, we left the hospital after midnight and slept at my in-laws' apartment in the city. Sometime during that long night I awoke drenched in sweat from the shifting waves of hormones, and my breasts, for the first time, were painfully engorged with milk. Here was a new outrage I hadn't prepared for, and it provoked a helpless anger.

Everything that was happening felt cruel and unbearable, though at the time I had little sympathy for myself and for my body, which now seemed a ridiculous, monstrous thing, with its swollen breasts, its slack belly, its out-of-control, hormone-fueled emotions. Something had gone wrong, and perhaps it was my fault. I replayed all of the things that might have caused such a disastrous misstep in the formation of Anna's heart: A glass of wine before I knew I was pregnant? Bus exhaust? Dry cleaners' fumes breathed in while walking to work? (While I was pregnant I had gotten into the habit of holding my breath when passing dry cleaners' shops and when buses went by trailing bursts of diesel exhaust.) To this guilty guessing game of potential causes, Jake contributed his occasional use of pot and hallucinogens in high school and college. The doctor in the neonatal ICU had told us there was no known cause of hypoplastic left heart, which occurred in roughly one in ten thousand births. Things go wrong, he said, amidst all the processes that have to go perfectly in the formation of a child. And he was right. Parents are shocked to learn that their infant has a congenital illness or defect for apparently no reason at all. It just happens, and the news has to be taken in somehow.

Yet parents—mothers especially—can't help feeling responsible when something goes wrong during a pregnancy, even when their fears are irrational. The sense of responsibility and personal failure may be largely why women who have lost a child in this way have been found to suffer a unique kind of bereavement, in which shame and social embarrassment play a role. In one study that compared about three hundred women who lost children to stillbirth, neonatal death, or sudden infant death syndrome to three hundred women who had healthy infants, the bereaved mothers showed significantly higher levels of psychological distress for at least two and a half years after the loss. A Vancouver study of parents who had experienced the death of a child up to age five found that both parents tended to remember the events surrounding the death with extreme clarity, while suffering prolonged grief and, in many cases, marital difficulties: "The process of mentally 'giving up' the child is very difficult and very slow," the authors wrote, and "parents may search for many months or years for a reason for the death and a meaning in life and death." It turned out that this was true for Jake and me as well. Our marriage never fully recovered from Anna's death and its aftermath, which widened cracks that were already there. After a series of painful separations and reunions, we filed for divorce a few years later.

FOUR YEARS INTO our marriage, I had grown dissatis-
fied with my life and was hoping that having a child would
make me happier. Late in my pregnancy, we moved out of our
cramped one-bedroom apartment in Manhattan into a house
about a half-hour north, with a view of the Hudson. I wanted
to move into a two-bedroom apartment in town. Jake, not a city
lover, argued for the economical choice: a whole house and some
outdoor space in the suburbs, for less than the price of a two-
bedroom apartment in the city. We could have a garden; our
child could play outside. While those two possibilities excited
me, I worried about being cut off from friends and felt strongly
that we were much too young for such a life. But, as with most
things, I gave in.

Living in the suburbs didn't feel comfortable to me at all—I
would have preferred that we both leave our jobs and move to
Vermont, which had always been the plan. We had met there,
at Middlebury College, when I was eighteen and he was twenty-
one. Jake worked summers and then full-time at his father's
Wall Street firm. By the time I graduated he had been made
a partner, and I reluctantly moved to Manhattan and looked
for a job in publishing. I didn't have any particular interest in
publishing, but that was where English majors usually tried
to find employment. The job that Jake intended to be temporary, a way to pay for the drafty farmhouse we had bought and
where we had gotten married, was beginning to determine our
life. He now made so much more money than I did that I felt
powerless. Most of the other partners belonged to country clubs
and had stay-at-home wives. Jake and I kept up our old ways,
spending our weekends shuttling between the city and Ver-

mont, where we tended a huge garden and pursued our back-to-the-land dream. All of this increased my sense of alienation. What had happened to my life, and why had I let it all happen? I had doubts about a marriage I had entered into with some ambivalence, deeply worried that I was closing off exploration and independence too early. But I loved Jake, and I had hoped all would work itself out. We moved just two months before my due date. We bought a crib and some tiny, beautiful clothes, we painted the bedrooms, and we looked forward to bringing our child home.

The shock of having no child to bring home would be difficult for any couple, and it was especially so for us, because we were experiencing the loss in very different ways. I couldn't stop thinking about this random developmental error that determined my daughter's life and death, while Jake kept insisting that we would get through it, and that we could of course have another child. I wasn't able to share in his effort to be resilient. It was as if a switch had been thrown in my brain and the lights had gone out. Looking back, it's easy to see that this was far from a normal expression of grief. Postpartum depression is associated with a number of risk factors, including previous depressive episodes, social isolation, and a lack of social support. By moving to a suburban town where we knew no one so soon before our child was due, we inevitably faced a degree of social isolation. It was heightened by the unexpected state of having no child in this new neighborhood, surrounded as we were by families with children or older adults whose children had grown up and moved away. A memory from the days before I gave birth makes me think I was already depressed during the pregnancy. My due date was imminent, and I was alone in the empty house. I felt so strange and miserable, and so guilty about being miserable, that I sat down on the stairs and cried.

When Christmas came, we went to be with my family. I was hollow-eyed, numb, and very thin, having already lost all the weight of the pregnancy. I stayed in the kitchen much of the time, preparing food or cleaning up so I could avoid conversation. It was hard for my siblings to comprehend what had happened. I was no longer pregnant, and there was no child. They had been away at college or living at a distance and had not attended our little funeral ceremony. Only my parents and Jake's parents had seen Anna. My older brother and his wife announced that they were expecting their first child in June, but because of what had happened only two weeks earlier, there was a pall over everything.

I was fixated on the meaninglessness of things—of my pregnancy, of my marriage, of my life. The most pressing problem was that I needed to find a new occupation. I had reached what felt like a dead end in my job doing book design and production in a midtown publishing house. Ours was a tiny department, and there was no position into which I could advance. Now I believed I could save myself from feeling so terrible by using my maternity leave to find work that would be more satisfying, something that would make me feel I was moving forward in life. To become an English professor required a doctorate and looked even more impossible in my present state of mind than it had when I left college. So I considered other careers, and I took the GRE. Landscape architecture could be a good fit for me, but the better graduate programs would require my moving away for a couple of years, and I needed to think about what would work with my marriage. I had looked upon the processes of pregnancy and birth with an awed fascination, and

I began to think I could try becoming a nurse practitioner like the midwife I'd been seeing. A good friend has pointed out to me that thinking seriously of such a career at such a moment was more a symptom of grief than anything else. I didn't see that at the time. I signed up for a chemistry course that was starting immediately at a college nearby because I needed to do some science prerequisites. For a couple of weeks I took meticulous notes on the movement of charged ions through cell walls and other complexities I'd never learned about, but soon realized that I was in no condition for studying or for making major decisions about graduate programs. I was often on the edge of tears, I had trouble talking to people I met in class, and it was getting harder and harder to concentrate. My mind seemed to be disintegrating. It didn't seem to be a good time to take on an intensive new challenge.

On the other hand, being idle was far, far worse. Jake had gone back to work immediately, eager to be distracted from his own grief and my dismal mood. He took on an extra project that kept him at work for longer hours. When not in chemistry class, I was spending my days alone in the sparsely furnished house or in the public library, trying to figure out how to jump-start a new career. As the weeks went by, the empty air in the house began to seem tense and fraught, even malevolent. I was supposed to be making decisions about furniture, fabrics, rugs, all the stuff that people who own houses have to buy. Instead, I would gaze out at the river and the bare trees in the wan winter light, stunned, unsure what to do.

One morning as I stood in this hesitating way, the mail clattered through the metal slot on the door. I looked down to see small black footprints showing through an official-looking envelope: Anna's birth certificate had arrived. I stooped to pick it up, tore it open, and stared at the intricacies that marked her brief, unique identity. I was shocked by the fresh cruelty of this arrival, as if there should somehow have been a sensitive oversight committee that sent the birth certificates of doomed infants to—ha!—the dead letter office. Coming out of the library in town a few days later, I stopped and stared at a half-empty baby's bottle that stood on a brick ledge. Its shadow, sharp and black in the winter sun, seemed to vibrate on the wall behind it, as if in a Hopper painting. Any given day, dangerous sights like these could appear without warning. It wasn't only that I took such incidents as jolting reminders that unknown forces had taken over my life; my mind now seemed to receive everything as maliciously intended, or as having some profound, damning significance. When I stood at the kitchen sink drinking tea, I stared at the enormous spruce tree looming on the lawn of the house across the road, whose dark and draping branches had a sinister look. A shudder of dread ran though me when, one day, three enormous crows arrived and strolled around in their glossy black, casually pecking the ground beneath the tree.

It's not that I was receiving messages from bottles and birds—I wasn't quite, yet, psychotic. But I was interpreting what I saw with an intense, self-lacerating negativity. What had happened to us was a rare event, and I kept coming up with answers to the agonizing "Why?" of Anna's death. I imagined that her death held some kind of judgment on me—almost as if she had chosen not to be my child. Reviving the God of my Catholic childhood, I was sure I was being punished for some inner badness that I had always managed to hide but which was now, through this punishment, revealed to all. I also believed that Anna's death was the outward sign that my marriage was doomed. And that her heart was faulty because I had a cold, unloving heart. It was a distorted, self-obsessed, and frankly crazy manner of reasoning. Almost immediately upon her death my mind was unbalanced. What I didn't know was that I was moving slowly toward full-blown depressive psychosis. Jake kept telling me, with the voice of sanity, that her death was an entirely random event. It meant *nothing*, he would say, apart from being a terrible thing that *just happened.* But it was impossible at the time to comprehend that he was entirely right.

It was becoming really urgent that I get out of the house. In early February, perhaps eight weeks after Anna's birth, I returned to work. My colleagues were very kind, and tolerant of my stricken look and withdrawn behavior. I started taking the stairs and avoiding the elevator, because after the initial questions about how I was doing, the silence inside the closed doors was awkward. In truth, this kind of disaster is hard on everyone. People feel terrible, and once they've expressed their condolences it's hard to know how to talk to the bereaved person. I felt like I was emitting a force field of bad luck, like a silent Ancient Mariner. My desk looked out on the office floor through a glass front wall, and my drafting table faced the solid back wall. I sat at the drafting table whenever I could, because I had trouble composing a public face for those who passed by. It wasn't a busy time at work, but I couldn't have been of much use. Sometimes at lunch I would go down to the bookstore in our building to look for psychology books that might help me. I worried about being so self-obsessed: Why was I? And how could I stop being so? A prominent book on the tables was Christopher Lasch's *The Culture of Narcissism*—a jeremiad against the "me" culture of the 1980s. I flipped through it and realized there was no way that I'd be able to concentrate enough to read even a chapter, but I certainly felt like an example of this endemic narcissism that Lasch was going on about. So I gave myself the advice that depressed people so often hear: try to focus on someone else's troubles instead of your own.

The following Saturday afternoon I volunteered at the pediatric ward of a local hospital. I faintly recall having to wear a pink uniform of some kind, and being assigned a small child in the playroom. The little boy, perhaps three years old, could not stop crying as I held him, read to him, tried to comfort him— all to no avail. His tears just kept flowing, along with the mucus from his nose, which I wiped every so often. We were a mess, the two of us. I was hopeless at helping. Needless to say, that was my last day as a hospital volunteer. I didn't have enough to offer anyone in need; I would have to fix myself first. Another Saturday I wandered over to the Catholic church in our town and looked at the bulletin board, thinking I would join a grief support group. I was trying to motivate myself to talk to a priest about my despair, but there was no one around, and I didn't go back.

None of my halfhearted efforts to return to life in the world had made me feel any better. Anxiety was becoming an overwhelming physical sensation, something rising from my gut, grappling at my ribcage, making it hard to breathe. Sometimes it was an involuntary clenching of muscles, tightening and releasing, over and over. I couldn't sleep for more than a few hours at a time. I awoke in the dark, at three or four in the morning, and sat up with my heart pounding, my body revved up and panicked, flooded with adrenaline. Then I'd realize that nothing was going to happen. This was just the too-early beginning of yet another day. I would lie down again and try to go to sleep, my mind churning with anguish, spinning its wheels through the various unlikely fixes for the unmoored condition I was in: get a new job, apply to graduate school, move back to the city, move to the country. Suicide began to press itself into this list of potential solutions. The powerful feeling of loss had turned into something else: a heavy, self-absorbed internal collapse, a constant thrumming of dread, a suffocating inwardness, a conviction that I was permanently cut off from the world and other people, marooned in the hell of my own consciousness. Living in time had become a torment. Each day felt endless, with no sense of forward motion, no anticipation of the future, no belief that I would ever feel better. Time was unbearable: time needed to stop. One morning I announced it would be better if I were dead.

I don't recall at what point I started seeing a psychologist near my office—my memory of that time is full of gaps—but it must have been once I started talking about being dead. I don't remember any of my sessions with her, except that one day she strongly suggested that Jake and I go to the hospital. As he remembers it, I needed sleeping pills, and as a psychologist she didn't have prescribing privileges. As I remember it, she sent us to the hospital because I was suicidal. I don't know which of us is right. After a visit to the emergency room at Roosevelt Hospital, we went home again that evening to our dark empty house. Jake's father was on the board of a Westchester hospital, and he put us in touch with a psychiatrist there. I began to see this doctor every evening after work. I didn't like him; I found him detached and unsympathetic. I didn't talk much—I too was detached and unsympathetic. He prescribed an antidepressant. When there was no improvement after a couple of weeks, he suggested that I be hospitalized. But we did not take his advice, mainly because of the fear and stigma surrounding mental illness.

My mother recalls that immediately after Anna's death I

was in a state of such bitter despair that she didn't understand it. She was devastated herself, but my despair seemed excessive to her. She was already distressed at the time because her father had been in a coma since a stroke at the end of October. She later told me that when I called her from the hospital to tell her that Anna was dying, she put down the phone and screamed at God, "You're taking the wrong one!" In all those weeks, as I was getting more and more depressed, my mother was driving to a Philadelphia hospital several days a week to join her mother in the vigil beside my grandfather's bed. One day, as they were talking about Anna's death and the terrible state I was in, they noticed that tears were running down my grandfather's face. This was the first time they understood that he was still present and could hear what they were saying.

He died at last on the first of March. I knew that at the funeral I wouldn't even come close to behaving like my former self. It was difficult seeing so many people I hadn't seen in a long time, and when I tried to talk it seemed that my words were coming too slowly. My body felt slow too, as if I wasn't moving normally. After the Mass and the funeral, there was a reception at my grandmother's house. I went upstairs and sat in one of the bedrooms, beneath the crucifix on the wall. My mother remembers, on coming up to find me, that I was numb, staring, and silent.

Gradually I had stopped feeling so much—so much grief, so much anger, so much shame—and had begun to feel nothing at all. I was convinced that my body was just a remnant, and an entirely pointless one since my mind and soul, whatever essences define a human being, were dead. My consciousness was in permanent exile from life as it proceeded around me. The negativity I felt about myself didn't extend to other people.

Other people were good; they were just fine. They knew how
to live. I was failing to grasp this most basic human instinct. It
was baffling, and also damning, that I should be lacking something so universal and necessary. My intense conviction that
this body needed to die was the result of my utter hopelessness
and inability to imagine a future, and of a belief that my own
life was broken, irreparable, and over.

IN THE NEXT FEW WEEKS, the days grew warmer. There
was a bench in the garden next to St. Patrick's Cathedral, and
I sometimes went to sit there on my lunch hour. One day I
brought along an old volume of T. S. Eliot's poems and read,
for the first time, the poem "Marina." I thought I couldn't feel
anything, but I could feel the beauty of the words. I went inside
the church and lit candles for Anna and my grandfather, then
knelt in a pew and tried to pray. I'd hardly ever been to Mass
since leaving home for college, but I hoped that God would
hear me. A few days later, trying to hold on to my life, I picked
up the psalter from the rack in front of me and turned to the
Twenty-Third Psalm. "Yea, though I walk through the valley
of the shadow of death, I will fear no evil, for thou art with me,
thy rod and thy staff will comfort me." I read the psalm several
times, hoping some miraculous shift in my state of mind would
allow me to keep living. But it made no difference, and I didn't
feel that God was with me.

Out of the shadowy interior of the cathedral, I emerged into a
bright March afternoon. Spring was returning, and the branches
of the big elm outside the bedroom window that morning had
been hazy with red buds. Tiny serrated leaves, sticky and bright
green, would soon unfurl. I suppose I had been trying to hold

on until spring, which had officially arrived the day before, but nothing in me seemed to be coming back to life. I left the church and returned to the office, where I picked up from my drafting table the silver X-Acto knife I used routinely, stripping lines of type and images onto page layouts. It was a good tool; I liked its simplicity and precision. It was about two in the afternoon, and I didn't tell anyone I was leaving. I walked to Grand Central Station through the tunnels under midtown buildings, anxiously eyeing the tracks and the slow trains entering and leaving the station. The trains brought the end of *Anna Karenina* to mind, but I never seriously considered death by train. That would be too public, and too messy. For weeks, suicide had come to seem so inevitable that each day I was preoccupied with figuring out not only how to avoid killing myself, but also how I might finally accomplish the dreadful thing, and what would happen to my parents and to Jake after I did so. There was so much guilt at the thought of causing lasting pain for my family that I would have chosen simply to vanish, to become vapor, if only it had been possible.

I sat as usual to the left on the northbound train, and watched the shining river appear and disappear until we arrived at my stop. Beyond the parking lot the Hudson spread out in its everyday grandeur, the Palisades rising on the other side, the wide span of the Tappan Zee in view. I felt no regret for what I would be leaving behind—this earth, this beauty—though I remember noticing crocuses in bloom as I trudged a half mile uphill from the station, my mind oddly divided as I tried to focus on the tedious necessity of my task. Yes, I remember this feeling: the tediousness, the nastiness of what could no longer be avoided. Once at home, I wandered around, trying to figure out what to do. The house was set sideways on a narrow lot.

The terrain fell away steeply toward the river, so that the front door sat slightly below the road while the basement in the back was well above ground level. Outside, I went down the garden stairs to the backyard. Along the steps, the daffodils I planted when we moved in were beginning to pierce the dead leaves while, down below, the terraced lawn still had that flattened, end-of-winter look. At the northwest corner of the house was a small doorless room with stucco walls that we had never used, a kind of storage place whose purpose was mainly to hold up the porch that sat above it. On the tamped dirt floor against one side stood a dusty pile of wood left by the previous owners. I had been thinking, in a vague way, that this might be a good place to do it—this out-of-the-way place would save anyone the shock of seeing my body right away. I could see myself there, lying curled up at the base of the woodpile. But I would be found eventually, and how awful that would be. The business of killing yourself raises all kinds of daunting problems if you want to be courteous to those you're leaving behind.

The poet Anne Sexton wrote, "suicides have a special language. / Like carpenters they want to know *which tools*." I had brought one good tool home from work but thought I might find a better one. I went back into the house through the sliding basement door, noting chisels, wood saws, fertilizer, pruning saw, and up two flights of stairs to search the bathroom cabinet. There was nothing in the way of pills. I was taking a tricyclic antidepressant, but Jake had hidden them on orders from the psychiatrist. (I hadn't known in those pre-Internet days that tricyclics can be fatal in overdose.) I did find some syringes that my allergist had given me to use for injections while I was away on vacation. He had taught me how to fill the syringe, and the importance of squeezing out the bubble of air at the top.

We injected water into an orange, which at the time I found amusing. Now I remembered that you could die by injecting air into a vein and removed a syringe from the bundle. Then I opened a drawer in the bedroom and took out my journal, an old-fashioned Boorum & Pease book with hard covers, just like my friend Elyse's. She had encouraged me to buy it one day when I visited her in Cambridge in the summer after my sophomore year, and she took me to the Harvard Coop especially for the purpose. It was always a little embarrassing, having a journal. I didn't come from journal-keeping people. Jake had teased a friend about his journal one day in college: "Oh, is that where you keep *your thoughts?*" So it wasn't something I shared with him. Since college I had used it only occasionally, as a commonplace book, where I wrote down poems and passages from books, and as a diary—the place I filed away all kinds of troubles and "thoughts" that I couldn't talk about. Unhappy, uncomfortable thoughts about myself, rebellious, remorseful, treasonous thoughts about my marriage or my family. Like many diaries, mine skewed strongly toward the negative and was visited mainly on bad days. Now I went downstairs again and ripped all of the pages out of the binding, tore them into pieces, and buried them in the outgoing trash in the garage. It seemed important to get rid of anything that would hurt the people I was leaving. I didn't write a suicide note.

Then, at the kitchen counter, I pulled back the plunger of the syringe, filling it with air, and injected it into a pale blue vein in the crook of my elbow. Nothing happened. Next, I took out the X-Acto knife and sliced vertically along the vein at the base of the thumb—first the left, then the right, having seen once in a stupid movie about a cult that this was the serious way to go about it. It was discouragingly difficult and painful.

Fine lines of blood seeped out, thin as paper cuts. To cut deeper would take more courage than I could summon. To stand there bleeding in the kitchen began to seem ridiculous. Wasn't a bathtub the place for this? I couldn't face the bathtub, all that nakedness and pink water.

I called Jake at work to tell him what I had done. When I look at the barely visible scars on my wrists I can see how tentative an attempt that was; perhaps I still wanted to be helped more than I wanted to be dead. Jake called the psychiatrist, who called the police, and two officers arrived a few minutes later and took me to the county hospital. Going out to the patrol car on the street with them I felt utterly ashamed, like a misbehaving child. Were the neighbors seeing this? In the suburbs, I felt the nearness of the neighbors and the windows of their houses in ways I had never been conscious of in the city. What was happening was embarrassing, but really, it was impossible to cling to dignity under the circumstances. I was no longer in control of myself—wasn't that the problem? In the emergency room a doctor bandaged my wrists (no stitches were necessary) while the policemen stood by. Jake arrived, having rushed there from work, and the doctor said he would discharge me only if we would just shift hospitals. It was very dark now on the wooded roads, and in the car the silence between us was thick with disaster. We drove directly to my new home for the uncertain future: the psychiatric branch of New York Hospital in Westchester. I didn't want to go into the hospital, much less stay there. The intake doctor at the hospital strongly suggested I sign myself in because otherwise he would seek a court order to commit me. So I signed the paper, humiliated that it had come to this at last, and thinking that I would never get out of there.

2

What Happened Next

Between the night I arrived in one hospital to give birth and the night I arrived in another to stay on one of its locked wards, a hundred or so days came and went. As I tried to adapt to my unexpectedly childless condition, it seemed to me that time moved too slowly. But the rhythm of the seasons was rolling along as usual: the dark closed in early, and Christmas came, and then the nights grew shorter again until the equinox balanced night and day. Human bodies are attuned to light and to seasonal change; mood and energy levels tend to rise in springtime. To me, time felt empty and nonprogressive, and when spring arrived it made no difference. I had entered a state of living death.

At some point along that span of days, amid the shock and grief, and as communication along certain pathways in my brain was shutting down, I arrived for an extended stay in what Susan Sontag called the kingdom of the sick. "Illness is the night-side of life," she wrote, in a book about her experience with cancer and the strange state of being ill. "Everyone who is born holds dual citizenship in the kingdom of the well and in the kingdom of the sick. Although we all prefer to use only the good passport, sooner or later each of us is obliged, at least for a spell, to identify ourselves as citizens of that other place." Sooner, rather than later, it was my turn.

Among the proofs of citizenship in that kingdom, at least where mental illness is concerned, is the experience of life in a psychiatric ward. Let's say that the diagnosis—the professional assessment of symptoms—is the official passport. Mine was stamped, as I later learned, "Major depressive episode, with melancholia." No one ever mentioned melancholia when I was in the hospital; I only knew they were treating me for depression. I *was* depressed, of course, but I believed what was really wrong with me was a grievous fault of character. Depression was just the outward manifestation of my inferiority and failure. Much later, I learned that these overwhelmingly negative, self-punitive, and delusional patterns of thought are classic symptoms of melancholia, an illness recognized and described for over two thousand years. So was my experience of slowed time: in the illness, distorted time perception and sleep disruption both result from a breakdown of the body's circadian clock. But this understanding of what happened to me was long in coming.

Many years later, I asked my psychiatrist to make me a copy of the discharge summary—an encapsulated version of my case—that was sent to her because I was to be her patient when I left the hospital. On the first page of the typewritten case file is the underlined heading "Chief Complaint," followed by a transcription of my own words: "I've felt like I've had to kill myself for the last two months and have been able to fight it off until now." I made this statement during the intake interview that was part of the admission process. This would be the first page of my chart. The nurses, my psychiatrist, the mental health workers, the social worker, all would add their notes as the record thickened with dated entries after that first day. Given the prominence of my chief complaint, I have to wonder why the hospital didn't take seriously enough the statement that I could no longer fight the suicidal urge that had landed me in their care.

The task of admitting me to the hospital fell to Dr. Reed, a resident who was on call and whom I never saw after that night. Judging from the date of his medical degree, he had probably received his B.A. the same year I did. The psychiatrist I had been seeing after work, Dr. Bennett, had called ahead to the hospital to arrange my admission. He conveyed to the admitting doctor his belief that I was suffering from an endogenous depression. "Endogenous" means "within the organism"; it suggests that what was wrong with me was driven by disorder in my body and was more than a psychological and emotional reaction to my bereavement. This kind of depressive illness used to be called melancholia. Dr. Reed concurred, and recorded Dr. Bennett's diagnosis: "major depressive episode, with melancholia."

In describing the types of depression, psychiatry set the term "endogenous" in a dichotomy with the terms "psychogenic" or "reactive," which were used interchangeably. The types reflect an understanding, now seen as far too simple, that depression can arise either from the mind or from the body. A diagnosis of my illness as purely psychogenic, interpreted through a psychoanalytic framework, would assume that it was a reaction to life circumstances: I hadn't been able to adapt psychologically to Anna's death, which triggered unconscious memories of earlier losses, resulting in rage turned inward upon the self. All of this ideally would be brought to consciousness, worked through, and resolved over the course of many therapy sessions. Sigmund Freud's famous essay, "Mourning and Melancholia," treats melancholia as a maladaptive response to loss. Freud writes, "The distinguishing mental features of melancholia are a profoundly painful dejection, cessation of interest in the outside world, loss of the capacity to love, inhibition of all activity, and a lowering of the self-regarding feelings to a degree that finds utterance in self-reproaches and self-revilings, and culminates in a delusional expectation of punishment." Freud's description is accurate; it is in his ideas about the etiology—or origin—of the illness, as well as the best way to treat it, that he differs from those who see pathology in the body as the root of the problem.

Biological psychiatrists understand melancholia as a severe mood disorder associated with dysfunctions along the body's hypothalamic-pituitary-adrenal (HPA) axis. People with melancholia have very high levels of the stress hormone cortisol, a disordered sleep-wake cycle, slowed speech and movement, and diurnal swings in mood, which is darkest in the morning and improves slightly as the day goes on. They express an overwhelming sense of hopelessness, failure, and guilt. Sometimes they are psychotic. Very often, they are acutely suicidal. A recent textbook defines the illness as "a recurrent, debilitating, pervasive brain disorder that alters mood, motor functions, thinking, cognition, perception and many basic physiologic processes." Postpartum and bipolar depressions can also take this form. The gloom is unremitting, and efforts to cheer up the patient have no effect. Sufferers are trapped inside a totalizing negativity, and it is hard to reach them with rational thinking. When they are very ill and delusional, psychotherapy is of no use at all. It might help them to know that their illness is unmistakably a *real* illness, not a manifestation of weakness, moral failure, or an inferior character, if they could only hear this truth. But usually they can't.

Major depressive disorder first appeared as a diagnostic term in 1980, in the newly revised third edition of psychiatry's *Diagnostic and Statistical Manual of Mental Disorders (DSM-III)*. The phrase "with melancholia" was then attached to MDD to specify a subtype. Some biological psychiatrists argue that in relegating melancholia to a subtype, the editors put out of sight one of psychiatry's most ancient terms and most recognizable illnesses. But melancholia had been gradually disappearing from view, and from common knowledge. The use of specifiers under the umbrella of MDD continues today in the most recent edition of the manual, the *DSM-5,* where the various diagnostic specifiers of MDD—anxious, melancholic, with mixed features, etc.—indicate different groups of symptoms and different treatment protocols. They also suggest different biological pathways of disorder, although these pathways remain unclear.

Until the early decades of the twentieth century, when the influential psychiatrist Adolf Meyer suggested that the profession shift to using the word "depression" for both endogenous and reactive types of illness, Americans were familiar with melancholia and its sometimes fatal outcome. A search in *The New York Times* archives turns up many nineteenth- and early twentieth-century articles where the word "melancholia" nearly always appears in the report of a desperate act of suicide, with headlines like "A Fatal Leap," and "Suicide in Central Park." Under a headline that reads, simply, "Brooklyn," I found a case similar to my own: a quiet, seemingly compliant patient takes an action that surprises her keepers.

Margaret Schmitt, aged 55 years, a lunatic, confined in the
asylum at Flatbush, committed suicide some time during
Thursday morning by strangling herself with a torn sheet
in her cell. She was visited several times during the night
by the nurses, and as she had always shown a quiet, inoffen-
sive disposition, suffering chiefly from melancholia, it was
not believed that she would make any attempt on her life.

While the status of major depressive disorder has come under
fire on the grounds that it is a loose and somewhat arbitrary
collection of symptoms rather than a discrete illness, historian
Stanley Jackson has written of the "remarkable consistency"
with which melancholia has expressed itself across more than
two millennia. He writes, "It is the clinical description that is
essential—the symptoms and the signs, the observations that
could be attested to by the sufferer or noted by another person." When I read Jackson's book and others, I realized that the
phrase "with melancholia" in my diagnosis best expresses the
experience I've been relating, and that melancholia is a more
specific and terrible ailment than what is implied more generally by major depressive disorder, the diagnostic drawer into
which it has been slipped. Reading accounts of melancholia, I
recognized that across expanses of time, countless people had
felt what I had felt. As described by sufferers and physicians
alike, the consistent symptoms and signs—the sleeplessness,
the anguish, the despair, the pathological guilt, the suicidal
impulse—appear again and again. These voices helped me to
place that bewildering period of my life in a longer, more communal perspective.

THE EARLIEST DESCRIPTION appears in ancient Greece in the fifth century B.C.E., when Hippocrates and his followers ascribed melancholia's prolonged sieges of fear and anxiety, aversion to food, sleeplessness and irritability, to an excess of black bile in the spleen. The word is a transliteration to Latin from Greek (*melan*—"black, dark, murky," plus *khole*—"bile") into Latin. While early writers thought the spleen was dominant in determining the temperament of melancholy people, they also understood that melancholia disturbs the mind because it affects the brain. Galen, a second-century Greek physician, was clear about the illness's distorting effect on thought, feeling, and social relationships, writing of despondent patients who "hate everyone whom they see, are constantly sullen and appear terrified, like children or uneducated adults in deepest darkness." In seventeenth-century England, Samuel Butler cast the melancholic in similar terms, as a person trapped in the echo chamber of his own distorted mind: "A melancholy man is one that keeps the worst company in the world, that is, his own, and though he be always falling out and quarrelling with himself, yet he has not [the] power to endure any other conversation. His head is haunted, like a house, with evil spirits and apparitions, that terrify and fright him out of himself, till he stands empty and forsaken."

For the deeply religious, the conviction of inner badness that accompanies melancholia slides all too readily into a belief that one has been cast out by God. The case of the seventeenth-century Englishwoman Hannah Allen provides an instance of severe melancholic delusion expressed as spiritual trial. She was already in a state of depression when she received the news that her husband, a sailor who was often away from home, had died at sea. Her severe condition became dramatically worse, and she tried to kill herself. She later described her experience to a spiritual counselor: "I would often say, I was a thousand times worse than the Devil. . . . My sins are so great, that if all the sins of all the devils and damned in hell, and all the reprobates on earth were comprehended in one man; mine are greater; There is no word comes so near the comprehension of the dreadfulness of my condition as that, I am the Monster of the Creation: in this word I much delighted." Allen's grandiose self-damnation sounds like a classic—if rather gleeful—expression of depressive psychosis. When she recovered, she agreed that she had been suffering from melancholy and that she had no moral reason to think herself so evil.

In 1682, the Presbyterian preacher Timothy Rogers found himself so disabled by melancholia that he had to leave his position in London and retire to the countryside. Once he recovered, he wrote a book in the hope that his experience and counsel would be useful to other sufferers, as well as their families and friends. He describes "what dreadful apprehensions a soul has, that is under desertion," and offers comfort to those convinced that God has abandoned them. Rogers understands that melancholia is an ailment of the body that afflicts the mind, and he emphasizes the distinction between a person who feels guilty and a person who is very ill: "There is a very great difference between such as are only under trouble of conscience, and such whose bodies are greatly diseased at the same time . . . Melancholy seizes on the brain and spirits, and incapacitates them for thought or action." It can overwhelm people who are naturally inclined to it "by the loss of children" or some "unlooked for disappointment that ruins all their former projects and designs." He writes, too, of the insomnia that is one of melancholia's chief torments: "It is very reviving to a man that is in pain all the day,

to think that he shall sleep at night; but when he has no pros-
pect nor hope of that for several nights together . . . he is then
like one upon a rack, whose anguish will not suffer him to rest."

As a former patient, Rogers advises friends and family
members not to argue with sufferers, nor to respond to their
complaints by asserting that it's "nothing but imagination and
whimsy. It is a real disease, a real misery that they are tormented with: and if it be fancy, yet a diseased fancy is as great
a disease as any other; it fills them with anguish and tribulation." The Puritan preacher Cotton Mather, across the Atlantic
in the Massachusetts Bay Colony, took a sharply contrasting
approach, seeing malingering and whining in cases where Rogers sees suffering: "These melancholics do sufficiently afflict
themselves, and are enough their own tormentors. As if this
present evil world would not really afford sad things enough,
they create a world of imaginary ones." Anyone in the depths
of the illness could only feel worse in the face of this exasperated "pull yourself together" response, whereas Rogers counsels
faith and patience. Since he knows of no medicine that can help,
he emphasizes that prayer is the only recourse for an illness so
frightening, one that can arrive without cause and stay so long.

Reading Timothy Rogers led me to wonder whether, on
those last days when I was sitting in the cathedral, reading the
Psalms and hoping to be saved, I might have avoided all that
came next had I been able to hold on long enough for the medication to begin to take effect. But I didn't have faith. I was
strongly enough marked by my Catholic childhood, in which
divine punishment was a constant threat, and bewildered
enough in my postpartum state of mind, to suspect that the
death of my child might well be a punishment. I've wondered
whether deeply religious people in my condition might be

slower to act on suicidal impulses. To feel compelled to suicide, a mortal sin, brings its own fears to believers: those in Rogers's time who could not resist would have been judged posthumously as self-murderers, their property confiscated, their bodies not allowed to be buried in sanctified ground.

Because the compulsion to suicide was for me the most agonizing aspect of the illness, I took a strange comfort in Robert Burton's *The Anatomy of Melancholy*, which has long been one of the most authoritative works on the subject. Burton was an Anglican cleric and scholar at Oxford who began this work, first published in 1621, in order to distract himself from his own dismal moods. His vivid depiction of people in the grip of melancholic illness seems to me strikingly accurate. He describes how the sufferer is pulled toward death against the tide of the rest of humanity and against the human instinct for survival: "In all other maladies we seek for help," he begins, "we will freely part with all our other fortunes, substance, endure any misery, drink bitter potions, swallow those distasteful pills, suffer our joints to be seared, to be cut off, anything for future health: so sweet, so dear, so precious above all other things in this world is life." When I first read this phrase—"So sweet, so dear, so precious above all other things in this world is life"—I was moved by its simple truth. Timothy Rogers expressed this feeling when he recovered, and so did I, most wholeheartedly, after I had survived. But to someone in the depths of the illness, the moment-to-moment experience of life in time is neither sweet nor precious. It's just too much broken, ruined, hopeless life.

Burton's extraordinary prose invites readers to understand why, for the unfortunate souls gripped by melancholia, their peculiar suffering leads all too often to the door to death, which stands open and inviting:

In the day-time they are affrighted still by some terrible object, and torn in pieces with suspicion, fear, sorrow, discontents, cares, shame, anguish, etc., as so many wild horses, that they cannot be quiet an hour, a minute of time, but even against their wills they are intent, and still thinking of it, they cannot forget it, it grinds their souls day and night, they are perpetually tormented, a burden to themselves, as Job was, they can neither eat, drink, nor sleep. . . . In the midst of these squalid, ugly, and such irksome days, they seek at last, finding no comfort, no remedy in this wretched life, to be eased of all by death. . . . 'Tis a common calamity, a fatal end to this disease . . . and there remains no more to such persons, if that heavenly Physician, by His assisting grace and mercy alone, do not prevent (for no human persuasion or art can help,) but to be their own butchers, and execute themselves.

To be their own butchers, and execute themselves. I had used nearly the same phrase in my journal, trying to put into words the strangeness and horror of what had happened to me:

How can a physical illness, acting on the brain, make people believe that their once precious lives are so unlivable that they become their own executioners? It's no wonder people in its grip believe God is punishing them, or that the devil is telling them to destroy themselves. Because what else could take over the mind so completely? It's like an evil spell: something you won't die of *unless you kill yourself.* But it will make you want to. Nothing else will seem so necessary.

The active anguish Burton describes brought back the vacillating condition that I experienced in my first few days in the hospital: I wished to be helped and believed I could not be helped. I was perpetually tormented with the thought of suicide, and even more tormented with guilt about what I was doing to my husband and family. My failure to live, and its impact on others, was the "terrible object" that troubled my mind.

〜✓〜

ON THE FIRST PAGE of the case file, right below my words describing my "chief complaint," is a note about how my case appeared upon my arrival on the unit:

PRESENT ILLNESS:

The patient is a twenty-seven-year-old, white, married and employed female who was admitted on transfer from the County Medical Center where she'd been taken the prior day by local police sent to her home by the psychiatrist with whom she was in treatment for Major Depressive Disorder. The patient, who is a book designer, had left work early with an Exacto-Blade instrument, intending to suicide and had inflicted bilateral wrist lacerations which did not require suturing.

At the time, she was two and a half weeks into an intensive outpatient treatment with Dr. B____ of ____ Hospital, seeing him daily and taking 225 mg. per day of imipramine. The patient had been ill for several months before beginning treatment with Dr. B____ and had had suicidal ruminations throughout that time but hadn't acted on these thoughts. She had no prior formal history of any similar episode in the past.

Next, a section called "Mental Status Examination on Admission" records Dr. Reed's impressions of me on the night I arrived, including a note that I "denied suicidal thinking" and expressed remorse and embarrassment about having cut my wrists.

> The patient was a neatly attired, plain-appearing, thin young female. . . . Attitude towards treatment was cooperative, hopeless regarding potential for improvement. There was a moderate degree of psychomotor retardation. . . . She was alert and oriented x three without impaired attention, concentration, memory or cognition. Insight seemed good and judgment was fair, impaired by marked depressive ideation. Patient seems quite intelligent with good fund of knowledge and ability to abstract. . . . Affect was restricted to the depressed range, tearful, with an infrequent but sincere-appearing brief smile appropriate to the content of speech. Speech was very slow with dampened prosody. Thinking was without disorder to form or apparent disturbance of content. Overall there was a slow and deliberate quality. . . . There were no hallucinations or delusions. The patient denied suicidal thinking, stated she "can't believe things could have gotten to the point of my wanting to die."

For years I've confronted the scar in the mirror and wondered why it was so easy for me to make a nearly fatal attempt on my life in the hospital. Chief Complaint: *I've felt like I've had to kill myself for the last two months and have been able to fight it off until now.* It's a serious complaint, and a life-threatening one: I arrived at the hospital just hours after cutting both wrists. Thirty years later, I look back at the two people whose encounter is preserved here. What are they thinking? What is impenetrable in each of them to the other? I try to understand what the intake doctor's day has been like—he is on call—and how he sees this new patient as he ticks off the headings of the intake interview and decides not to place her on the twenty-four-hour watch reserved for the most high-risk patients. She is young, plain, thin, neatly dressed. With no prior formal history of mental illness, she presents with postpartum depression and bereavement. Her lacerated wrists are bandaged. She appears to be cooperative, though hopeless that treatment will help her. She is not psychotic. She is "alert and oriented x three"— she knows who she is, where she is, and what time of day it is. She has moderate psychomotor retardation, the slowing of thought, speech, and movement that is a classic symptom of severe depression. Tearful as she explains what brought her to the hospital, she manages a brief smile. Despite her statement that being suicidal for over two months has brought her to the hospital, she denies feeling suicidal during the interview, and expresses some disbelief that she has come to the point of wanting to die.

Thinking of myself in this interview brings to mind an image: a miner, at the end of his shift, lies down in a wheeled wooden cart on iron tracks. In this way he is carried up through a tunnel from deep underground, back to the surface of the earth and to daylight, blinking and black with soot. To speak to the doctor under those fluorescent hospital lights, I had to pull myself back from a very deep and isolated place to engage in an arduous social act. I had that slowed-down sensation while speaking that I'd noticed at my grandfather's funeral. Still, I can see myself trying to come across as socially "normal" in the scary new setting of the psych ward. The brief smile was a sign of that effort; it would have been the way I expressed remorse and embarrassment at my predicament. Meanwhile, part of me was standing outside all of this, shaking my head. It was as though I were a spectator at a bizarre melodrama, while I was also the desperate, pathetic person at center stage. *Unbelievable, what is happening. Unbelievable, that I've gotten to the point of wanting to die. Nevertheless, believe me.* The patient is two people now: one is without hope, walled in and suffocating, fixated on death as the only escape. The other, the remnant of the healthy self, badly wants to be made well and is envious of people who are going about their professional lives, like the doctor. Perhaps I was trying to assure the doctor that I still wanted to be like him, a person who could function in the world of the living.

During the intake process I signed a legal form called "Request for Voluntary Admission," where I had to indicate the reason for my request. There on the photocopy, in my familiar handwriting though smaller and more cramped, I see three words sitting alone on a field of many blank lines: "I need help." Even from this distance, I can feel the desperation behind that muted statement, the brief mental scan for what I could possibly write down. Dr. Reed filled out a form called "Initial Screening and Evaluation Note." On the line reading "Patient's Statement of the Problem" he recorded my verbal response: "I can't work. I'm suicidally obsessed." On the same form, under the heading "Tendencies," he circled the words "Depressed" and "Suicidal." He did not circle "Disturbed" or "Assaultive." The admission forms all indicate that I'm a suicidally depressed patient who is not suicidal at the moment.

I'M TRYING TO REMEMBER that evening accurately, but it's possible that I don't. Maybe I was being deliberately dishonest when I denied feeling suicidal at intake, just biding my time until I could try again. Suicidal patients often keep their intentions to themselves because they don't want to be stopped. Writing this account has led me to remember more, and also to ask more questions, as I reconstruct how things must have been. The reason I had left work early that day, I now remember, was to avoid meeting Jake at the station for our regular train home. Since I had become actively suicidal, he was with me all the time except when I was at work. According to psychiatrist Kay Redfield Jamison, "Were suicidal patients able or willing to articulate the severity of their suicidal thoughts and plans, little risk would exist. But this is not the case. Patients determined to die may present a clinical picture greatly at variance with how they actually feel or what they intend to do. They may move quickly and with desperate ingenuity." Emil Kraepelin, a late-nineteenth-century German psychiatrist who made significant progress in the diagnosis of mood disorders, noted that suicidal patients in asylums often deluded their keepers while managing to find ingenious and sometimes blood-curdling methods to do away with themselves: "Only too often the patients know how to conceal their suicidal intentions behind an apparently cheerful behaviour, and then carefully prepare for the execution of their intention at a suitable moment." In England in the 1880s and 1890s, physicians who wrote textbooks on mental disorders emphasized the most salient point in treating melancholia: "Melancholics are by far the most suicidal of all lunatics," and the risk of a patient becoming suicidal "should never in any case be left unprovided for." Why was the provision for me, a patient with melancholia one hundred years later, so lax by comparison?

Trying to understand what went wrong in the hospital, I wrote to Jake. We've remained friends since our divorce, and he was willing to help. He sent me several email messages about what he remembered and how he perceived what was happening at the time. Here he recalls our arrival at the hospital and my mother's visit the next day:

> I took you to the hospital. The place scared the shit out of both of us. I walked you down the hallway of the ward and it felt like a movie set of a mental hospital. I remember feeling like I was leaving you in a bad place. I think this was on a Thursday. Your mom was on her way to stay with us and she came to see you the next day. She brought you clothes and personal items including a glass bottle of lotion or face wash.

To fill in other missing pieces of the story, I needed to get access to the complete hospital record. The brief discharge summary that I've quoted didn't give any details of the second suicide attempt apart from its being "highly lethal." I wrote to the hospital to request my file, giving my long-ago dates, without much hope of receiving it. When the thick envelope arrived in the mail, I flipped through it quickly with a sense of dread. Its pages are filled with information I had forgotten or never known. The names of the doctors, the nurses, the mental health workers, the rules and routines, the group therapy, the line-up for meds, the cafeteria, the board games, the boredom: all began to swim into consciousness again. As I skimmed through the packet more slowly, it was as though I had re-entered the hospital and could see my former self through the eyes of those watching me, assessing the condition of my mood and affect, making notes about all of it. I learned more about what happened shortly after I committed myself to the hospital's care, on a day when I came closer to death than at any time before or since.

On the night I was admitted, a nurse wrote in my chart, "Patient denies present suicidal ideation and agreed to tell staff if she does." Everyone who worked on the unit was constantly asking us patients to communicate our feelings. This seemed to be a component of their therapeutic protocol as well as a way of keeping tabs on us, especially those of us at risk for suicide. But the trouble with a doctor or nurse eliciting promises or agreements from a critically ill depressive patient is that the patient's core hopelessness is far more powerful than any agreement made with someone who is, after all, a stranger. So overwhelming is their mental suffering that suicidal patients also break promises to their loved ones, and to doctors they've known for long periods of time. One small study showed that in 78 percent of patients who killed themselves while in psychiatric hospitals, the person's last communication with staff on the question of suicidal ideation was a denial. Of those, 51 percent were on fifteen-minute checks or one-to-one observation, and 28 percent had agreed to a "no suicide contract." The study concluded, "Tools used to assess risk have failed to predict risk in the short run." For patients with mood disorders, "the risk of suicide is highest if the depression is very severe, hospitalization has been required, or suicide has been attempted at some point." In all settings, the single most powerful indicator of suicide risk is a previous attempt.

It's possible that I was one of those deliberately misleading patients that Kraepelin and Jamison mention. I have no doubt that a part of me sincerely wanted to survive, but the hopelessness was overpowering. The medication I'd started taking two weeks earlier had given me more energy, and this combination of increased energy and hopelessness is a well-known formula for suicide attempts in the extremely depressed. Psychiatric units have protocols for monitoring patients in danger of self-harm or of harming others. Every patient's chart includes the observation status assigned by the psychiatrist, a notation for the degree of surveillance under which that patient should be kept. Most units use four levels of observation, depending on the degree of safety the patient needs: 1) within arm's length of a member of staff, 2) within eyesight of a member of staff, 3) intermittent checks, and 4) general observation (my unit was locked, so all patients were under general observation all the time). At admission, Dr. Reed assigned me to the third and second of these levels: standard observation (SO) during the day, which meant that someone checked on my whereabouts every fifteen minutes, and constant supervision (CS) at night. He didn't put me on the highest level of surveillance, round-the-clock supervision within arm's length (CO, or constant observation). The practice of heightened observation varies, and studies have shown that experienced nurses sometimes elect to modify orders as to the observation status of the patient.

The notes of various staff members emphasize how cooperative I was, which may explain why I was not watched more closely. Here is a nurse's note, the day after admission—the day before my second suicide attempt: "Patient appeared to be very upset during earlier part of day. Attended group. Tearful. Feelings of low self esteem. Mood improved as day progressed." Another nurse's note, that evening: "Patient remains on restrictive status but has remained cooperative to same. Affect appears brighter. Continues to deny suicidal ideation. Visited by husband and interacted appropriately." I can't help thinking that all this emphasis on cooperation and acting appropriately, and on asking whether the patient feels suicidal, would elicit the compliant response, which is obviously "No," the patient does not feel suicidal at the moment. But I don't remember lying about it, either.

That same day, my first full day in the hospital, I met Dr. Young, the psychiatrist who would be in charge of my case and who would also be my psychotherapist while I was there. Like Dr. Reed he was a resident and, judging from the year of his medical degree, he too was about my age. He had not been present when I arrived the night before, but it was he who created the case file I've been quoting from. He typed up Dr. Reed's intake interview and my responses, and his remarks in the file throughout my stay convey all medical decisions about my case. He writes well, and thoughtfully. That day he also met with Jake and my parents and took a family history, eliciting information about my life, my character, my habits, the economic status of the family, the employment and marital status of my siblings, and so on. He also checked in with Dr. Bennett, the outpatient psychiatrist I'd been seeing after work. Dr. Young's first note in the chart reads, "Patient continues on CS and very cooperative. Patient's outpatient therapist was contacted. . . . Regarding the patient's diagnosis he has felt she has an endogenous depressive illness and stated that at the outset of treatment the patient had had the indications of psychosis that are no longer appreciable. . . . Patient has had imipramine in therapeutic range for about 2½ weeks. Appetite has improved and she has gained some weight back. Will continue imipramine @ 225 mg/day for one additional week. . . . Individual insight-oriented therapy 3x week, Group therapy 3x week."

He mentions only a single observation status, CS, which means that I'm within a staff member's sight at all times. He writes this during the day, because he only works during the day. But Dr. Reed put down CS for night, and SO (intermittent checks) for day. Is this discrepancy a clue to what went wrong, or merely an oversight in record-keeping? A meeting of six staff members assigned to my case, including two doctors, two nurses, a social worker, and an occupational therapist, agree on the plan to continue the antidepressant. Given that Dr. Bennett has mentioned the indications of psychosis in the days before I entered the hospital, this was a fateful choice.

I slept late the next morning, went to lunch but didn't eat, and returned to my room. I then apparently decided to take a shower—or rather I decided to take that small glass jar into the shower. Jake recalls what happened when he came to see me later that day:

> When I came during visiting hours they couldn't find you. I was agitated because you were supposed to be on suicide watch and it seemed very strange to me that they didn't know where you were. They found you in the shower. You had broken the bottle and used the glass to cut your throat. We went to an ER for stitches and you were once again contrite and resolved not to hurt yourself. The hospital put you under 24-hour watch. For the next several months you had no privacy: someone watched while you slept, showered, and used the bathroom.

The fact that my watcher had lost track of me makes me wonder about how seriously my restrictive status was being taken. On the other hand, it may be possible that I was free to go to the bathroom unattended at any time, which seems to defeat the purpose but allows the patient some dignity. They might have been short-staffed at the moment, and my nurse might have decided that since I was so cooperative, she trusted me to take a shower alone. But when Jake arrives, he thinks I'm on suicide watch, and *they don't know where I am.*

Here's what I see in memory: the shower room was empty. Light from a barred window on the left showed a row of five or six stalls along the opposite wall. Everything was tiled in a tone of institutional green. In one of the center stalls I turned on the water, stepped in, and closed the curtain. I dropped the jar from standing height, then crouched and rinsed off the most suitable-looking piece of glass while feeling with two fingertips for the place of the strongest pulse along my throat. I don't remember the pain, or being found, or being in the emergency room, or returning to the unit. Perhaps I was in shock. Afterwards, I was aware that my nurse was in trouble because of me and resented me for it. But now I had conveyed to the staff that I needed to be on the status called CO, constant observation. A woman came to sit in my room, never further than arm's reach away. I didn't mind being watched. I didn't care about anything at all.

In Dr. Young's report I later discovered further details, like what I said to the doctor on call that day, who examined me when I was found in the shower. I never knew what a close thing it was. The artery was visible but intact, and I was disappointed to find myself still among the living:

Examining physician reported visualizing the unlacerated carotid artery, the patient having apparently narrowly escaped successful suicide. She reports having made multiple passes in the neck area and sitting "waiting" to die, soon realizing she felt "no change" and was "unable" to continue cutting herself, feeling she was a "failure" and a "coward."

While at the initial interview the patient was clearly clinically depressed she had managed to present herself such that there was not at all any indication of the potential lethality she soon demonstrated.

He wrote the referral for my transfer to the emergency room: "27-year-old white female with depression cut left side of throat w/ glass (?) in bathroom several minutes ago. Carotid appears okay, active bleeding stopped, but cut is deep and jagged." (That question mark in parentheses is the *only* indication in the entire hospital record that a glass jar in the possession of a suicidal patient might have been a serious oversight.) Jake recalls that we went to the ER in an ambulance with Lisa, the nurse who was in charge of me. That must have been awkward, but I don't remember it. I wondered whether my memory of what happened in the shower room was accurate. Jake says it must have been: "I keep having this impression that you were wearing a hospital gown with a sweater over it (you were wet and it was winter). I am sure your hair was wet."

Here is the surgeon's note: "Ragged, stellate laceration of L anterior neck, 3 cm. in length, deep to platysma. No evidence of major vascular or nerve injury. Wound debrided and skin edges trimmed. Repaired in two layers." The wound was deep and jagged, through the muscle covering the artery. There wasn't much bleeding. I again failed to cut deeply enough, and for this my present self is immensely grateful.

While just about everything in the hospital record is disturbing, reading the surgeon's note is more than that. It provokes a feeling that is oddly surreal; it is remote and also intimate. After he carries out this sewing task in the middle of the day—the two layers requiring two different gauges of thread—he pauses to write the details in the patient's chart. Here is the cut, here is the repair: both actions shaped the jagged scar that is such a familiar and unwelcome mark on my body, a different kind of permanent record.

I've often wished I could undo my own act (if indeed "I" and "my" are accurate words for a self in the condition I was in). So too have I often wished that the decisions and indecisions, the actions and inactions, the misunderstandings and human errors that led to the wound and the scar *had all not taken place.* It's so easy to want things to be other than they have been. I could wish Anna's heart perfectly formed, so that she wasn't born to die. I could wish her alive on the earth today as a thriving young woman. I could wish all the awful aftermath of her death undone, spooling time back and letting it run forward again. And what then? I don't know how the pieces fit together again when I erase these catastrophes from the timeline of my life. I don't know who I am.

I've long felt that this act of violence against myself is too awful to talk about, and certainly too shameful to write about. Even now I find it shocking. Looking back at these events in the hospital record provokes a complicated response: I am angry on behalf of the patient and her husband, who trusted the hospital to keep her safe. I'm appalled at the quick, desperate act of the patient, who needed so badly for her ordeal to be over. I want to turn away from the sight of that pathetic woman crouched in the shower stall; I want to disown her. I want her to stop embarrassing me; I want her to pull herself together. I also want to protect her; I want the staff to understand what's happening to her; I want to speak on her behalf.

DR. YOUNG RETURNED TO WORK on Monday and learned
what I'd done on Saturday. Now the treatment plan had to
change, and fast. The doctors had to confront their mistaken
judgment and change tack. "Current thinking is to proceed
ASAP with bilateral ECT and not pursue completion of tricyclic antidepressant trial." Jake says they strongly implied that
even if we refused ECT, electroconvulsive therapy, they would
go ahead, pursuing a court order. I think his fear was greater
than mine, but the record notes that on the morning of my first
treatment I was extremely anxious about the procedure. The
widespread public disapproval of shock treatment at the time
may have been the reason that it had never been recommended
to us before. But it is often effective in breaking the hold of
suicidal depression. Today, given my acutely dangerous condition, many doctors would urge immediate ECT as a first line
treatment rather than waiting for the second suicide attempt to
make that decision. Now the tricyclic antidepressant, imipramine, needed to be quickly tapered and an EKG, an EEG, and
a complete physical had to be done before I could be cleared for
treatment. Jake and I signed the release forms, which explained
the details and included many caveats:

> Fatalities are extremely rare. Complications, although
> infrequent, may include fractures and /or adverse reaction
> to intravenous medication. . . . Although the results in
> most cases are gratifying, not all cases will respond equally
> well. As in all forms of medical treatment, some patients
> will recover promptly; others will recover only to relapse

again and require further treatment; still others may fail to respond at all.

It was scary, but was there anything scarier than what I had done? ECT was our last resort.

The full-blown, savage power of mental illness is hard to face. Oddly, this seems to have been so even for the hospital staff who wanted to believe I was compliant and cooperative, a nice girl who wouldn't give them trouble—even though on admission I had told them plainly, twice, that my reason for coming to the hospital was that I was acutely suicidal. The cuts I'd made on my wrists "did not require suturing"; perhaps they were taken for a lack of conviction. I've come to believe that there was an unbridgeable gap between my mind, with its unbearable compulsion to suicide, and those who were looking at me and talking to me—my husband, my mother, even the doctors and nurses.

The eye-opening effect of this latest event was unavoidable, too, for Jake and my parents. They needed to confront this new reality that I was no longer the person they knew, but it continued to be difficult. My parents, especially my mother, wanted to keep believing that I was grieving for my child, and not that I was disappearing into mental illness. This is why it would never have occurred to her that she was bringing me a weapon when she brought me that glass container of moisturizer along with my toothbrush and shampoo. I had never asked her about it, but I've always known that she blamed herself when the responsibility belonged to the hospital, and to whoever didn't think to go through the things my mother brought me when she visited. Very recently, to my great surprise, she told me that someone at the desk *did* look through the bag that day, and let the glass bottle pass without comment.

My own and my family's inability to understand that my depression was far from normal caused the delay in pursuing treatment. It's very likely that had I begun taking imipramine within the first few weeks after Anna's death I would have responded, and this whole disastrous chain of events would not have come about. We should have sought help much sooner. I have long thought that our inaction shows a lamentable degree of either cluelessness or denial. On the other hand, how do you recognize what you've never seen before? I had never been the least bit suicidal in my life, nor had I ever been very dramatic in my moods. I had been depressed, and clinically so, for periods of time since I was sixteen or so. I hadn't talked about it because I assumed it was just what it felt like to be me, and I only recognized this history once I was experienced in distinguishing what depression feels like. The depression I now had was so engulfing and dangerous that it was nothing like those earlier episodes. If we were familiar with psychotherapy or with psychiatry, it would have been natural to seek help much sooner. But my four grandparents were Irish immigrants, and my family was steeped in Irish ways of thinking and behaving. Our culture was one of self-suppression, stoicism, and silence. We did not talk about feelings, and no one we knew had ever been to a psychiatrist.

Jake and I did talk occasionally about what we were feeling; the impact of Anna's death made that unavoidable. He was energetically trying to move past his own grief, and we were puzzled at how debilitating, how paralyzing, my reaction was. One weekend we spent some time in the psychology section of our local library, reading about possible explanations for what was wrong with me. Clearly, I was depressed, or maybe I had borderline personality disorder, a new diagnosis at the time that was associated with unstable, suicidal women. It was probably mid-February when I began to see a psychologist near where I worked, and by then I was already deep in a cycle of insomnia, dread, and hopelessness that would continue to intensify. Jake recounts what that period was like, and how difficult it was for him to fully comprehend what was happening:

> I remember waking up one morning and you telling me that you thought it would be better if you were dead. Even then I don't think I understood how depressed you were becoming.
>
> At some point you started seeing a woman psychologist in NYC. One day you decided you couldn't face going into work and I took the day off and we both went to see the psychologist together. She and I clashed. She felt like there were issues in your life and I think between us that were causing you to be "depressed" and I felt that you had depression and needed medication. You had not been sleeping and since she was a psychologist she couldn't prescribe anything so she referred us to the hospital. I think it was called Roosevelt.
>
> We went through the ER and eventually had a brief consult and were given a prescription for some sleep meds. I remember we went home and cooked dinner together and life felt very dark. It didn't help that by this time it was mid-winter and it was physically dark.
>
> The sleep medication didn't help much and you became worse and started to focus on suicidal thoughts. I slept holding on to you so I would wake with you in the night.

One night went especially badly and you asked me to let you go so that you could kill yourself. At dawn I called my father who very quickly came up with the name of a shrink in Hartsdale (I think). I called him and he told me that the meds from the hospital were inappropriate for someone who was depressed and that we could come in and see him that day. You were somewhat nonverbal at that meeting. I think I described what was going on. He prescribed antidepressants but warned that it could take a while to find the right dose and even the right drug. It was a tricyclic drug but I don't recall which one.

The doctor started to think that it would be best if you were hospitalized but you didn't want to do that and I was totally freaked out by the idea. I think it was the stigma and perhaps the sense that it would make it all too real and also perhaps that "we" would lose control of the situation.

One day I found you had thrown away some personal items including a picture I had taken of you when you were pregnant. I also found a razor blade, which you confessed you had been contemplating using on yourself but immediately felt foolish about. It seemed that after that incident you had decided you really couldn't do yourself in.

Several elements stand out here. First, the psychologist wants to examine the causes of my unhappiness, which at this point was like telling a person in the midst of a heart attack that she needs to go home, improve her diet, and get more exercise. Second, my vacillation is striking: I was compelled toward suicide, resolving to live, incapable of feeling alive, contemplating the act again, seeking the method, backing away. I think I wanted to deny how unrelenting these feelings were, and Jake wanted to believe that I couldn't do myself in. The idea that I could actually kill myself was simply unthinkable. It was much easier to think of my depression as a reaction to Anna's death, which had so recently been the unthinkable thing. Third, Jake recognizes in retrospect that the "we" he assumed he could rely on was gone. My half of the "we" was non compos mentis, no longer a fully rational or responsible actor in the partnership. Possessed by mental illness, I had lost critical aspects of my personhood—my powers of will, intention, and self-control. I was no longer someone who could promise with any certainty.

I speak of being "possessed," and it's true that being ill in this way is like being occupied by a force that makes you act and speak in ways that do not arise from your accustomed self. This was most obvious when I made statements that exposed just how delusional I was. What does a statement like this one, recorded by a nurse the night of the shower incident, say about my state of mind: "She is talking more and more this evening. She says, 'I am a bad person. I should not live'"? This kind of extreme self-accusation is typical of depressive psychosis. The nurse's note continues, oddly, "Her husband visited this evening. The visit went well." What would explain why I sometimes seemed like myself, like a person who was lucid and cooperative toward my hospitalization, and then say crazy things like "I should not live"? I think there is a continuum between the normal self, recognizable even when expressing the delusional negative thinking of melancholia, and the self engulfed, expressing full-blown psychosis. Although I looked and spoke like a very depressed version of myself, I was sometimes slipping into madness.

Dr. Bennett, the psychiatrist who counseled us to go to the hospital, was aware that my illness was acute and dangerous.

He communicated his accurate diagnosis to the admitting doctor, and it appears in the record. Diagnosis on admission: *Major depressive episode, with melancholia.* The word "melancholia" is a key indicator, and a long tradition of clinical observation existed to understand the exigencies of patients in that condition. But once I was in the hospital, it seems that the meaning of "melancholia" no longer mattered. I was just another patient on the unit, and I seemed to be compliant and cooperative. The absence of any reference to melancholia after admission has made me wonder whether the doctors and nurses on the unit didn't think in terms of this unique and dangerous syndrome, and didn't register how closely I was exhibiting the full range of its symptoms.

The hospital's main approach to treatment was through psychotherapy, which may explain the lack of interest in melancholia. In therapy one day, Dr. Young commented that my superego was "the most powerful"—or maybe he said "most punitive"—that he had ever seen. The remark suggests that he was looking at me through a Freudian lens rather than a biological one. In Freud's tripartite model of the psyche, the superego represents the conscience; it reins in the aggressive drives of the primitive id by enforcing moral and social laws. Is it possible that I was the first patient with melancholia that Dr. Young had treated? An overwhelming sense of guilt, sinfulness, and even criminality, as well as the expectation of terrible punishment, are symptoms expressed again and again by melancholic patients across the centuries. But despite my delusional frame of mind, the hospital's treatment model required us to examine the origins of my cruel superego.

In his book *Unhinged*, Daniel Carlat writes about his very first patient, a college junior named Dave, who arrived on a psychiatric unit after taking an overdose of Tylenol and was put on suicide watch. It was 1990 and Carlat was in medical school, doing his fourth-year rotation in psychiatry. Dave explained that he became depressed when he and his girlfriend broke up—a normal sort of event that Carlat could identify with. But when Carlat asked Dave why he felt so bad about the breakup, and why he felt suicidal, Dave replied in words that I myself had spoken. He said that it was his fault: "I thought I loved her, but I don't think I can love anyone. I don't deserve anything. I don't deserve to live." When Carlat pressed him to explain what he could have done that would explain his guilt, "Dave continued to simply declare that he was a 'bad' person." He was on a tricyclic antidepressant and was soon found to be hoarding his pills in order to make another suicide attempt. The attending physician suggested ECT, which Dave refused. They made sure he swallowed his pills and put him on Haldol, an antipsychotic, because his guilt was so extreme that it qualified as psychosis. (I too was put on Haldol about two weeks into my ECT treatment, and for the same reason.) Dave did not improve, and didn't respond to psychotherapy. When Carlat left the unit after his six-week rotation, Dave was still there, "on round-the-clock suicide checks." Although the care Dave received was conscientious and compassionate, "We were very frustrated with our inability to do much more than provide a safe place for him," Carlat writes. "For some patients, the best we can do is to keep them alive and hope that something changes within them to ease their suffering." Dave's case brought home to Carlat the central challenge of the profession he was entering: he realized that "the underlying science of psychiatry was in a shockingly primitive state in comparison with the rest of medicine." Because the neurobiological processes causing mood disorders are poorly understood, treatments can't precisely target the underlying dysfunction. The illnesses remit and recur or linger chronically, and can be managed but not cured.

Carlat doesn't mention that Dave's symptoms are clearly those of melancholia, nor is the word mentioned in his book, a critique of his profession's move toward fifteen-minute psychopharmacology consultations, away from the intensive knowledge of patients that the earlier psychodynamic model had provided. Carlat's psychiatric training began in the early 1990s, after the paradigm had shifted, and about a decade after that of Dr. Young. Neither of them uses the word "melancholia," although their education must have made them aware of its symptoms and dangers. People hospitalized for depression are usually there because their suicidal urges need to be addressed in a safe environment, and the practical management of symptoms from day to day is, I presume, of far greater importance to doctors than diagnostic terminology. It's also likely that in the world of the *DSM-III*'s major depressive disorder, the word no longer mattered to them.

Does it matter what we call someone's illness, so long as that person receives compassionate care and the best possible treatment? I don't know whether the fact that the word doesn't appear in my chart after the first day has any relation to the grievous lapse in care that took place. But I believe it does matter that melancholia has been hidden from view in the public mind, and perhaps even in the medical mind, under the name of major depression. It matters that a fairly uncommon and dangerous syndrome shares a name with a common condition—depression—that in many people is not a state of illness.

Like Timothy Rogers and other Christian writers, Robert Burton assumed that melancholia will always be with us because illness and suffering are the lot of human beings since the fall of Adam and Eve. Indeed, as a first cause of the illness Burton offers, bluntly, "God." Our own skeptical and scientific age doesn't accept this proposition, and we have treatments that ease, but do not cure, melancholic depression. And in the out-moded belief that all this spiritual suffering comes down to out-of-balance neurotransmitters in the brain, we have pills that promise to fix that. But they don't—not completely. Research in mood disorders is moving to molecular biology and genetics, and there is reason to hope that in time Burton will be proven wrong. But it's unlikely that will be soon.

3

How to Save a Life

Few who have seen Milos Forman's film *One Flew Over the Cuckoo's Nest* are likely to forget the scene in which its hero, Randle McMurphy, undergoes shock treatment. As a spokesman for England's Royal College of Psychiatrists ruefully put it, the film "did for ECT what *Jaws* did for sharks." ECT—electroconvulsive therapy—is what the medical profession calls shock treatment. Handcuffed and waiting on a bench with his friend Chief Bromton, McMurphy is summoned into a treatment room by a white-capped nurse. He looks around, curious but wary, as a doctor's voice says, "This won't hurt and it will be over in just a minute." A nurse inserts an improbably large wooden object into his mouth—"to keep you from biting your tongue," she explains—and places what looks like a set of cotton-covered headphones on his temples. Six young men, neatly dressed in white shirts and bow ties, hold him down as the doctor turns a knob on a machine. Then the camera focuses on McMurphy's face as electricity surges through his brain and his entire body begins to convulse. He gasps and struggles to breathe as the nurse holds the crown of his head and his chin together to keep the enormous bit in his mouth, his body arches and shudders, the three assistants on each side press down on his thrashing legs, hips, and shoulders. The only sympathetic presence in this frightening clinical scene is McMurphy, whose character is brought to life by Jack Nicholson in one of the most memorable performances of his career. Since the camera refuses to look away, we watch the simulated effects of a grand mal seizure on a human body for thirty slow seconds.

Forman's film was greeted with critical and popular acclaim when it premiered in 1975, and went on to win the five major Academy Awards. It has terrified many a prospective inmate of a psychiatric institution ever since. Shot on location at the Oregon State Hospital with patients and staff as extras, the film's slippage between patient and prisoner is deliberate. Like Ken Kesey's 1962 novel on which it is based, the film is an antipsychiatry and anti-authoritarian polemic, and portrays the men on the ward as prisoners of a repressive social machine. They are all in some way deviant, and they will be held until they become the conformist, emasculated, deadened individuals that American society demands. McMurphy is a gambler, a Korean War veteran (with a dishonorable discharge for insubordination), and an all-around hell-raiser who has gotten into trouble with the law yet again, this time for statutory rape. He decides to avoid the hard labor of a prison farm by pretending to be psychotic. "If it gets me outta those damned pea fields," he says, "I'll be whatever their little heart desires, be it psychopath or mad dog or werewolf." He moves into the psychiatric hospital and becomes the rebel-hero who urges the broken men of

the ward to rise up against the sadistic and man-hating Nurse
Ratched, called "Big Nurse" by her patients.

Because McMurphy has challenged her regime in outra-
geous ways, Big Nurse has a plan in store for him: "The Shock
Shop, Mr. McMurphy, might be said to do the work of the
sleeping pill, the electric chair and the torture rack. It's a clever
little procedure, simple, quick, nearly painless it happens so
fast, but no one ever wants another one. Ever." The Shock Shop
is the threat that ensures compliance. Chief Bromden describes
how a character named Ruckly looks upon returning from "that
filthy brain-murdering room": "You can see by his eyes how
they burned him out over there; his eyes are all smoked up and
gray and deserted inside like blown fuses." McMurphy emerges
from the Shock Shop unbroken, much to the amazement of his
weaker comrades. He jokes that his electrified body can only
enhance his sexual magnetism: "When I get out of here the
first woman that takes on ol' Red McMurphy the 10,000 watt
psychopath, she's gonna light up like a pinball machine and
pay off in silver dollars!" But after he nearly strangles her to
death, Nurse Ratched destroys McMurphy with the deadliest
weapon in her arsenal: a lobotomy. In an off-camera surgical
procedure that the novel refers to as a "frontal lobe castration,"
the nerves to the frontal lobes of his brain are severed. We see
him afterwards, head lolling, eyes vacant, two incision marks
on his forehead. Chief recognizes that his friend is gone, though
his body is still living. He suffocates McMurphy with a pil-
low, throws a massive marble hydrotherapy machine through
a window, and makes his escape from the hospital. In the film,
shock treatment and lobotomy are two instruments of the same
soul-killing institutional practice. In reality, lobotomy *was* an
irreversible mutilation of the brain's frontal lobes, while ECT

is often a life-saving intervention in the worst cases of drug-resistant depression, especially when the threat of suicide makes the situation urgent.

Kesey's novel was inspired by his experience as a night-shift aide at the Veteran's Hospital in Menlo Park, California, where he had volunteered to test the effects of hallucinogenic drugs. He didn't know that in doing so he was contributing to a clandestine CIA program called MK Ultra, whose purpose was to find drugs and mind-control techniques that could be useful in interrogation. The novel's central ideas—that people labeled with mental illness were just people who didn't or couldn't conform, and that those who did submit to psychiatric treatment were betraying their authentic selves—did not originate with Kesey. Several books of the early 1960s presented challenges to psychiatric diagnosis, treatment, and confinement, including *The Myth of Mental Illness*, by the Hungarian émigré psychiatrist Thomas Szasz; *The Divided Self*, by the Scottish psychiatrist R. D. Laing; and *Asylums* and *Stigma*, both by the Canadian sociologist Erving Goffman. The works of Szasz, in particular, provided the intellectual basis for a patients' rights movement. In the San Francisco Bay Area, a group of activists, including people calling themselves survivors of psychiatric commitment, issued a quarterly journal called *Madness Network News*, printing testimonies from people who had been denied "even the most basic aspects of personal choice, self-determination and human rights." One issue included an article called "Tom Szasz, Freedom Fighter," and another included one called "R. D. Laing, Superstar." Laing's position on insanity was that it was a rational response to an insane world. Other articles focused on the horrors of shock treatment. In 1982 the residents of Berkeley, California, voted to criminalize ECT, although the ban was soon overturned.

As a psychiatrist who had turned against his profession
while holding a tenured position at SUNY Upstate Medical
University from 1956 until 1990, Szasz became a leading voice
in the American antipsychiatry movement. He taught psychiatry, he said, as an atheist would teach theology. In 1969 he
joined forces with the Church of Scientology to create the Citizen's Commission for Human Rights, which still commands
a highly visible position on the Internet to oppose psychiatric
treatment of all kinds. Szasz's attacks came at a bad time for
psychiatry. His central claim, that there was no such thing as
mental illness, dovetailed with an ongoing problem for the profession: the lack of clear physiological evidence for the psychiatric illnesses. Szasz argued in book after book that mental illness
cannot exist because the mind is not a physical organ. His final
book argues against psychiatric treatment for the prevention of
suicide because to end one's life is a voluntary act, the right of
every human being. He refused to countenance the idea that
mental illnesses result from pathology of the brain and nervous system, and his primary concern was to oppose diagnostic labeling, coercion, and confinement by what he called "the
therapeutic state."

Many viewers of Forman's film and readers of Kesey's novel
would have been aware that in real life, the mentally ill were
sometimes abused instead of helped. *One Flew Over the Cuckoo's Nest* raised an undeniable truth: shock treatment had been
used as a form of punishment in state hospitals that warehoused helpless mentally ill patients. ECT was introduced to
the seven-thousand-bed Georgia State Sanatorium in 1942,
where it was called "the Georgia Power cocktail" by patients
and staff. Peter Cranford, who worked as a psychologist there,
remembered, "The words 'punish' and 'shock treatment' were

often synonymous to the disturbed." Abuse by attendants was common in large institutions like this one, where the doctor-patient ratio was less than one to one hundred. In a 1985 report for the National Institutes of Health, the medical historian David Rothman wrote, "ECT stands practically alone among the medical/surgical interventions in that misuse was not the goal of curing but of controlling the patients for the benefits of the hospital staff." So it is with McMurphy and the men on the ward; shock and other therapies are used solely to intimidate or punish.

Szasz was delighted that *One Flew Over the Cuckoo's Nest* aligned with his philosophical position. He even wrote a letter to Kesey asking permission to quote from the novel, which he commended as a "tremendous achievement." Kesey replied,

> Mr. Szasz: I took your letter to my next door neighbor, who is getting his Doctorate in Psychology, and he was much impressed: "Oh, man, Szasz? Yeah. This book of his [*The Myth of Mental Illness*] is the Catch 22 of the syke world!" Just to give you some idea of your impact in these distant parts. Certainly you may quote my book. I would consider it an honor.

Kesey explained to Szasz that he wrote the entire novel while working night shifts at the VA hospital, except for the shock treatment scene: "I did that scene after, the day after, in fact, I took a treatment with an apparatus that a friend of mine had rigged up for me." It's unclear why Kesey felt the need to have a friend give him a makeshift treatment, but the detail under-scores just how bold he could be in experimenting on him-self. Elsewhere Kesey wrote, "Peyote . . . inspired my chief narrator"—the paranoid, visionary Chief Bromden—"because it was after choking down eight of the little cactus plants that I wrote the first three pages." In a 1990 interview, Kesey speculated on the harm he might have done himself in his long love affair with hallucinogens: "If I could go back in time and trade in certain experiences I've had for the brain cells presumably burned up, it would be a tough decision."

Psychiatrists who tried to recommend ECT to frightened patients in the wake of *One Flew Over the Cuckoo's Nest* faced the task of convincing them that neither the film nor the novel conveyed an accurate representation of the treatment. The audiences flocking to see *Cuckoo's Nest* in 1975 witnessed a scene of shock treatment given without the anesthesia and the muscle relaxant that were both used routinely from the mid-1950s onward, and many viewers assumed that it was always given that way. These modifications had been put into use as soon as they became available, because when ECT was given without muscle relaxant, compression fractures of the patient's vertebrae sometimes resulted from the body's violent movement during the seizure. These could occur even when the patient was lying on a padded table and held down by leather restraints.

Sylvia Plath's autobiographical novel *The Bell Jar* draws on her experience of a suicidal depression in the summer of 1953 and includes a memorable passage in which the protagonist, Esther Greenwood, receives shock treatment without being anesthetized: "Then something bent down and took hold of me and shook me like the end of the world. Whee-ee-ee-ee-ee, it shrilled, through an air crackling with blue light, and with each flash a great jolt drubbed me till I thought my bones would break and the sap fly out of me like a split plant. I wondered what terrible thing it was that I had done." The inexperienced young psychiatrist to whom Plath's family doctor had sent her gave her ECT as an outpatient, without anesthesia and without her informed consent. Gordon Lameyer, Plath's boyfriend at the time, wrote, "Sylvia felt so traumatized . . . that she felt, not so irrationally, as if she were being electrocuted for some unknown crime." From the novel's opening sentence, Esther is preoccupied with the imminent execution of Julius and Ethel Rosenberg— "It was a queer, sultry summer, the summer they electrocuted the Rosenbergs"—and Esther's traumatic experience of ECT blurs the distinction between electrocution and shock treatment.

The vivid account in *The Bell Jar*, with its great jolts and crackling blue light, is often cited on anti-ECT websites, useful in its description of the treatment as a form of electrical torture. But Plath's novel also includes a rarely cited fictional reference to the much more successful round of ECT that she received at McLean Hospital later the same year, after which she returned to complete her final year at Smith College: "All the heat and fear had purged itself. I felt surprisingly at peace. The bell jar hung suspended a few feet above my head. I was open to the circulating air." While this sense of relief has been felt and recorded by many people who have emerged from suicidal depression after just a few ECT sessions, the public perception of shock treatment continues to be fed by images in film and on television that are jarringly at odds with the experience of people who have been helped by it.

Contrast Plath's description or the scene of McMurphy's torment with what ECT looks like when given with the muscle relaxant, anesthesia, and oxygen that are now standard components of the procedure. Here psychiatrist Daniel Carlat describes what happens once these preparations are in place for his patient Michael, who is unconscious:

"Treatment!" I called out, and pushed the red button.

After one or two seconds the machine had drawn the necessary voltage and let out a loud *beeeeeeep,* signaling that current was now flowing. Michael's jaw clenched, and I soon noticed a very fine tremor of his right arm. I looked at the brain wave tracing to confirm that he was having a seizure, and indeed, Michael's brain waves [were] indicating rhythmic activity of large swaths of the brain—in other words—a seizure.

Emphasizing the ordinary medical aspect of modern-day shock treatment, one practitioner said, "We like to keep it as boring as possible." A patient concurred: "It is a nonentity, a nothing. You go to sleep, and when you wake up, it is all over. It is easier to take than going to the dentist." The undramatic nature of present-day ECT can be seen on YouTube in short explanatory videos posted by people who hope to defuse the stigma surrounding the treatment. Since the seizure is notable only by the slight tremor, there is almost nothing to see, which is probably why movies and television dramas don't represent it realistically.

This was brought home in the popular television series *Homeland,* whose bipolar heroine, Carrie Mathison, looks like she is undergoing something dreadful when, in the finale of the first season, she lies on an ECT treatment table and, once the anesthetist has inserted the IV drip, begins counting backwards from one hundred. Suddenly she awakens, her descent into unconsciousness having been interrupted by the memory of a critical plot detail, and she fears she will forget it. Then she lapses into sleep once again, but as the doctor's latex-gloved hands place the electrodes on her temples and the machine releases its electrical pulse, Carrie's whole face clenches as if she is suffering and her body shudders violently until the screen blacks out for a season-ending cliffhanger. While one of the show's producers, whose sister has bipolar disorder, has said that she wanted to show the illness realistically, the scene of Carrie's treatment bends to the drama's demands, showing ECT as more nightmarish than benign.

～

MELODRAMATIC SCENES of shock treatment like the one in *Homeland* continue to appear in television and in movies, and elicit in audiences a *frisson* of horror that can be traced back to Mary Wollstonecraft Shelley's 1818 gothic thriller *Frankenstein*. Shelley's novel reflects popular interest in the relatively new science of electricity. It also features both electricity and a convulsion, just as ECT does. In Shelley's tale, the scientist Victor Frankenstein hopes that an electrical charge will "infuse a spark of being" into a human-like form he has made from body parts stolen from graveyards. The monster's moment of awakening, narrated by his creator, is marked by a dramatic convulsion: "It was already one in the morning; the rain pattered dismally against the panes, and my candle was nearly burnt out, when, by the glimmer of the half-extinguished light, I saw the dull yellow eye of the creature open; it breathed hard, and a convulsive motion agitated its limbs."

At the time, people were fascinated with the question of whether the dead could be reanimated. Shelley took her inspiration from Giovanni Aldini, who carried out experiments based on the discovery in 1791 by his uncle, Luigi Galvani, that muscles and nerves communicated through electrical signals. Seeking a way to revive those who had been drowned or asphyxiated, Aldini conducted electrical experiments in 1803 in London's

Newgate Prison on the body of a man who had been hanged for the murder of his wife and child. During Aldini's macabre public demonstration, onlookers reported that "Forster's eye opened, his right hand was raised and clenched, and his legs moved." To some, it appeared that the dead man "was on the eve of being restored to life." Aldini also reported some success with the trial of his electrical apparatus on the head of a farmer suffering from "melancholy madness"—a use for electrical shocks that had been suggested by Benjamin Franklin and his friend the Dutch physician Jan Ingenhousz. ECT is a later refinement of these early hunches that electricity could have an enlivening effect. If severe depression is a kind of living death, ECT *can* return the dead to life. After his first session of shock treatment, the talk show host Dick Cavett sat up in his hospital bed when his wife walked into his room and said to her, "Look who's back among the living."

Aldini, with his uncanny effects upon the body of a murderer, was just one of several scientists who contributed to the rapid development of electrotherapy in the nineteenth century. Electrical stimulation became a standard treatment in private clinics for those suffering from nervous illnesses, and continues today in such technologies as the pacemaker, cardiac defibrillation, and ECT. Yet ECT alone among these medical innovations retains an aura of stigma. It is curious that ECT provokes such horror while television shows like *ER* and *Grey's Anatomy* routinely feature the dramatic effect of electricity when applied to a heart in cardiac arrest. We've all seen it again and again: a doctor places the paddles on the patient's chest and calls "Clear!" The patient's body visibly receives the jolt, while everyone glances anxiously at the monitor for the return of the regular waves of the heartbeat. First used during an open-heart surgery in 1947 by Claude Beck, defibrillation can restore a stopped or arrhythmic heart to its normal rhythm. The amount of current sent through the heart is much greater than what is sent through the brain in ECT. Nonetheless, a jolt of electricity comes across as heroic and lifesaving when used in a medical emergency room—at least in the movies and on TV—and no one questions the need for it.

The two treatments were not always viewed in such opposite ways. In 1952, *Time* and *Newsweek* underscored that the new technology used to shock the heart was essentially the same as the one already in use for the brain: "Electric shock, which has brought back to sanity hundreds of bewildered psychotics, has saved the life of a pretty Chicago nurse whose heart had stopped beating." But it is not precisely true that the technologies are alike. ECT uses electricity to induce a therapeutic brain seizure, and it is the seizure, not the shock, that is the crucial element (thus, although colloquially useful, the term "shock treatment" is inaccurate).

Several plausible theories have emerged as to how ECT may work. It appears that severe depression results from a lack of connectivity in some areas of the brain and hyper-connectivity in others, particularly in an area called the left dorsolateral prefrontal cortex (DLPFC). ECT decreases connectivity in the DLPFC, which is associated with negative emotion. Bilateral seizures may address an imbalance of connectivity across the brain's two hemispheres. ECT has been found to trigger a surge of hormones that alleviates the dysfunction along the HPA axis and halts the overproduction of cortisol. In animal studies, seizures enhance neurogenesis—the generation of new neurons—in the hippocampus.

The history of what would emerge as electroconvulsive

therapy, like so many advances in medicine, can make for disturbing reading. During the first half of the twentieth century, scientists made dramatic experiments on the bodies of the mentally ill as they tried to heal disordered minds. Some of these methods were based on the observations of doctors over the centuries that high fevers, seizures, and even comas could bring about positive changes. In 1917 Julius Wagner-Jauregg injected malaria-infected blood into a patient suffering from dementia paralytica, a condition caused by syphilis, to bring on a high fever. Wagner-Jauregg won the Nobel Prize for medicine in 1927, despite the fact that his treatment killed 15 percent of his patients.

During the 1930s, Manfred Sakel experimented with rendering patients comatose with overdoses of insulin, sending their bodies into insulin shock and often into seizures as well. Sakel would revive them with an injection of glucose, repeating the process daily for weeks. Both coma and seizure appeared to have a calming effect on schizophrenics, sometimes returning a psychotic patient to a state of lucidity. The treatment was widely used through the 1940s and '50s before it was finally acknowledged that insulin shock and glucose injections were doing more harm than good. An American psychiatrist remarked on his experience of the insulin treatment ward, "With all these people—tossing, moaning, twitching, shouting, grasping—I felt as though I were in the midst of Hell as drawn by Gustave Doré for Dante's *Divine Comedy*."

Psychiatry's enthusiastic adoption of therapies later proven to have no benefit is no different from what has happened in other branches of medicine. Innovation is born from the desire to find a cure. Until the mid-twentieth century when effective antipsychotic and antidepressant drugs became available, psychiatrists were the helpless caretakers of patients who were psychotic, catatonic, or immobilized by profound depression, and who spent years wasting away in asylums. The resistance of the major mental illnesses to any treatment at all made doctors willing to use desperate measures to bring about even temporary improvement. Only in light of what historian of psychiatry Edward Shorter has called "half a century of nihilistic hopelessness" do experiments with fever, coma, and seizures make sense as bold, if dangerous, measures.

꒰ꪆ꒱

IN 1932, A YOUNG NEUROPSYCHIATRIST named Ladislas Meduna sat before a microscope in Budapest, comparing fine slices from the postmortem brains of epileptics and schizophrenics under a microscope. Meduna was a pathologist by training, but he was soon to find himself attending patients in a psychiatric clinic. Looking through his microscope, he noticed a striking contrast in the respective density and scarcity of glial cells, which form connective and insulating tissue for neurons. Because epilepsy appeared to be uncommon in schizophrenics, doctors had long suspected a biological antagonism between epilepsy and schizophrenia, and hence between seizures and psychosis. As early as the sixteenth century, the Swiss physician Paracelsus had used camphor to produce epileptic convulsions in so-called lunatics. Working from the antagonism hypothesis, two Hungarian doctors that Meduna knew had recently tried injecting epileptics with the blood of psychotic patients, with no success. Reversing that logic, Meduna wanted to find a safe way to induce seizures in schizophrenics, and began his experiments using camphor injections in guinea pigs.

Since October of 1930, a thirty-three-year-old electrician

whose name was Zoltan L. had been living in the Royal Hungarian State Psychiatric Institute where Meduna was working. Zoltan was brought to the hospital because he had been trying to strangle his wife, although he didn't remember having done so. His diagnosis on admission was schizophrenia, and his preoccupations centered upon jealousy of his wife and his doubt that he was the father of their young daughter. He sometimes heard voices coming from his stomach, he sometimes perceived people passing in front of his face, and sometimes animals "sneaking" in front of his feet. Four weeks before his admission he had asked his wife for some poison so that he could kill himself. After his admission, during which time he was mute and motionless, the doctors treated him for several months with opium, and later for a couple of weeks with strychnine, which was then used as a stimulant. Neither approach had the desired effect.

On January 23, 1934, Meduna was ready to try inducing a seizure in a patient. He chose Zoltan, who since his admission over three years earlier had stopped eating, was fed through a tube, and was in a continuously catatonic state. Before an audience of his colleagues, Meduna injected Zoltan with a solution of camphor and oil and, according to Meduna's autobiography, "after forty-five minutes of anxious and fearful waiting the patient suddenly had a classical epileptic attack that lasted sixty seconds." As Zoltan returned to consciousness, Meduna nearly collapsed in anxiety: "My body began to tremble, a profuse sweat almost drenched me, and, as I later heard, my face was ash gray." At the time, physicians could experiment on disabled patients without their permission, so it's reassuring to know that Meduna was himself frightened during the seizure, and relieved that Zoltan was apparently unharmed.

Each injection Zoltan received resulted, after a long delay, in a seizure. But there was no change in his condition until the fifth when, according to Meduna, "He spontaneously arises from bed, is lively, and asks for something to eat. . . . He is interested in everything going on about him, asks about his illness and realizes he has been sick. He asks how long he has been in the hospital, and when we tell him that he has already been there four years he cannot believe it." Meduna's autobiography presents Zoltan's case as an unqualified success, and punctuates it with a memorable anecdote. When one morning Meduna asked the nurse how his patient was doing, she replied, "We had quite a time with him. He escaped last night from the institution, went home and found out that the 'cousin' living with his wife was not a relation at all but a lover of his wife." After beating his wife's lover and then beating his wife, Zoltan returned to the hospital, saying he preferred living there rather than in the "crazy world." Meduna's autobiography then closes the case of Zoltan: "From then on I considered this patient cured, and he remained well at the time I left Europe in 1939."

Medical historians have accepted this version of events, with Zoltan miraculously well, the first patient to prove the success of Meduna's innovative convulsive treatment. When he published the results of his trial in a medical journal, Meduna reported that of twenty-six patients, thirteen had remarkably improved or recovered. By 1938, his technique for the induction of seizures was adopted in European and American psychiatric hospitals, and Meduna himself emigrated to America in 1939, taking a position at Loyola University in Chicago.

While doctors adopted the treatment enthusiastically, it was harrowing for patients. Early on, Meduna had switched from camphor to a faster acting chemical agent called metrazol, but even then a delay of about a minute remained between the injection and the onset of the seizure, a delay filled with extreme anxiety for the patient. American psychiatrist Solomon Katzenelbogen reported in 1940, when metrazol convulsive therapy was being used for schizophrenia, mania, depression, and even alcoholism, that "while the patients' statements obviously reflect some of the content of their basic psychotic conditions, they contain nevertheless one common and outstanding feature, namely, the feeling of being tortured, and of intense fear of imminent death."

And what became of Zoltan? It seems odd that a fully recovered patient would be allowed to continue living in a state institution. Recently, several Hungarian scholars unearthed Meduna's case notes in the archives of the Institute, which closed in 2007. They found that Meduna treated Zoltan over a longer period than had been thought, from 1934 through 1937, and that after his brief remission in 1934, Zoltan was never well and could never be discharged. He died in the Institute in 1945.

IN 1938, JUST FOUR YEARS AFTER Zoltan was subjected to Meduna's convulsive therapy in Budapest, the Italian police picked up a man who had been wandering in Rome's train station. He couldn't tell them his name, nor where he lived. Since the man was speaking incoherently and seemed to be hallucinating, the police took him to the university's psychiatric clinic. It happened that the head of the clinic was Ugo Cerletti, who had been working for several years to develop a method of using electricity to induce seizures. A neuropsychiatrist born in 1877, Cerletti had studied with some of the leading figures in biological psychiatry, including Emil Kraepelin and Alois Alzheimer.

In the early 1930s, Cerletti began investigating what happened to the brain during epileptic seizures, based on an observation that the mood of epileptic patients who were also depressed seemed to improve after a period of frequent convulsions.

Cerletti was sensitive to the moral revulsion people would feel about his research, and wrote that "the idea of submitting a man to convulsant electric discharges was considered as utopian, barbaric, and dangerous; in everyone's mind was the specter of the electric chair." Nonetheless, he proceeded. For two years Cerletti and his assistants experimented with inducing seizures in dogs, and found that by placing the electrodes on the temples, they could induce convulsions without killing the animal. Seeking a safe method to deliver electrical current to a human brain, they carried out further experiments at Rome's slaughterhouse, where pigs were stunned with electricity before being killed.

Cerletti's colleague Lucio Bini built a small box that would transmit the current. The challenge was to find the proper variables of voltage and duration that were strong enough to cause a seizure, and not so strong as to cause death. Once they determined that the gap between a seizure-inducing dose and a lethal dose of electricity was wide, they felt it would be safe to take their experiment to the next level. The police had just unwittingly delivered them their first human subject. At the clinic, the man from the railway station had been diagnosed with schizophrenia. Cerletti wrote, "He expressed himself exclusively in an incomprehensible gibberish made up of odd neologisms and, since his arrival from Milan by train without a ticket, not a thing had been ascertainable about his identity." One of Cerletti's assistants, Ferdinando Accornero, described the patient as "unemotional, living passively, like a tree that does not give fruit." He felt that the man's mind "had completely unraveled," and there was little hope of his recovery.

On the eleventh of April, they were ready to proceed. They put a gauze-covered rubber tube between the man's teeth and placed electrodes, moistened with saline solution, on his temples. Bini flicked the switch, and 80 volts of current ran for a quarter of a second. The man's body jumped, and he cried out. With the next pulse, he sat up and began to sing a bawdy popular song. Another slightly longer pulse still didn't produce a seizure, but the patient protested in perfectly clear Italian, "*Che cazzo fai?*" or, "What the fuck are you doing?" Cerletti was pleased that the man's speech was no longer incoherent. One more attempt, and the patient cried out that another would be deadly ("*Non una seconda! mortifera!*"). Now the doctors looked at each other nervously, fearful of proceeding. Cerletti nodded, Bini gave the pulse, and since the patient still did not have a full seizure, Cerletti ended the trial for that day, heartened that the patient was unharmed and speaking.

They tried again with this same patient nine days later (these first two trials, on two separate days, were combined in Cerletti's record to make for a more dramatic story of immediate success). This time, Bini applied enough current to send the man into a full epileptic seizure, and the doctors looked on as he violently convulsed, turned blue, and stopped breathing for forty-eight seconds. Much like Meduna during Zoltan's first seizure, they were terrified that they might kill the patient. According to Cerletti, when the seizure ended, "The patient sat up of his own accord, looked about him calmly with a vague smile, as though asking what was expected of him. I asked him, 'What has been happening to you?' He answered, with no more gibberish: 'I don't know, perhaps I have been asleep.'"

The man—his name was Enrico, as he now remembered—
received several more treatments and was discharged, "thought
and memory unimpaired," according to Cerletti, and aware that
his paranoia and hallucinations were symptoms of an illness
from which he had recovered. However, his wife wrote to Bini
nearly two years later to report that her husband's illness had
returned, and that he had been admitted to a psychiatric hospital in Milan. She asked that Bini contact the doctor there. Bini
forwarded the letter to Cerletti, but Cerletti never responded.
In this disappointing detail Bini and Cerletti seem less interested in patients than in their larger project. Having served his
purpose as the first human subject of a pathbreaking medical
technology, was Enrico now to be ignored because his relapse
would not be convenient for Cerletti to acknowledge? Like
Meduna, whose narrative of Zoltan's recovery was misleading,
Cerletti allowed the story of his first cure to go untainted by the
disease's recurrence. Cerletti was widely praised for the breakthrough therapy he called *l'elettroshock*, which was soon adopted
in European hospitals. He had proven that placing electrodes
on the patient's temples and giving an electrical stimulus produced an immediate seizure, and was far more efficient than
Meduna's slower and more painful chemical induction method,
which Cerletti's method now superseded.

Lothar Kalinowsky, a German psychiatrist who had been
present at Cerletti's first treatments in Rome, brought the
method to the New York State Psychiatric Institute in 1940.
The use of ECT in American psychiatric hospitals didn't become
widespread until the 1950s, however, for two reasons. First, psychoanalytically minded psychiatrists were opposed to it because
an intervention on the physical brain didn't support their theory
that the causes of mental illness were psychogenic. Second, the

possibility of broken bones (especially in frailer patients) was a powerful disincentive. When the muscle relaxant succinylcholine began to be used in 1952, ECT became a highly effective treatment for melancholic depression, mania, and for catatonia and depression in schizophrenia. By 1959, it was considered such an acceptable procedure that Group Health Insurance of New York City allowed coverage for up to ten electroshock treatments annually for each subscriber.

Even as the treatment was gaining widespread acceptance, the forces of antipsychiatry were gathering. Very soon, activists would work to brand ECT with the mark of shame—even to associate it with Nazi torture techniques—and to force it out of use alongside the abandoned, harmful practices of lobotomy and insulin coma treatment. In the 1960s and '70s, shock treatment came to be associated with coercion, mind control, and "all that was brutal and inhumane in clinical medicine." These negative associations were powerfully reinforced for the many people who saw *One Flew Over the Cuckoo's Nest*. In the wake of the film, one psychiatrist complained in a letter to the *British Medical Journal*: "What to me is inexplicable is that no responsible medical body appears to have made any effort to allay the fear engendered among filmgoers by the demonstration of punitive, unmodified ECT in 'One Flew Over the Cuckoo's Nest.'" Even worldly and well-educated people continue to associate ECT with mind control and punishment. The film contributed to a steep decline in the use of ECT during a period when new and effective antipsychotic and antidepressant drugs had already reduced the numbers of patients in need of the treatment. Data gathered by the National Institute of Mental Health shows that between 1975— the year *Cuckoo's Nest* premiered—and 1980, ECT use fell by a remarkable 46 percent. Still, the opposition continued.

In 1985, the National Institutes of Health held a conference on ECT. Max Fink, an early practitioner of the treatment who has long been a devoted advocate, recalled that activists interrupted his presentation, shouting, "Everybody who does electroshock should be in jail!" By this time, the NIH reported that, far from being a treatment used on nonconsenting involuntary patients, those patients that the antipsychiatry movement felt needed protecting, ECT was used overwhelmingly "for patients who are white, voluntary, and paying their way in private institutions." Seventy percent of them were women. The downward trend in the use of ECT only began to reverse itself in the late 1980s, with numbers rising through the 1990s. Today, roughly 100,000 people receive ECT annually, nearly triple the number cited for 1980 in the NIMH study, though in some parts of the country it remains under legal restriction. The lack of treatment centers and skilled psychiatrists continues to limit access for many people.

DURING THE 1980S, in the aftermath of *Cuckoo's Nest*, clinicians were reluctant to suggest ECT and more likely to face opposition by the patient's family if they did. Most medical schools, and even most psychiatry residency programs, didn't include electroconvulsive therapy in their curricula. In the hospitals that still did provide ECT, it was often used only after a long drug trial had failed.

Take, for example, a young psychiatrist in 1984, whose female patient remained suicidal after four weeks on an antidepressant. Having seen *One Flew Over the Cuckoo's Nest*, her husband was alarmed when the doctor suggested ECT. But he acquiesced when told that if he resisted, the hospital would seek a court order to overrule him. So the psychiatrist jotted down the new plan: "In this acutely suicidal patient, bilateral ECT is felt to be the modality of choice with the highest potential for rapid clinical improvement. Projected number of ECT treatments is 7–10 with hope of response evidencing around 4th-5th treatment."

I was that patient. When I first stepped into the treatment room four days after the shower incident, the use of ECT was in the trough of its long decline, while in the wider culture it carried a powerful stigma. The antipsychiatry backlash meant that progress in refining the techniques had drastically slowed. In the trial-and-error approach that my hospital record reflects, certain aspects of the treatment were not so distant from the experimental early days of Meduna and Cerletti, despite the four and a half decades that had passed.

It was late morning when one of the aides came for me, and we walked through long, polished corridors to another part of the hospital. A nurse and two doctors—an anesthesiologist and the resident who would perform the procedure—were waiting in a large tiled room. They were kind and reassuring, and although I was anxious about what was now going to happen, I felt that I had nothing to lose. I lay down on a gurney and the nurse started an IV for the anesthetic. Behind me was the ECT machine, a small electrical box with knobs and switches. The nurse placed an oxygen mask over my face and told me to count backwards from one hundred. I don't think I ever got further than ninety-seven. The next thing I remember, someone helped me off the table and walked me back up to my room.

There was more going on before and during the treatment than these few details that I recall. Bilateral ECT means that the current passes between electrodes placed on both sides of the head, and the resulting seizure affects both sides of the brain. This was considered the most effective treatment for someone in the terrible shape that I was in. It causes greater temporary cognitive deficits than unilateral placement because the current passes through the brain's speech and memory centers, but is more efficient in bringing about a recovery. The memory loss is usually temporary, though this is a matter of contention and an issue that still gives pause to potential patients. The electrodes would have been moistened with conductant gel, positioned over my temples, and held in place with a rubber headband. My pulse, blood pressure, and brain waves would have been monitored. The muscle relaxant succinylcholine was given through the IV to keep my body from moving during the seizure. Because the diaphragm is temporarily paralyzed by the muscle relaxant and cannot expand and contract the lungs, oxygen is necessary. Today, a nurse or doctor manually ventilates the lungs because the anesthetized body's inability to actively take in oxygen means the brain is not getting enough, and this increases the cognitive side effects. According to the record, they also gave me atropine. Seizures can cause a temporary interruption or slowing of the heart's rhythm, and atropine was used to prevent that. The fast-acting sedative that sent me to sleep in three seconds was pentobarbital. ECT is a simple procedure, but many precautionary measures must be taken before the pulse of electricity can be given to produce the seizure.

For the first few treatments, given the settings he marked down, it seems that the doctor was working with the variables of current and voltage in order to induce a seizure of adequate strength and duration. Seizure thresholds vary according to the patient's age, gender, medications, and other factors, and the current can be impeded by faulty contact of the electrodes and other issues. He would have needed to begin with a setting based on given parameters and modify according to the results.

ECT seizures should end without intervention, but my first two seizures lasted more than two minutes, and the doctor stopped them with additional pentobarbital. After the third treatment he seems to have arrived at the result he was seeking, and from then on most seizures were in the range of forty-five to sixty-five seconds. Because I knew he would have been familiar with the treatment protocols of the mid-1980s, I consulted ECT expert Max Fink, who told me that notations on my treatment record indicate the use of a then recently introduced machine that delivered a brief-pulse current, as opposed to the sine-wave current of earlier machines. Since the early 1980s, brief-pulse machines have replaced the earlier sine-wave ones. After the fourth session a nurse reported, "Patient talks about feeling like she is cured, that she would never hurt herself again, is in good spirits and talking to patients and staff." (I found this hospital euphemism "to hurt oneself" annoying, since I had never been interested in hurting myself. I had only been interested in dying, as quickly as possible.) Dr. Young, too, noted my brighter mood. He raised my observation status so that I was no longer being watched twenty-four hours a day.

Side effects were troublesome. In the aftermath of anesthesia came headache, nausea, and vomiting, sometimes into the next day. Another problem appears in the notes: they suspected that one of the drugs used during ECT was exacerbating a rash I'd had for several weeks. It began as a reaction to the antidepressant imipramine, which gave me hives. Although that drug had been tapered quickly before the ECT began, a very itchy, angry rash was now spreading up my back and neck. I was taken to a medical clinic in another wing of the hospital, where a blood test indicated a strong allergic reaction. They discontinued the atropine, which can cause a rash in some people, and gave me Benadryl, which eventually solved the problem. Much of the physical discomfort I had with ECT treatment resulted from complications of drug sensitivity, and these diminished with adjustments in the first couple of weeks.

Immediately after each treatment I had some loss of memory, which cleared as the hours passed. As the number of treatments mounted, the amnesia increased. This aspect of the bilateral ECT I was receiving was very strange, since it separated me from the feelings that had brought me to the hospital. On the day of the third session Dr. Young wrote, "Patient has been disoriented and confused with treatments. As yet this pseudo-dementia is transient though will become a more persistent feature with bilateral treatments. Patient showing some early improvement but unable to recognize this herself as her cognitive features of depression persist and are severe." "Pseudo-dementia" was a term then used in psychiatry to refer to problems with memory, concentration, and attention that are reversible but similar to those of dementia. Prolonged severe depression causes cognitive symptoms too, which result from a loss of neural connections in the brain. That day, I couldn't remember why I was in the hospital. A nurse wrote in my chart, "She says something happened to her although she doesn't know what it is. Confused after ECT and not really understanding what has happened to her or what she is doing here." I had forgotten about Anna's death and all that followed. I was still having melancholia's variation in mood, feeling very dark in the morning and better as the day wore on. Dr. Young commented on how this diurnal mood shift made it hard for me to hold on to feeling better: "It is difficult for her to experience subjective improvements and be confronted soon after with these renewed feelings of hopelessness."

Whatever mild improvement Dr. Young had noticed then reversed itself, and I entered a state of true depressive psychosis. He put me back on twenty-four-hour surveillance. Now I was talking freely about my terrible thoughts: "Patient had a talk with nursing staff member and explained her problem as a 'moral illness.' She feels disloyal to husband and family in wanting to kill herself. She has been suicidal for a long time and has prayed but her prayers were not answered so she feels she's evil and full of sin and can't change. She feels suicide is inevitable and has no desire to live." The next day I was begging to be allowed to go home, since I believed that there was nothing more they could do to help me. Dr. Young noted my "significant loss of reality testing," and added the antipsychotic Haldol to my regimen. The next day he wrote, "Patient currently firmly believes that she is 'not human,' is not depressed but rather 'depraved,' 'evil,' and would like 'a brain transplant.' " I could feel and express nothing but guilt, hopelessness, and self-condemnation. He increased the dose of Haldol.

How much more disastrous could things get? My parents, too, had had enough: during visiting hours one day, a nurse wrote, they were asking me to "snap out of it." It was unbearably frightening for them. Jake was bringing books from the library and reading to me about patients having the same delusional thoughts I was having. But I continued to believe, he says, that I was evil, not depressed. In psychiatry there is a term for this: I lacked "insight" into my state of mind. Like so many people in the state of what used to be called madness, I believed in the truth of my delusions.

On the day of the eighth ECT treatment Dr. Young wrote, "Patient continues to be markedly delusional—today unhappily is her birthday, and she is involved with the fact that it is Friday the 13th, as it was on her actual day of birth." Recent events had proven that I was very unlucky indeed, and I now believed it was no coincidence that I'd been born on that particular day. Dr. Young noted that the treatment plan was to be re-evaluated, since the ECT didn't appear to be making any difference in my condition. They had abandoned the antidepressant trial, and now they were considering abandoning ECT for a new medication trial combining an antipsychotic and an antidepressant. Jake remembers feeling that the doctors were "grasping at straws," since none of their proposed treatments were helping. He worried that I was having too much shock treatment: "Your short term memory got bad and you continued to be depressed. . . . The ECT continued well beyond the half dozen sessions that had been proposed. It was spring and getting quite nice out. You weren't allowed out of the ward. I wanted them to take you outside." I had been indoors continuously for over three weeks. So many aspects of our life had become very strange, and to Jake my situation seemed too much like imprisonment. The doctors then decided to press on with more ECT: "Patient continues not to show any clinical improvement with this treatment but nonetheless a full course of ECT will be pursued." They added a drug called Cogentin, which was supposed to protect against the neurological side effects, like rigidity and muscle spasms, that could result from prolonged exposure to the anti-psychotic Haldol.

Over the next ten days or so my condition continued unchanged as the number of ECT treatments mounted. The cognitive side effects of the shock treatment were taking a toll.

A nurse asked me to recite my home phone number one day, and I couldn't. I had been writing occasionally in a notebook, and Dr. Young suggested that given the increasing short-term memory loss, I record what feeling better was like so that I could read it when I felt hopeless. In one such lucid moment I wrote, "Feeling hopeful again today that there must be some way to recover from this and return to my old, better self. There is so much to live for, if only I can convince the doctors here that I'm capable of it." At other times, Dr. Young observed, I seemed detached, lethargic, "generally blunted affectively"— possibly Haldol side effects—and worried about what would happen when they finally realized that they couldn't help me.

In my guilty frame of mind, the anxiety was overwhelming. I was tormented by the seeming inevitability of suicide. I was unable to reverse the mental process that had brought me so low, and now the experts, too, were stymied in their efforts to reverse it. I worried about how my suicide would affect Jake and my family. I felt responsible for the crime of not being able to carry the burden of my own life, and thereby transferring the burden of my death to the people who loved me. My trouble seemed to me unnatural and perverse: everyone should be able to stay alive, at the very least. I couldn't see that illness was driving me to suicide, and not my own moral failing or weakness of character.

By the third week of April I'd been in the hospital for a month, and Dr. Young put in a transfer request to longer term care. He was ready to give up on ECT, noting that after the twelfth treatment I would be considered "ECT nonresponsive," and they'd have to try another plan. After the twelfth treatment, the nurse noted that I was "extremely confused, disoriented, babbling." She did neurological checks throughout the evening as these cognitive and speech disturbances gradually cleared. But cumulative exposure to bilateral treatments and a daily antipsychotic grew more and more debilitating.

Instead of switching to an antipsychotic/antidepressant combination for the next phase of treatment, they again decided to press on with ECT. Today the number of treatments in an effective sequence can range from four up to twenty or so, but because these are usually unilateral—given on the right side of the head only—or with ultrabrief pulses of current, they don't cause the degree of memory loss that I experienced. They took me off the antipsychotic and switched to an older-style ECT machine that used sine-wave current (the kind of current in wall outlets). For whatever reason, my recovery began with the use of this more primitive machine. It may be a coincidence, but within two treatments there was noticeable improvement. According to a National Institutes of Health study on ECT from 2007, the treatment I had would not now be recommended because of its heavy toll in cognitive side effects: "Sine wave stimulation, for the use of which there is no justification at this point, and bilateral electrode placement, produced the most persistent long-term deficits."

I did lose memories, but most of what I forgot I eventually remembered. Episodes from my childhood and my more recent past were inaccessible for quite a while, though after the treatments were over I had no trouble retaining new information, and I started graduate school the following year. What happened while the treatments were ongoing remains mostly a blank. My older brother visited and gave me a dress for my birthday, but when I got home I had no idea where the dress came from. Friends wrote letters I have no memory of receiving. What I do remember about the time during treatments,

I've been able to retrieve because the hospital record jogged the memory, or because I wrote it down in the notebook at the time.

The problem of memory loss remains the most contentious issue with ECT. Some people refuse treatment for fear of it, while others agree to treatment despite the chance of it. It all depends on what you're willing to lose: your memory or your life. Ernest Hemingway protested, shortly before his suicide, that shock treatment had destroyed him: "What these shock doctors don't know is about writers . . . What is the sense of ruining my head and erasing my memory, which is my capital, and putting me out of business? It was a brilliant cure but we lost the patient." Hemingway's alcoholism and his very severe depression could also have impaired his memory, but it was simpler to blame ECT. A very different perspective on ECT and writers comes from David Foster Wallace, whose friend Donald Antrim was in the depths of a suicidal depression. Antrim's doctor told him, "You're very sick, and you're very psychotic, and we can take care of you." They told him he should have ECT. Antrim was terrified, "because he believed it would mean the end of him as a writer. That his talent would be scattered. His brains scrambled. The mechanism disassembled." Wallace, having been in these circumstances himself, called Antrim at the hospital. He said, speaking writer to writer, "I'm calling to tell you that if they offer you ECT, you should do it. You'll be all right." For the great majority of people, any lingering amnesia clears as the brain heals in the months after treatment, but a small and vocal group claims that important moments in their lives—the birth of a child, a wedding, the death of a parent— are lost forever.

By the end of April, after seventeen treatments over a period of six weeks, the worst was over. The nursing notes are studded with a new, positive language: "Patient seems brighter, alert and motivated, interacting with staff and peers"; "Status raised to CS. This made her very happy"; "Patient able to concentrate long enough to play chess"; "Patient continues in great spirits, smiling and verbal"; "Patient socializing with peers. In good spirits. Affect brighter. Pleasant." Dr. Young wrote, "Affect is bright and full-range. Patient continues to have euthymic mood, punctuated with mild persistence of diurnal mood variation. Denies suicidal ideation, no longer expressing hopelessness and worthlessness, no evidence of psychotic thought process"; "Patient to receive 14th ECT today. Plan is to administer additional 2–3 more ECT treatments to consolidate response"; "Socializing appropriately with other patients. Went outside to courtyard and played volleyball." Volleyball? Chess? Great spirits? Even now I can feel the relief and happiness conveyed by these words and what they meant for me, for my family, and for my doctor, who had been expecting improvement much earlier.

Suicidal depression is difficult to treat, and I imagine it can be nearly as distressing for the doctor as for the patient. For some reason, I didn't get better as quickly as Dr. Young's optimistic projection suggested I would. I assume that psychiatrists will think it unfair of me to look back and question the technique or the experience of the resident who performed the ECT, and to wonder whether it might have been more quickly effective with another person in charge. The truth is, I just don't know whether the treatment could have, or should have, gone better at the time. Certainly it is much better for the majority of people having ECT today. The American Psychiatric Association claims that ECT can bring about a dramatic improvement in 80 to 90 percent of patients with mood disorders. The improvement is not necessarily permanent; these are relapsing and recurrent illnesses. But because of continuing stigma and fear, ECT is often not suggested until a lengthy course of medication has failed to bring relief. Some people kill themselves in this interim. In my case it's easy to recognize some of what went wrong: the belated realization that I was ill and not merely grief-stricken, the belated diagnosis and prescription of medication, the switch from medication to ECT only after a nearly lethal suicide attempt. Lithium could have been given as soon as I arrived in the hospital, since it has a proven record of reducing suicidal impulses.

Despite the discomfort and the temporary memory loss it caused, I would have ECT again without hesitation. People voluntarily undergo much more invasive and damaging medical interventions to save or to prolong their lives—chemotherapy, radiation, open-heart surgery, blood transfusions, bone marrow transplants—and speak freely about those experiences, but continue to think about cancer and heart disease differently from mood disorders that can be equally deadly. In telling my own less than ideal story thirty years after the fact, I don't want to discourage anyone from having this potentially life-saving treatment. What was difficult in my experience would now be unusual because the treatment protocol has improved over the years to greatly reduce the side effects. And my situation was extreme not only because of the perilous condition of my mind, but because my body was already hypersensitive and aggravated by drug allergies.

But now ECT was behind me. The serious work of returning to life could begin.

4

The Paradise of Bedlams

On the morning of August 8, 1894, a long line of horse-drawn carriages raised the summer dust on Broadway, turned right at the porter's lodge at 115th Street, and entered the spacious grounds of the Bloomingdale Insane Asylum. In front of West Hall, a large brownstone building that was home to the female patients, thirty women of varying ages stood waiting, dressed in traveling clothes. With them stood Dr. Samuel Lyon, the superintendent of the asylum, along with the physician in charge of women and several attendants.

Some of these patients had lived in the Bloomingdale Asylum for many years (one had been there for nearly half a century), others for only a few months. The asylum's property, thirty-eight acres of prime real estate, had been sold. After seventy-three years on Manhattan's West Side, the asylum was moving twenty miles north to the village of White Plains in Westchester County. Dr. Lyons had chosen the most "tractable" and cooperative patients for this first trial day of the exodus. In all, some three hundred patients suffering from a variety of illnesses including mania, melancholia, dementia, and alcoholism, had to be moved.

Under the watchful eyes of the two doctors, the attendants helped their charges into the carriages. The drivers set out to the northeast, crossed the Harlem River into the Bronx, and pulled up next to the stone railway station at Mott Haven. There, private cars had been added to the train especially for the asylum's use, and when all the women were seated the attendants locked the doors. In less than an hour they arrived at the White Plains station, the patients entered closed horse-drawn carriages once again, and were driven to the new asylum buildings where the staff waited to settle them into their assigned rooms. For those patients likely to be troubled by unfamiliar surroundings, the furniture from their old rooms had been moved into place.

Dr. Lyons returned to the city to prepare for the following morning, when the next group of patients would be moved. The process continued through August and September. More elaborate plans had been made for special cases: ambulances would transport bedridden patients; those who were agitated, violent, or unpredictable had to be taken separately, accompanied by strong guards. Wealthy patients, whose families paid for special treatment, could travel with their private attendants apart from the group. The very last patients to go, because their new residence was still incomplete, were the dozen or so men who lived with their servants in a handsome brick house at the Bloomingdale Asylum called Macy Villa. The villa, only recently finished, was built to accommodate patients who wished to live in the style they had known before coming to the asylum. These patients would be moving into a new building much like it, which would be connected by an underground passage to the residence of Dr. Lyons.

The transfer of a major urban institution to a new location was a task of serious magnitude. Planning had taken five years, construction had taken two more. By October the move was complete, and the new asylum held an open house. Journalists arrived, along with the curious public, the families of patients, and the board members of the Society of the New York Hospital, whose funding had been necessary to the whole process. The next day, under the headline "New Home for the Insane," *The New York Times* reported that "Everything was found in the best of order, and the buildings and their admirable arrangement were praised by everyone." The thirteen redbrick buildings were designed with secure access to one another as well as to sunlight and fresh air: "This new Bloomingdale is of the class called pavilion hospitals . . . which afford convenient and protected access to all parts of the wards from every other ward." The connecting corridors looked out onto the grounds so that patients, "in being transferred from one section to another, will get as much change of view as possible to break the monotony of their daily routine." A ward for suicidal cases was designed so that the staff could see all patients at all times.

A great deal of thought had gone into creating a pleasing social atmosphere for both patients and staff, who would spend time together in the dining rooms and in the living areas located in the central part of each hall. The asylum's therapeutic effect depended in part upon the patient feeling comfortable in the community. Each patient's day would be structured with activities and exercise, and the facilities, which included a theater, a library, and a social amusement hall, would provide many choices. The buildings would amply accommodate over four hundred patients, as well as the doctors and staff who would live there. Like the asylum it replaced, the new Bloomingdale had a fine view. It stood on the ground occupied formerly by a three-hundred-acre hilltop farm, and this generous acreage, now reduced by a third, provides a buffer for its proximity to the busy Cross-Westchester Expressway. The firm of Frederick Law Olmsted created a landscape design that included gardens, a golf course, and tennis courts.

Almost ninety years on from the August morning when the patients first set out for White Plains, I was allowed access to that inviting outdoor space after eight weeks of confinement indoors, once shock treatment had returned me to something like my former self. It was early May, and the grounds were vivid with bright green lawns and flowering trees. The formerly rural asylum stood at the edge of the busy White Plains business district, and traffic zipped along the tall fence at the property's limit. While the surrounding countryside had disappeared, other aspects of the 1894 asylum were unchanged. My long walks with one of the staff to and from the shock treatment room in another building had taken me along those connecting ground floor corridors mentioned by the *Times* reporter, giving a view to the outdoors along the way. I remember the calm of those corridors, strangely quiet and empty, and their gleaming, immaculate floors. At the time, I vaguely knew that this was supposed to be a very good hospital, but I didn't know of its importance as one of the first institutions in America to provide care for the mentally ill.

Everywhere, the hospital's grounds revealed traces of its long history, although modern buildings had been added and old spaces adapted to new therapeutic uses when their original uses proved outdated. The tiled surroundings I noticed in the shock

treatment room suggest that the room was designed for hydrotherapy, where agitated patients were wrapped in wet sheets or
restrained for hours in supposedly calming baths. Psychotropic
drugs, ECT, and psychotherapy now took the place of hydrotherapy, insulin coma treatment, and other superseded treatments
of the asylum's earlier decades. Some of the illnesses had new
names: bipolar disorder, major depression, obsessive-compulsive
disorder. Gone were the terminal patients with general paresis;
with the advent of penicillin, syphilis was no longer a cause
of insanity and death. And the asylum had been renamed: in
becoming the Bloomingdale Hospital for Diseases of the Mind
in 1910 and then New York Hospital—Westchester Division
in 1936, the former Bloomingdale Asylum for the Insane had,
nominally at least, sloughed off the stigma of insanity.

We who were patients there in the mid-1980s felt that
stigma nonetheless. Cultural attitudes are pervasive, and we
tend to be unconscious of having absorbed them. Without
knowing anyone who had been in a psychiatric hospital, I had
resisted my psychiatrist's urging that I sign myself in, for fear
of what the words "mental patient" would do to my sense of
self and my future prospects. When I was a child we would
occasionally drive past the notorious Byberry state hospital in
Philadelphia, and a shiver of morbid curiosity ran through us
each time because our mother had told us that the best man at
her parent's wedding—a man we knew from the photograph,
dressed in 1920s finery—had been confined there. I was much
luckier than he, with a private room in a private hospital. Looking back on the impact of having lived for three months in a
former asylum I can see that the worst time of my life had some
redeeming aspects because of where I spent that time.

Historically, for both good reasons and bad, the mentally

ill were kept apart from society. The belief that the insane required not a space for imprisonment but one of sanctuary, a protected place for recovery in which nature would play a healing role, only emerged in the nineteenth century. My experience of a fairly extended stay has more in common with nineteenth than twenty-first century treatment in this respect. Today patients are treated more briskly, often on an outpatient basis. It's expensive to stay in a hospital for any length of time, and insurance companies want to limit costs as much as possible.

By 1894, the Bloomingdale Asylum was subject to a different kind of economic pressure from that faced by psychiatric hospitals today—not from health insurance companies but from real estate investors. The fear of a stigmatized institution's effect on local property values was what forced the move. The day after the asylum's opening in White Plains, *The New York Herald* published a detailed description, like that in the *Times*, full of praise for the new arrangements. But as the voice of business interests who wanted access to the asylum's valuable land, the *Herald* had campaigned tirelessly to force it out. As the neighborhood grew more urban, the *Herald*'s crusade appealed to many who wanted the insane to be not only out of sight, as they had been in this quiet location for many years, but out of the way.

In 1821, when the asylum opened as the psychiatric branch of the New York Hospital, the plateau between the Hudson River and the Harlem valley was rural countryside, seven miles north of the city. There were open views to the Palisades across the Hudson, and across Long Island Sound to the east. The asylum was named Bloomingdale after the locale, which Dutch settlers had called *Bloemendaal*, a flowery dale. In an early print, the wide Federal-style building stands on an open knoll. A sailboat can be glimpsed on the Hudson immediately to the west, two figures stand on the sloping lawn, and several deer browse amid wildflowers in the foreground. In 1846, the writer of a guidebook to New York City described the "lunatic hospital" as a surprisingly beautiful place, praising it as a model of land-scape gardening that would help to "relieve the melancholy mind from its sad musings." Because fresh air and quiet sur-roundings were believed to be curative, early asylums placed a strong emphasis on their gardens and enclosed as much outdoor space as possible. By the time of the move to White Plains, sev-eral more buildings had been added to accommodate the grow-ing number of patients, but the property held on to traces of its rural beginnings. A pasture, vegetable gardens, and some barns were features to the north and south of the cluster of buildings.

By the 1880s, the rapidly expanding metropolis pressed right up against the property. A row of brownstones stood at the southern edge of the asylum's land, along with some ram-shackle wooden houses. The country homes of wealthy mer-chants dotted the high ground above the river's edge. With the city's street grid filling in as construction pushed north, real estate developers and investors wanted to get their hands on the asylum's very fine views and extensive acreage. The *Herald* began to draw negative attention to the asylum in 1886. Under the headline "Remove Bloomingdale!" the paper declared that the presence of "the famous madhouse" was causing people seek-ing to walk from Morningside Park to Riverside Park to make a considerable detour because streets ended at the asylum's fenced enclosure. Real estate brokers complained that people wouldn't risk having the asylum as a neighbor, and politicians urged that there could be "no neighborhood, no development . . . so long as lunatics are stored in that madhouse." Why not move what was essentially a human storage facility out of the way of progress and profit-taking? *The New York Times*, too, voiced that obsession with real estate that continues to excite the minds of New Yorkers: the *Times* agreed that the asylum was standing in the way of the creation of "the most magnificent park and residence district in the known world." In response, the hospital's board of governors was implacable. "We will go, but we will not be driven," said one of the governors to a *Herald* reporter. Capitalist aggression was not in line with the ethics of the hospital, whose mission had always included providing care for the insane, and whose governors came from old money families and looked down upon the upstarts flooding their city.

Among the possible new locations that the governors explored was the White Plains farm they had bought in 1868 in the knowledge that rapid urbanization might eventually force their relocation. The farm supplied fresh meat and vegetables to the asylum, and patients and staff stayed in cottages there on visits to the countryside. When the governors decided to move the institution to that property, they chose someone they trusted to oversee the project. Charles Nichols had spent a few years as superintendent of the Bloomingdale Asylum in the 1840s before being hired away to take on the creation of a national asylum in Washington, D.C., known today as St. Elizabeth's. Returning to New York as superintendent during the transition, he would lead the task of planning the new asylum. In 1889 the hospital board sent him to visit the best European institutions, seeking models for what the Bloomingdale should provide its patients. He returned from Europe and made his report before dying of cancer within months of his return, and it fell to Dr. Lyons to implement Nichols's suggestions for creating a fully up-to-date asylum.

This project reached its completion with the transfer of patients in the autumn of 1894. Shortly before the move, the agitators of the Morningside Park Association learned that the New York Hospital had sold the asylum's property to Columbia University for two million dollars. The university, which would move north from Madison Avenue and Forty-Ninth Street, would increase the value of surrounding property, but no one would be able to buy and sell the many building lots the asylum's land would have yielded. The sole architectural vestige of the original asylum, the brick residence for wealthy men called Macy Villa, is now Buell Hall on Columbia University's campus—a five-minute walk from where I live.

BY THE TIME I WAS admitted to the former Bloomingdale asylum, the New York Hospital had been caring for psychiatric patients for nearly two hundred years. The approaches to treatment in this single institution reflect the faltering, trial-and-error path of psychiatry itself. If mental illness, varied as it was, still lacked surefire cures in my time there, treatment methods were far more humane than they had been at the time of the Hospital's founding in 1771, when New York was still a British colony. Right from the start, the building plans included "wards or cells for the reception of Lunatics" in the basement of the hospital. Fire, a yellow fever epidemic, and the Revolutionary War interrupted construction, but in 1791 the hospital opened at Pearl Street and Broadway, then the northern edge of the city. By 1792 it was taking in mentally disturbed patients along with those in need of medical and surgical treatment. Those cells set aside in the general hospital quickly grew overcrowded, and a new three-story building, called the Lunatic

Asylum, opened in 1808 to accommodate mentally ill patients separately from medical ones, so that "the sick are not incommoded by the lunatics."

Among the early documents from the New York Hospital are receipts for the purchase of chains, leg irons, and iron staples for attaching chains to the walls, and there is at least one reference to these chains being used for lunatics. We have an idea what confinement was like for Colonial-era insane patients from a description of Philadelphia's hospital. According to a visitor, the cells were "partly underground," and "made as strong as a prison. . . . In each door is a hole, large enough to give them food, which is closed with a little door secured with strong bolts." In warmer weather, the patients in Philadelphia could take the air in an outdoor barred enclosure, much like a cage in a zoo. Going to gaze at the lunatics became such a popular entertainment that in 1762 the hospital decided, supposedly in an effort to discourage such visits, to charge admission. Nonetheless, visits by the public continued until the 1830s.

In the Colonies, as in old Europe, there was no question that the social order trumped the good of the disordered individual. Philadelphia's Pennsylvania Hospital set aside space for the insane in 1751 in the hope that "the wretched maniac, sequestered from society, might be made subject to such regiment and regulations, which if not always the means of recovery, would at least insure safety, decency and order." The New York Hospital followed suit, providing "a place of safekeeping" where the mad would be "disabled from injuring themselves and others." Until the early nineteenth century (and beyond, in less progressive institutions), binding in chains was standard treatment for the so-called raving maniac, the person who was agitated, violent, or uncontrollable.

Two strands of philosophical and religious thought emerged in the late eighteenth century to bring about more humane practices. One was a belief in the rights of man, exemplified in post-revolutionary France by Philippe Pinel. The other, promoted by the Quakers, was a belief that all human beings share the divine inner light, and that the loss of reason does not alter a person's essential humanity or spiritual being. Enlightened doctors of the time came to believe that insanity could be cured or diminished through a shift in the mode of treatment: to house the insane in home-like settings designed to be calm and healing, and to replace beatings and chains with a doctor who would listen to them and treat them well. This idea that madness could be alleviated through kinder treatment, and in a special sort of institution, was the impetus for a wave of asylum building.

Philippe Pinel usually gets the credit for beginning this revolution. When Pinel was appointed to be physician in charge of the men's hospice at Bicêtre outside of Paris, criminals and the insane were imprisoned together, chained in stone cells on beds of filthy straw. This was in 1792, during the Reign of Terror. In that revolutionary moment, the story goes, Pinel had his assistant Jean-Baptiste Pussin remove the chains from all but the most violent patients. Many had been immobilized for so long that they could not walk. According to Pinel's son Scipion, an official of the Commune visited and asked Pinel, "Look here, citizen, art thou mad thyself, that thou wilt unchain such animals?" Pinel reportedly replied, "These lunatics are so unmanageable only because they are robbed of air and liberty; and I dare to hope much from the opposite means of treatment."

Unfortunately, there is no evidence that this dramatic meeting ever occurred, but Pinel expressed much the same belief in his writings. He called this opposite means *le traitement moral*—the French phrase conveys something like "treatment of the mind" or "psychological treatment." Pinel was certain that bleeding, purging, and other bodily remedies of the time were useless. English and American asylum doctors soon followed Pinel's lead and adopted his term, "moral treatment." What was most important about Pinel's approach was his belief that the insane should be treated in a way that did not deprive them of their human rights.

In 1790, two years before Pinel arrived at Bicêtre and just before the New York Hospital opened its doors in lower Manhattan, Hannah Mills entered the York Asylum in England. She was a young Quaker, poor, recently widowed, and suffering from melancholia. After a few weeks had passed, her family, who lived at some distance from York, asked some acquaintances to go and see how Hannah was faring. The doorkeeper refused to let them in, saying that she was not in a condition to be seen. Within six weeks of her admission, and before anyone could see her, Hannah died. The cause of death is unrecorded: it's likely that she committed suicide or contracted a contagious illness in the asylum.

The death of Hannah Mills awakened the Quaker community in the north of England to a grim realization: any one of their members could fall ill and be lost to them, to die alone without the solace of their faith. The case also led many to believe that the practices of the York Asylum were corrupt. Founded in 1777 as a charitable institution that would take in patients in "low and narrow circumstances" whose families would have difficulty looking after them, the York Asylum was meant to be a humane alternative to confinement in the poorhouse or the jail. But an investigation found that the physician in charge was skimming money from the public funds meant for the pauper patients, whom he neglected, while taking in paying patients to whom he gave the best food, rooms, and care. The investigators found that abuse of poor patients included "fatal neglect," rape, and whippings.

Soon after Hannah Mills's death, William Tuke, a Quaker tea and coffee merchant already active in support of abolition and prison reform, sought donations to build an asylum that would protect others from a fate like hers. The name of the new Quaker asylum, "The Retreat," was meant to convey the idea of "a quiet haven in which the shattered bark might find the means of reparation or safety." The Retreat opened its doors in 1796 just a mile from the York Asylum, and stood as a public rebuke to that institution during the years it was under investigation.

Like Pinel, Tuke called his method "moral treatment." Also like Pinel, he did not believe medical treatment effective in cases of insanity. Instead, he believed that if patients were treated with kindness they would come to like and admire their keepers and wish to be esteemed in turn, which would encourage them to exercise more self-restraint. Moral treatment assumed a childlike quality in the insane and emphasized the paternal role of the caretaker, who might wield the power of fear, shame, or kindness as needed to bring a patient under control. The atmosphere was domestic, and at the outset about ten attendants lived with and cared for thirty patients. The superintendent and his wife lived in the house as well and acted in a parental role. A medical doctor visited, but did not live on the premises.

The results at The Retreat were remarkable, and English and foreign visitors were soon convinced of the value of the Quakers' innovation. (It has been noted that the Quaker culture had, from birth, instilled in these patients a willingness to

cooperate and to exercise self-control; in the larger, secular, and
diversely populated asylums modeled on the Retreat, positive
results were not so reliable.) News of the Retreat's success spread
quickly to Quakers across the Atlantic. William Tuke's grandson Samuel wrote a small book on the experiment that would
have an enormous impact in the history of psychiatry, providing
a conceptual foundation for the ensuing era of asylum-building.

～⌒⟩

THE HOSPITAL IN WHICH I was treated was indebted to these
emerging ideas of moral treatment and originated in the efforts
of Thomas Eddy, another Quaker merchant, who was on the
governing board of the Society of New York Hospital. He had
corresponded with Samuel Tuke and had read his book. Because
the freestanding Lunatic Asylum adjacent to the general hospital in lower Manhattan was overcrowded after only five years,
Eddy urged his fellow board members to create a new rural asylum that would offer "a course of *moral* treatment for the lunatic patients." His recommendations came almost directly from
Tuke's book: "the patient should be always treated as much like
a rational being as the state of his mind will possibly allow"; no
patient would be confined in chains, although in violent mania
a straitjacket might be used; kindness would prevail, but if necessary the power of fear might be used; and the asylum must
accommodate poor patients.

In architecture and landscape design, this New York asylum
would be closely modeled on Tuke's York Retreat. Moral treatment called for a peaceful environment with opportunities for
fresh air, exercise, and useful work, and to that end Eddy urged
the board to purchase a site in upper Manhattan with extensive
grounds that avoided, "as far as possible, the aspect of a prison."

For patients who had experienced more prison-like arrangements, or who had been confined in their family's homes, it must have been a pleasing change. The Bloomingdale Asylum, begun with such humanity and optimism, seemed certain to set a new standard in the care of the mentally ill.

For its first thirty years the New York Hospital received money from the state legislature, and in return the asylum agreed to take patients from the city almshouse. As time went on, the asylum grew crowded and new buildings were added to handle the overflow. Despite the annual contribution from the state, the asylum always operated at a loss. Crowded conditions eased when, in 1839, the city opened a municipal public asylum, the nation's first, on Blackwell's Island in the East River. Here the city consolidated its prison and welfare institutions, both swelling with inmates as the city received wave after wave of immigrants.

Once the city's yearly contribution ended, the Bloomingdale superintendent emphasized that it would serve "the wealthy," as well as "indigent persons of superior respectability and personal refinement," including "families of clergymen and other professional persons . . . teachers and businessmen who have experienced reverses . . . [and] dependent unmarried females." The asylum did not, however, refuse to accept patients who could not pay the full cost of their care: a sliding scale applied, and the gap was filled by charitable contributions. But laborers and the desperately poor had to make the best of Blackwell's Island. When Charles Dickens visited during an 1842 tour of New York, he found that "Everything had a lounging, listless, madhouse air, which was very painful. . . . The terrible crowd with which these halls and galleries were filled, so shocked me, that I abridged my stay within the shortest limits, and declined to see that portion of the building in which the refractory and violent were under closer restraint."

Although less crowded than the so-called pauper asylum on Blackwell's Island, Bloomingdale also had trouble maintaining a hopeful atmosphere. At midcentury the medical superintendent was Pliny Earle, who was keenly interested in figuring out why his profession did not have better success. He found that the asylum's cure rate was inflated because it did not account for patients who had been admitted again and again. Instead, each time a patient was discharged as "improved" and returned some time later after a relapse, that person was counted as a new patient, and upon improvement and release, counted as another successful case. Earle noted too that as time went on, the incurable and chronic cases comprised a greater percentage of the patients, so that unless the asylum were to take in more and more curable cases, the atmosphere of hopelessness could only intensify with the years. Earle was clearsighted about treatment's limited effects. He wrote, "If insanity is to be diminished it must be by prevention and not by cure." As to diagnosis, the classification of illnesses was so muddled that "there are scarcely two physicians who would classify a series of cases, such as are admitted into any institution, in precisely the same manner."

The Bloomingdale Asylum's reputation suffered a setback in 1872, when the muckraking journalist Julius Chambers, pretending to be insane, was admitted to a padded room on one of its back wards. He reported that violent, raving patients howled all night. On admission, he wrote, the physician took his pulse but didn't speak with him before locking him in. The attendants were brutish, and the famous amenities of the Bloomingdale Asylum were only available to the most well-behaved patients. He described in detail (and included a drawing) how one patient was subjected to the "cold-water douche," a punitive treatment that looks much like a form of waterboarding. Abuses in asylums were a popular news item, for there had been several habeus corpus cases brought on behalf of patients who argued that they were not insane, whose families had had them committed. "The Bloomingdale," Chambers wrote, "had always been considered a place for 'genteel' lunatics," where family and friends of the inmates need not worry about anything like the conditions at the pauper asylum on Blackwell's Island: "Here was an aristocratic insane asylum, with pleasant grounds, bowling-alleys, and other means of making a patient's time pass agreeably. Here were supposed to be books and papers and easy chairs, skilled physicians and kind nurses—the very paradise of Bedlams." But he had infiltrated the place and exposed its abuses, "for nothing that the public deserves to know can be effectually barred against the press any more. . . . And then the paradise of Bedlams was a paradise no longer." If the most disturbed patients were being cruelly treated, the asylum had moved far from its roots in Quaker kindliness.

When Charles Nichols arrived to manage the relocation, he introduced a high internal standard once again. In his report of 1887, Nichols noted that of 202 patients admitted, he classed the prognosis of 80 as favorable, 61 as unfavorable, and 61 as incurable, of whom 35 had the insanity of late-stage syphilis. It must have been a frustrating career, given the unpromising prognosis for so many. And yet, judging from the intelligence and dedication of such figures as Nichols, Pliny Earle, and Samuel Lyon, Bloomingdale attracted some of the profession's best doctors.

The move to White Plains presented an opportunity for the institution to reinvent and modernize itself, while staying true to the original mission set out by Thomas Eddy in 1818, to diminish the suffering of the mentally ill and "to restore many of them to the bosom of society, to their former usefulness and to the affections of their families and friends, redeemed from a calamity the most awful and severe which can befall humanity." In the design of its landscape and living areas, the new Bloomingdale asylum was faithful to the tradition of moral treatment even while implementing each innovation in psychiatric care as the decades passed. Talk therapy developed the directives of Pinel and Tuke that patients need conversation with empathic doctors. The greatest breakthrough in treating mental illness did not arrive until the 1950s, with the introduction of antipsychotic and antidepressant drugs.

~⁄⁓

LOOKING BACK AT my own stay in the former Bloomingdale Asylum, I have decidedly mixed feelings about the care I received. I retain a sense of lasting harm, but I was also helped. Because I expected that the hospital would protect me from the danger of being suicidal, the word "asylum" takes on a certain degree of irony in this regard. It's taken all this time for me to realize that the shame I've so long felt about the scar is unwarranted, and that what happened was not my fault. But I still needed to be there. I needed ECT, and I needed the time and space to recover. To be fair, most of the people who worked on the unit did seem to embrace the spirit of Thomas Eddy's vision of moral treatment. My three-plus months there felt like ages, but because the period immediately after discharge is the most dangerous time for patients who have been suicidal, my caretakers needed to be relatively confident that I would be safe if discharged.

In the United States in 2016 there were nearly 45,000 suicides, a number that has surged more than 28 percent in the
past two decades. While very few of these deaths—perhaps 6
percent—occur in hospitals, one small study estimated that a
psychiatric nurse will be confronted with a suicide every two
years or so. Most inpatient suicides are the result of inaccurate
clinical assessment of the patient. Malpractice suits often cite
"inadequate monitoring and protection of new patients with
moderate or high suicide risk." Even when a patient is correctly
assessed as very suicidal, surveillance isn't foolproof. One way
to ensure that no patients attempt suicide, short of immobiliz-
ing them with drugs, would be to return to the use of physical
restraints like the straitjacket. It can be very hard to save the
life of someone who is determined to die.

Taking care of suicidal patients was a perennial challenge for
the Bloomingdale Asylum. In 1880, while in a storeroom with
the attendant who was guarding her, a suicidal woman found a
piece of glass from a broken window, quietly hid it in her cloth-
ing, and later made a fatal gash in her throat when the attendant
allowed her to go into a bathroom alone. In 1914, a thirty-
nine-year-old patient escaped from attendants and was found
the next day, drowned in the pond on the hospital grounds.
In 1916, a wealthy woman suffering from "melancholia with
suicidal tendencies" went missing after living in the asylum for
four years. Police speculated that she had been hiding in the
woods or in barns for a week when she lay down on the rail-
road tracks near the White Plains station and was killed by the
train. This grim catalogue includes many entries over the years,
though the numbers decrease as time passes. These patients
were suicidal despite their time in the asylum because there
was no effective treatment for the illnesses fueling their desire

to die. Especially in the years before ECT, antidepressants, and other drugs that could diminish the power of self-destructive impulses, the asylum's role was to guard patients and to provide long-term care if they were unable to live at home.

Shock treatment had brought my own suicidal crisis under control. The nurses observed me closely, and each day their notes in my record include their asking about, and my denial of, suicidal thoughts. In early May my demeanor was returning to normal, and the nurses recorded my "good spirits" and social interactions with patients and staff. On the day of my final ECT treatment, I had improved so much that Dr. Young wrote, "Patient is felt to be fully treated for her Major Depression and course during next week will shape what the nature of further treatment and transition out of hospital should consist of."

I no longer needed to be checked on every fifteen minutes, and I began to attend therapeutic activities like art classes, games in the gym, and the required group therapy. I was allowed to enjoy the grounds, though not unaccompanied, and I was able to engage in the communal life of the unit and pay more attention to my fellow patients. My short-term memory wasn't working well because of the ECT and the "at least moderately severe organic brain syndrome." One nurse noted that sometimes I asked the same question several times. By the time evening came I had trouble remembering what had happened in the morning, and even in the afternoon. Writing things down helped me feel more clear-headed, and when Jake visited after work I could remember enough to tell him about my day.

In the spiral notebook that was my hospital journal, the people I knew and our days together emerge from the fog of time with surprising clarity. The notes I wrote on a single day, "a crazy day on the unit," bring back the feeling of living there, and the shifting array of people with various presentations of mania, depression, obsessive compulsions, and psychosis.

A young woman named Rita, her nails bitten to the quick, believed there was something wrong with her body, something she called "a cosmetic problem." She talked about it constantly, and desperately needed to have it fixed. Instead, her father had forced her to come to this hospital. She was worried that they'd make her take all kinds of major tranquilizers and that she would become crazy. Rita was talking to me all the time, so I asked Dr. Young about her. He said that her beliefs about her body were delusional.

An older woman called Mrs. Cole was confined to her room, but at fifteen-minute intervals she was allowed to take a walk in the hall. On every tour of the corridor, she talked in loud and anxious tones about a laundry bag. Within a day, Mrs. Cole was transferred to another unit. I never understood why some people stayed while others passed briefly through our midst. Presumably this had to do with the doctors' assessment of what kind of treatment they required, and perhaps it had to do with what sort of insurance coverage they had.

Another woman, tall, very thin, and dark-haired, called herself the Queen of Israel. She clattered up and down the hallway in a bathrobe and high-heeled mules, stopping occasionally to aim her pronouncements at other patients. This time she fixed on a Cuban man named Luis and shared her predictions about the doomed state of Israel and of the world itself, which she said would end tomorrow. Luis was playing cards, as he often did, with a woman from Puerto Rico, and they always spoke Spanish together. Like Rita, the Queen of Israel talked incessantly to whomever would listen. Luis nodded a few times, and she moved on to where I sat talking with two new friends, Meg

and Paul, on the sofas in the hall. In her bathrobe and high-
heels, she walked with a provocative wiggle. She sat down next
to me and said, "Have you been to these nudist camps where
they have the parties? They started them in America, back in
1956, when Sputnik went up." We shook our heads—no, we
hadn't ever been. She told us how great the nudist camps were,
and then walked on, her heels clacking away down the hall. We
smiled to each other, murmuring about how that woman was
"really nuts." But we knew that we were nuts too—why else
would we be here in the nuthouse with her?

By then I felt better off than many of the people on the
unit. I wasn't obsessed anymore with my own evil, and I wasn't
obsessed with the end of the world, or nudist camps, or a laundry bag. Those of us who were more or less able to think ratio-
nally and to speak in the mode of normal social conversation
considered ourselves not as "crazy" as those who couldn't. People were passing through, so we didn't often see the full development of one person's case from crisis to remission. Those
who were there on the day of my suicide attempt would have
been aware of the time when I was perhaps the *most* crazy,
or at least the most troublemaking, person on the unit. But
for those who arrived later, the only evidence of my crazi-
ness was the still raw wound on my neck. Now it was others'
turn to make trouble—by not calming down, by making a
lot of noise. In doing so they gave the rest of us something to
talk about.

Meg was one of the quiet ones, and we became close. Like
me, she was in her twenties, and she was scheduled for shock
treatment. Like me, she came from a Catholic family, and she
seemed to be going through a similar kind of crisis. She had
lost one sister to cancer and another to an accident. She was her

parents' sole remaining child, and she had been depressed for most of a decade. She was engaged, and she worried that she couldn't go through with getting married if she was only ever going to be hopelessly depressed. Dr. Young and the staff asked me to talk with her about ECT and to calm her fears about it. I spent time with her and with her parents, telling them it would be okay, emphasizing the fact that suddenly one day, I had gotten better.

I always enjoyed sitting with Paul, a painter who had bipolar disorder. I don't know whether mania or depression brought him to the hospital, but by the time I met him he was extremely calm and companionable. He smoked a lot, and once I was allowed outside, we would sit together on a bench by the tennis courts. Sometimes we played tennis in a desultory way, because neither of us had much energy. Paul was an old hand at being hospitalized and seemed resigned to his life with illness. What I found comforting about him was that, unlike me, he wasn't panicking about his future, and he wasn't terrified. It was a relief to be around him. He was stoic, enduring yet another stint in the hospital, waiting it out.

The difference between the Queen of Israel, in her chatty psychosis, and Paul, in his subdued and patient depressive state, was the difference between drama and stillness. The more voluble people seemed to be having more fun, if that is the word, while the quiet ones seemed to be waiting for a prison term to come to an end. For both groups, the illness that had brought us to the hospital was what we needed to be released from. We just didn't know how long it might take, and whether it would all just keep happening over and over.

Jacob, perhaps twenty, was one of the liveliest presences during his stay on the unit. He was bipolar as well. His kippa and the fringes of his prayer shawl hanging beneath his shirt marked his identity as an Orthodox Jew. He played the guitar, which he had brought with him to the hospital, and he wrote poems and songs. He loved to talk about the many books he had read. He came by while Meg and I sat talking to tell us he had lost the capo for his guitar, and complained about how manic and upset he became when he lost things. He told us about visiting Auschwitz and Treblinka with his father, a Holocaust survivor, and about his sister, who had killed herself in Israel. I was struck by the fact that Meg and Jacob were both traumatized by what their families had been through: in their illnesses they seemed at once to suffer and carry on their families' pain.

Shortly before he was discharged, Jacob handed me a poem. It was written in pencil, in English, with Hebrew letters at the top and at the bottom. When I recently found the poem tucked inside the hospital notebook, I looked into the meaning of the Hebrew. The four letters at the top indicate the Jewish year 5744, which was 1984. In Hebrew, numbers can spell out words, and the four Hebrew letters for 5744 read as *tashmad*, or destruction. In Israel in the years leading up to 1984, visionaries and astrologers had been predicting destruction, disaster, even the end of the world. Jacob had written this word, *tashmad*, above the poem that begins, "In ebon-topped waves / you glide by," as he, "post / deep sea dive," imagines rising "immaculate" from the depths, with "her as my beacon." At the bottom was his name, in Hebrew. Was I the beacon of the poem, despite the shift from "you" to "her"? Maybe handing out poems was one of Howard's ways of being crazy. It was a way of expressing his creativity, and perhaps also a way of expressing his longing for escape from illness, from the pressures of his family's worry that he might not be able to get married and have lots of children. But disaster, *tashmad*, was his family's history and, so far, his own.

We were all feeling the pressure of our families; they were worried, and in some cases distraught. When they visited, they brought with them their understandable desire that we get better *right away*. I think all of us had experienced the sense of slipping under the waves that Jacob expressed. We were desperate to be saved, even as some of our loved ones failed to recognize that we were going under. While some of my new friends had plunged more dramatically into madness than I had, my own less noticeable descent was something like what Stevie Smith captures in her poem "Not Waving but Drowning." Swimming far out, a man has been waving as those on shore mistake his desperate call for help as no more than a casual, playful gesture. He is "the dead man" who says, "I was much further out than you thought / And not waving but drowning." I had drifted into those waters, much too far out, sometime after Anna died.

Smith's poem is powerful in registering the way that many people, some of them with undiagnosed depressive illness, move through life. If they are practiced, as I was, at the cheerful demeanor necessary to social life (the "poor chap" in the poem "always loved larking"), they may not reveal, as I didn't, just how much danger they're in until it's too late. Being in the hospital—the asylum, the madhouse—meant that the deception was over. Our families and friends might not have been keenly perceptive, but they were used to the selves we presented to them. Now the game was up. We had failed to keep the secret of just how far out we felt. The hospital took us in when we could no longer function in the world.

THE INITIAL EXCITEMENT about my recovery was short-lived. Although I was much better, I wasn't at all well. A week after ECT was over, I was writing about the extreme physical anxiety I was feeling: "I'm so nervous and anxious sometimes throughout the day, my muscles clench and unclench and I can't relax. My life is unreal. There's no visiting today, and I don't know how I'll get through it. Sometimes when I'm reading or writing the backgrounds reverse themselves and the white background looks dark. I can't imagine myself ever having a life, being at ease in it, having a home that I feel comfortable in. That's what I'm so afraid of." Thoughts like these circled endlessly when I was alone. I worried I would become suicidal again, and that I would need to stay in the hospital indefinitely. And as I sometimes did when I was full of fear, I tried to pray.

I looked through the Psalms just as I had done on my last day at work, trying to tether my agnostic, spiritually alienated mind to these ancient pleas for help. Thinking it might calm me, I wrote down some verses:

> Be not far from me, for trouble is near, for there is none to
>   help. . . .
> I am poured out like water, and all my bones are out of joint:
> my heart is like wax; it is melted in the midst of my
>   bowels. . . .
> In my distress I called upon the Lord, and cried
>   unto my God.
> He heard my voice out of his temple, and my cry came before
>   him, even into his ears.
> For thou wilt light my candle, the Lord my God will
>   enlighten my darkness.

If I was slipping back into illness as I feared, the language of the Psalms promised more effective help than shock and seizures, or talking to a young psychiatrist. But if there was no God, and prayers were only a heightened form of pleading, I was sending these words from my anguished self out into the emptiness. I was relieved that several people were praying for me who were better at it than I was. If prayers are most effective when the person praying is most sincere, my mother's mother, Bridie, would certainly be heard. Her prayers, coming from a place of absolute humility and faith, might have real power.

My mother had given me a book called *Beginning to Pray* by a monk named Anthony Bloom, and I was reading it in my room on that anxious evening of no visitors. To my surprise, the author immediately addressed the feeling of sending prayer into the void. He wrote, "Obviously I am not speaking of a real absence—God is never really absent—but of the *sense* of absence which we have. We stand before God and we shout into an empty sky, out of which there is no reply. We turn in all directions and He is not to be found. What ought we to think of this situation?" People expect God to be there only when they need Him, he wrote, but prayer should arise from a relationship in which we seek the presence of God regularly. I was ruminating on all of this—my lack of belief, my despair, my suspicion that my marriage was part of my problem with the future—when one of the mental health workers came in doing room checks. Teddy, a Jamaican man who was the kindest of all the staff, asked me why I was crying. When I told him that I was feeling hopeless and scared, he suggested I try to use my experience to feel stronger rather than weaker—something Jake was always telling me as well. I didn't understand why that was so difficult, but it seemed that the whole foundation of my life had disintegrated. Love, marriage, work, self, all were in ruins. Doubt and fear were all I knew.

Teddy mentioned that he would have to note my fragile condition in my chart. This was three weeks after shock treatment ended. I had not been on any medication since then, and Dr. Young now tried to halt my downward slide by putting me on an antidepressant. I had been telling him about my fear of relapse, my feeling of being "other than human," and of being "in a black box." I was having trouble getting to sleep, and was waking very early. Reading the record, it's clear to me that the symptoms of melancholia had returned. Because I was a patient who had no prior contact with psychiatry and no history of depressive illness, I think Dr. Young and the attending psychiatrist assumed that postpartum bereavement had caused the crisis—that it was situational, and not the eruption of an unrecognized disorder that had been quietly present for years. The pessimism and self-deprecation that I had long believed to be aspects of my character I now see as the familiar indicators of a syndrome that emerged when I was in high school, if not earlier. Anna's death had caused it to leap into visibility: unavoidable, urgent, and deadly.

Depression has been viewed as a complex "biopsychosocial" illness; it can have biological determinants, but psychological and social stressors contribute as well. It was the biological component, very powerful in melancholia, that I assume Dr. Young felt that ECT had resolved when he wrote "Patient is felt to be fully treated for her Major Depression." We had been addressing the psychological issues in talk therapy and family meetings. My fragile emotional state was what concerned him now, and the way my marriage and career situation continued to cause stress and anxiety. He thought I would need another three weeks in the hospital for my mood to stabilize before I went home.

When Jake visited, we talked about things I could do to help myself feel better when I got home. We made plans for the garden. We talked about trying to have another child. We made lists. A list in Jake's handwriting includes items to address my sense of uselessness and my fear of suburban isolation, like "make new friends" and "get new job" and schooling for potential new careers: landscape architecture programs, the Botanical Garden's horticulture program, graduate school in literature, the nurse-midwife program. The occupational therapist at the hospital gave me an aptitude test and found, not much to my surprise, that I wasn't suited for a career in nursing. Part of the appeal of midwifery was the potential for being employable when we moved to Vermont, where otherwise my only plan was to teach high school English. In the years that followed I would continue to believe that feeling miserable about myself and my future—core symptoms of depression—could only be fixed by finding the profession in which I would finally feel comfortable, useful, and hopeful.

My hospital notebook contains drawings too. I made a sketch of Ellie, who was one of my minders when I had to be within arm's distance of a staff member at all times. Sitting on the bed, I drew her in colored pencils as she sat on a chair beside me, as if we were roommates: her close-cropped Afro, her calm and benevolent face, the details of her sweater pattern. There is an unfinished profile of Lisa, the nurse who after my suicide attempt continued to dislike me, writing in my chart that I was "passive aggressive" and "acted condescending to staff." There is a drawing of our house and its outer hedge, where the privet made an archway over the entry path. There are diagrams of garden areas to be created. There's a self-portrait by Jake, to amuse me. He's drawn his curly dark hair and glasses, given himself a beard, a goofy face, and an arrow through his head, like the arrows you see through hearts on valentines. In its way, that drawing carries its own sense of *tashmad*. In the journal's drawings and written observations of goings on, its plans and lists, I can feel the slow time of the hospital, the pressure and desire to get well.

While the hospital provided a space away from the world, most of what happened there was intended to return patients to it, better able to cope with their lives. Each patient on the unit had a treatment plan focused on getting the illness under control so that he or she could return home. Recovering patients were sent on day and weekend passes to their homes, to practice getting ready for discharge. Our social workers and the psychiatrists talked with our families, gauging the support that they could provide. They arranged for residence in half-way houses for patients whose families were likely to exacerbate the illness.

Family meetings took place once a week, and in those meetings we patients felt the sharp pressure of our families' concern, along with their impatience and even their incomprehension. I was usually pretty shaken after these meetings, since until I was much, much better I couldn't help but disappoint Jake and my parents. My social worker made a note about my parents' "denial," in the context of their requests that I be released as soon as possible. Our status as *patients* points to our trouble in the presence of our impatient families. The word, as both adjective and noun, comes from Latin *patientia*—"patience, endurance, humility, submission." We had no choice but to submit to our circumstances, our suffering, and our possibly long-term or recurring illnesses.

Living in the hospital, compounded with the harrowing experience of having been suicidal and psychotic, seemed to mean that I was now fundamentally different from people outside. Erving Goffman, in his book *Asylums*, writes about the shift in identity that first-time mental patients undergo, passing from a "normal" to a "discredited" social status. While Goffman's work focused on patients in state institutions and I was lucky to be in a much better kind of place, his observation describes the way I now thought of myself, and the way I feared others would see me. I worried that if it were known that I'd been hospitalized for a psychiatric problem, I might have difficulty being hired in the future. Worse, if the illness were to recur unpredictably, I might have to leave any job that I had. It was to suppress this damaged identity that I avoided talking about my illness or my hospitalization afterwards, except to close friends who already knew about it. But the fact that I had made a mark on myself, a scar on my neck, during my time there, meant that the stigma—literally, a mark or brand of pain, punishment, or difference—would be for me a permanent reminder of that identity.

Given that when I was alone I just swam round and round my worry tank, it was better to go and sit with other people who were in similarly bad shape. That way we could distract and amuse each other. In our free time on the unit and in our group therapy sessions, we patients provided each other some relief from family pressure and a sense of being understood. We chatted and gossiped in the hours we were sitting around, but being together in group therapy was different, and the tone was

more serious and respectful. I was in a women's group that met
three times a week, and there I began to talk about Anna's death
and the feelings that had brought me to the hospital. One day a
new patient who was a psychiatric social worker spoke. Several
years earlier, she had been diagnosed with a rapid-cycling form
of manic-depressive illness and spent eight months in another
hospital. Now she was hospitalized again, and her husband had
left her amidst all the upheaval. I was moved by the stories of
people like this woman, who gave me a glimpse of what it was
like to move in and of mental disorder, in and out of normal
adult life. I admired people who had learned how to accept the
disruptive nature of their illness, and still carried themselves
with dignity.

In our therapy sessions, Dr. Young was honing in on painful matters. Doubts about my marriage were coming out into
the open, and the scrutiny by a third party only made things
worse for Jake. I felt like a traitor, but I knew that marrying
too young had weakened me. I was in mourning for my unful-
filled potential, and I was having to talk about it with someone
roughly my age who was already a doctor. Leaving college, I
had lacked the confidence to think I could become a professor
and had not pursued graduate work in literature. Our move to
the suburbs, where I was miserable and disoriented, made me
realize that I needed to claim some independence. I had to pursue what would make me feel happier, even if I could no longer
fit into the life Jake and I had made together.

I had written about my dissatisfaction in the journal that
I destroyed the day I came to the hospital, but I hadn't talked
about it much with Jake until it became a huge issue in my
post-ECT psychotherapy. Given the crushing event of Anna's
death, I had been hoping to salvage the life I had chosen and

the marriage I had promised to be faithful to. But I had trouble summoning any optimism about it. It was hard to know what I could trust about these feelings and what was the pervasive negativity of depression. When I went home a couple of times on passes I was devastated to have to acknowledge how disconnected I felt. I told Dr. Young I felt "like a stone," and was afraid I would always feel this way. Feeling like a stone was symptomatic, though. It was how depression felt. He focused on my marriage as a major source of stress, writing in my record that when we talked about it, "it appeared on many occasions that the affective symptomatology was recurring."

The medication Dr. Young put me on to address the return of symptoms was nortriptyline, another of the tricyclics, but one that didn't give me hives. It helped me sleep, and I began to sleep a lot. The sleep was wonderful. I gained five pounds in a week and I didn't care, because it quieted the runaway anxiety so much that my life began to feel bearable. "Today for the first time I don't feel completely hopeless," I wrote in my notebook, "and I think the drug is beginning to work. I hardly trust these hopeful feelings." Twelve days later, the positive response continued: "I'm alive. I can talk to people." Instead of being a sleepless, hollow-eyed, suicidal wraith, on nortriptyline I was becoming a cheerful, sociable, chubby person.

With this improvement, I was restored to the highest level of privilege, meaning I could again spend time on the grounds with other patients and with my visitors. One visit I remember clearly: I went out to the hospital's nine-hole golf course with Jake's parents, and we played on the putting green. I realized that despite the stress of the visit and my guilt about the pain I was causing their son, we were kind of having fun. They were golfers and I was not, but I was pretty good at putting that day. I imagined that I would be safe if I just stayed in the hospital forever, and my friends and relatives would visit me here. I would entertain them on the putting green; we would take walks and play tennis; we would avoid talking about whether I was getting better. This was how I could protect the people who loved me from my inevitable suicide.

Early in June, my peers on the unit elected me their representative. My social worker had told me (in an effort, no doubt, to counter my negative self-perception) that I was one of the most well-liked patients. If the other patients thought I was functioning well enough to represent them and communicate their concerns at the weekly meeting of staff, doctors, and patients, then perhaps I was more together than I felt. I was honored that they chose me. We had created a community of support for one another. I was getting stronger, going on more frequent visits home, getting in touch with friends, and my time of asylum was winding down. Soon I would be leaving them.

Dr. Young recommended a psychiatrist who would see me through the transition to life after the hospital. Dr. Waters had a private practice in Manhattan, and I went to meet her on one of the days she was working at the hospital. I immediately felt comfortable with her, and in telling her about my situation I had to explain Anna's death. I noticed with surprise that as I talked about it, her eyes filled with tears. She told me that she had also had a baby recently. This was a quality of empathy I hadn't experienced before, and I felt more hopeful in her presence. We agreed that when I was released I would see her twice a week.

On the discharge summary, Dr. Young wrote his diagnosis of my marriage: "While on admission and for many weeks thereafter the marital relationship was presented as ideal, and both patient and husband seemed genuinely to believe their marriage was an excellent one, very major problems in the relationship surfaced in the course of this hospitalization. . . . In reality she was highly controlled by him and unconsciously greatly resented him although she submitted to the domination. Consciously her knowledge of the relationship in which she was deeply involved was extremely shallow and she conducted herself within the relationship as if true harmony prevailed." Reading this for the first time over thirty years later I was struck by its accuracy, although I wasn't as unaware of this dynamic as he says. In my years with Jake I had come to feel more and more insignificant, and I had never learned how to insist on what I needed as a separate person. To be in therapy was to begin to make space for myself, and to find my own way forward.

This was the beginning of a years-long process of coming to understand how undiagnosed depression had, for a decade at least, affected my perception and decisions, paralyzed my desire and ambition. I'd begun to speak truthfully about the most difficult aspects of my life, and to see more clearly. But I was far from well, according to the discharge form. On a 100-point scale called the Global Assessment of Functioning, Dr. Young recorded a grade of 45, which indicated "serious impairment" of functioning. He noted my prognosis as "good" and my condition "improved," choosing neither "much improved" nor "recovered." In a final family session, Dr. Young recommended that I continue long-term intensive treatment with the outpatient psychiatrist, and my social worker suggested that Jake and I join a bereaved parents group and see a couples' therapist. I received my medication, with dosage instructions. On my last day on the unit, I said goodbye to everyone during the hall meeting, which felt strangely like a graduation. Being in the hospital had been an education, and graduation is not so odd an analogy.

Asylum, as I experienced it, was ultimately about the camaraderie and support of my fellow patients. Thrown together as strangers in terrible circumstances, we had no choice but to share our suffering, but we shared our humor and resilience too. In doing so we began to bring ourselves back into the human community. While ECT was vital to my recovery and antidepressant medication was even more so in the long term, these medical interventions were not sufficient in themselves. The acceptance and affection offered me by the other people there, both patients and staff, helped me to recognize my own value and begin to find an alternative to despair. In this commitment to helping patients reconnect with others, the Bloomingdale hospital in my time carried on the humane principles of its early Quaker lineage.

5

Where Do the Dead Go?

Imagine 2 percent of the world's population disappearing at the same moment on the same day. An infant suddenly goes missing from its carrier in the backseat of a car while a distracted mother talks on her cell phone. A young woman vanishes from the hotel room in which she and a married man who is cheating on his wife are having passionate first-time sex. Another woman's two children and husband disappear from the breakfast table on a harried morning, just after her little girl has knocked over a glass of orange juice. This is how *The Leftovers*, the HBO television series, begins. Because of the unexplained loss of so many people at once, the drama plays out like a thought experiment or a terrible dream.

None of those left behind, the so-called leftovers, knows why this vanishing has occurred. Was it the Rapture long awaited by evangelical Christians, their chosen loved ones transported to heaven while they, the not-so-good, are left to face a period of tribulation? Or was it somehow a scientifically plausible event?

The series, refusing to say, focuses narrowly on the aftermath. Those who are gone are simply gone; those who remain are devastated. Whether or not they have lost someone in their immediate circle, the survivors are enraged, or empty, or they fall apart. The leftovers split into two camps: those who try to cope with their grief and move on, and those who refuse to forget. Among the latter group is a cult called the Guilty Remnant. They live together, dress in white, chain-smoke, and generally make a nuisance of themselves. They want everyone to remember, and they behave nihilistically because they believe the world is ending. Their message is that there can be no recovery, no hope, no resumption of normal life after the event, for anyone.

The Leftovers is about the peculiar kind of suffering of people bereaved by unexplained disappearances. It shows their bafflement and loss of equilibrium. The division between those who seek to rejoin the current of ongoing life and those who don't aligns roughly with the difference between mourners and melancholics set out in Sigmund Freud's landmark essay "Mourning and Melancholia." The mourners work to heal themselves and carry on the business of living, however diminished their world is. The melancholics, on the other hand, are much like the Guilty Remnant: their grief has become grievance, and they won't move on.

I was fascinated by this divide because it reminded me of the period after I left the hospital, when I occupied both sides at once. I was mourning, but trying to accept what had happened and trying to re-enter the world. Traumatic memories were still with me, and I had trouble laying Anna to rest in my mind. It was as if her death and the aftermath had stripped away my accustomed pose of a normal, functioning person and left me revealed in my true nature—empty, drifting, without value.

My mood was fragile, and I continued to be haunted by the meaninglessness of things.

The British psychoanalyst Darian Leader points to what may have been the reason for my continuing sense of blankness and devastation. "In mourning, we grieve the dead," he writes, "and in melancholia we die with them." In mourning we work through our grief, find the words to talk about it, share it with others, and gradually relinquish it to the past. In melancholia we remain in the trauma of loss, so that what Emily Dickinson called "the hour of lead" extends indefinitely into the future. My new psychiatrist, Dr. Waters, encouraged me to return to the work of mourning that was left undone when illness shunted my mind onto a looping track of despairing, suicidal thoughts.

Psychoanalysis, as many have observed, is a sort of secular religion, and it was a radical departure from my family's long reliance on submission and prayer as the response to death, illness, and personal disasters of all varieties. In conversation, through an investigation into the source of intolerable feelings, it promised an alternative to the crisis of despair. For generations my family had said the Rosary on their knees each evening, prayed to patron saints for relief from affliction, and included the sick and dying in their prayers at Mass. But for me, Catholicism had been more powerful as a source of guilt and self-castigation than of comfort. As the grandchild of four Irish immigrants, I had done things that were unthinkable in the world they came from: I had gone to college, I had stopped going to Mass, and now I was in therapy. To most members of my family, psychotherapy seemed like self-indulgent nonsense. They blamed the psychiatrists for my disruptive new ideas—that I was unhappy, that I might need to get divorced.

One of my siblings and a couple of my friends became parents not long after I did, and the arrival of their healthy babies reinforced the rarity of what had happened to Anna. Since those days, I've met many people who have suffered more terrible losses, and even then I understood how lucky I was in not having had more time with her. Losing a child one has loved for two years, or twelve, or twenty, in the intimate attachment of daily life, is exponentially worse. So wasn't my reaction overblown? I can see how it might look that way. But losing a child you've never known is strange. I didn't know her, and neither did anyone else.

I was seeking solace and trying to make sense of things that just didn't make sense. After nine long months of sharing my body with her, her fatal secret ticking like a time bomb, my acquaintance with my daughter outside the womb had been so brief that my most potent memories were of her dying. A line I knew from Samuel Beckett's play *Waiting for Godot* expressed the absurdity of what had happened: "They give birth astride of a grave, the light gleams an instant, then it's night once more." To be born with her half-formed heart was to begin to die. And if this was so, wasn't her existence a pointless mistake? Who was *she*, apart from the error that ended her life? Didn't she matter as a child, as a person, as a soul?

The answers offered by religious traditions—both my own and Jake's—were not reassuring. Catholic teaching had maintained for centuries that if the sacrament of baptism wasn't performed before its death, the newborn remained in the state of original sin and was condemned to limbo, a sort of eternal waiting room. Although the concept of limbo wasn't official doctrine and is no longer taught, it underscored the Church's insistence that the sacrament of baptism is necessary for salvation.

Judaism's approach to neonatal death has been in place since the medieval Jewish sage Maimonides wrote, "We do not mourn for fetuses" or "anything which does not live for thirty days." If the child was a late miscarriage, or stillborn, or died before a month was out, it would go unmourned and be buried in an unmarked grave. But as with the view of limbo in the Catholic Church, it's a tradition that hasn't gone unchallenged. Recently a group of Conservative rabbis voted to revise it for their congregations, acknowledging the psychological reality that bereaved parents *do* think of their dead infant as a person. New ritual observance, as of 1992, obligates parents to say the mourner's Kaddish, to hold a burial with full rites, to sit shiva, and to observe the anniversary of the child's death. Orthodox Jews continue to observe Maimonides's rule, which no doubt reflects a point of view across ancient cultures: the death of a child was something that happened all too frequently, and parents were encouraged to move on rather than grieve. Historians of premodern eras have argued that because death claimed children so often, parents did not become as attached to them as we do today.

The poetic record, however, tells another story. Even in the plague- and disease-ridden days of the sixteenth century, an age of faith when mortality was unimaginably high, the Polish poet Jan Kochanowski could express how wrong it felt to survive his two-year-old daughter in this verbal epitaph:

> Stonecutters, hone
> the chisels sharp and cut the words in stone:
> "Ursula Kochanowski lies beneath,
> Her father's joy that slipped his loving hands.
> Learn from this grave the ways of careless Death:
> The green shoot is mown down—the ripe crop stands."

His daughter's death struck him so forcibly that in his effort to cope with it he wrote a cycle of laments, poems that registered so powerfully with me that when I came across a few of them in the *Times Literary Supplement*, I cut them out and saved them. In the final one, Kochanowski describes a dream in which he sees his dead mother holding Ursula in her arms: "my never lovelier Daughter . . . Rose petal skin, eyes bright as a new day." His mother says she has come from a "distant shore" to comfort him:

> We are alive
> Beyond the flesh. The dust returns to dust,
> But spirit is divine, a gift that must
> Return to its Giver.

The poet's dream mother informs her son that he should "Trust and understand / This Mystery: she sits at God's right hand," and concludes her long speech with a pointed assertion: "There is— / Never forget—one Lord of light and bliss." The last poem, and thus the entire *Laments*, ends on a note of uncertainty: "She vanished, and I woke, uncertain what / I had just seen: was this a dream or not?" His mother's return, dream or not, is partly comforting and partly scolding: Why is he so weak in his faith? If doubt leaves him in such a state of anguish, isn't this his own doing? It's as if his mother has had to remind him to accept the simple solution he hasn't arrived at on his own: the consolation of religious faith. I don't know whether Kochanowski was convinced by his mother's final statement, but the dream confirms that what is emotionally comforting may not withstand rational scrutiny.

Four centuries later, I was another grieving skeptic who had to be counseled by elder family members. My mother's mother,

Bridie, then my last living grandparent, wrote several letters to me while I was in the hospital, and among them I recently found a Mass card she sent me. For those unfamiliar with this practice, these are often sent as sympathy cards and represent a certain number of Masses that will be said for the soul of the deceased. The text of this particular card was a reminder that a child who dies is with Jesus and Mary in eternal life, awaiting the day when she will joyfully welcome her parents into heaven. The text on the card even spoke in the voice of the departed: "Do not grieve too much. We are living and are still with you." I assume that such a belief must have sustained my grandmother when her only son died in infancy, because she continued to attend Mass every day for more than a half century after that loss. In one of her letters, Bridie had written of her certainty that Anna was in heaven with my grandfather, who died just weeks before I entered the hospital.

In the face of the ancestral consolation held out to me, I was sure only of the material facts of the case. I knew that Anna was dead. I had seen her die, and seen her coffin slide into a wall of flame. I knew that if she were anywhere, she was in the container that held the ashen remains of her body. But when I was asleep other possibilities, and other possible children, took the stage. For several years after Anna's death, my nights were so troubled with dreams of pregnancy and childbirth that I often wrote them down. In one such dream, impatient to see the child, I scooped a baby boy out of my enormous belly and looked at him as if through a scrim of sheer stocking stretched taut. He was toddler-sized and fully dressed, in pale yellow suspender shorts and a white T-shirt. I decided to call him Andrew.

In another dream, a doctor told me I was carrying twin boys. In another, I was standing naked under an enormous sky, holding a newborn girl. The stars above were flickering in all colors, and I felt whole and at peace. In another, I was in a wide clearing, living outdoors without a tent. There I gave birth to three babies—two girls and a boy. They all died. I looked at them in their pine coffins and felt nothing, as if this were just what I expected to happen. Sometimes I dreamt about an infant that I'd lost or found. One night, I found an abandoned baby girl in an empty tenement building. Carrying her out of the building, I realized that two men were chasing me. Jake was there, and he quickly hammered slats of wood across a doorway as we escaped. Out on the street we caught a bus that took us to Canada, so that I could not be arrested for kidnapping.

In most of the baby dreams I was alone, which perhaps reflected the fact that Jake and I were sometimes living apart in the three years that followed my release from the hospital. After trying to stay together for a time, we separated for about a year. Then I moved back in to try again, and during that final period I became pregnant again and miscarried at eight weeks. The uncertain future of the marriage was captured in another vivid dream of that time: I was seated like the Mary of Michelangelo's *Pietà*, looking down at Jake's body lying across my arms. And I was sitting not on a chair but on a bicycle, moving slowly along the tree-lined sidewalk outside the office of Dr. Bennett, the psychiatrist I was briefly in treatment with before entering the hospital. The bicycle, like the tents and the camping gear of other dreams, seemed to represent our marriage. We did a fair amount of hiking and camping, and more often we covered miles and miles of hilly Vermont terrain on bicycles. As for the *Pietà*, it had been shipped from Rome for the World's Fair in Queens, where I saw it with my family when I was eight. A replica occupied a place in my parents' dining room cabinet.

The dream is a bizarre tableau: a grieving mother named Mary seated on a bicycle, her husband lying dead in her arms instead of her child. Did Anna's death foretell the death of my marriage? Ultimately, and in retrospect, it did.

The most vivid dream of all was one in which I was anxiously searching for my child, running along the corridor of a docked ocean liner and looking into the cabins. At last I found a familiar room with empty sleeping bags on the floor, but just then a ship's horn sounded. I rushed back to the dock, where a smaller ship was just pulling away. On a bench on the top deck were three of my grandparents, the three who had died. On the lap of my father's father sat Anna—a toddler with dark curly hair. She looked relaxed, and raised a chubby hand to wave at me. My grandfather had his familiar pipe clamped in his teeth. I stared in disbelief as the gangway was pulled back and the water widened between us. Too late. They were leaving me. But they seemed content, as if they looked forward to their journey and to being together.

Seeing Anna with my grandparents was consoling, even though I didn't consciously believe, as my grandparents had, in heaven or an afterlife. But my dreams—unlike my secular, intellectual daytime consciousness—sometimes presented hopeful visions about what happens after death. My grandparents had crossed the Atlantic when they were young, and they were powerful presences in my life. The dream suggested that they were going to a place that, like the Greek underworld, was on the other side of a body of water that no one but the dead can cross. Anna was with them, and they were looking after her.

Clearly, my unconscious mind was working hard at producing its own consolation. It was telling me that Anna was cared for and loved, and that the departed members of my family

were together. It wasn't yet time for me to be with them, and I
needed to get on with my task of living on this side of the sea
that kept us apart. However far I felt from the Catholic faith,
the image of an afterlife where we can be reunited with our
beloved dead just stayed with me. Another potential consolation
that people kept suggesting to me—having another child—
was fraught with difficulty in my dreams and in reality alike.

There were good reasons that getting over this loss took a
long time. Along with Anna, I'd lost the stability of mental
health, and I feared the lonely and childless future I might be
facing. I needed to accept her death and move on, but I also
needed to distill some meaning from the experience. I wanted
to turn what felt chaotic and random or, worse, like an inten-
tional blow from some divine punisher, into a story I could
accept. Amid so much uncertainty, psychotherapy offered a regular structure as well as reliable support in helping me to face
my losses and look to the future.

⌇

TO SOME DEGREE the mourning process had begun in the
hospital, where I was constantly being encouraged to talk about
Anna's death, as if talking were the best way to relieve myself
of it. Everyone wanted me to let my despair and emptiness give
way to the rage they were certain I was harboring. In the treatment plan for my first week of shock treatment, for instance,
my psychiatrist listed two goals: "Patient will be less delusional," and "Patient will be able to express angry feelings." Dr.
Waters was also interested in the anger I wasn't expressing. I
kept insisting that I didn't feel angry—I felt empty. Though
neither she nor Dr. Young ever said so, they were working from
a Freudian principle. The ideas that the melancholic is full of

rage, and that mourning should be an active and verbal process, come from "Mourning and Melancholia," where Freud gave the work of mourning a name: *Trauerarbeit*, or grief work. In that essay, Freud proposed that people must, by juxtaposing memory after memory with their present situation, come to accept the reality that their loved one is truly gone. This process allows the grieving person to free up the libido, the part of the self that was so deeply invested in the attachment, so that eventually a new object of love or desire can be accepted as a substitute for the lost object. Other psychoanalytic theorists developed variations on this model, but all of them emphasized the necessity of working through the memories and hopes attached to the loved one, and particularly those that elicited negative emotions.

The principle that depression is anger turned inward is based on Freud's theory of what happens to the psyche in melancholia. In Freud's memorable phrase, "the shadow of the object has fallen upon the ego": through an unconscious identification, the melancholic has taken the image of the lost person into herself. In this way, anger against the loved one is turned against the ego. Indeed, the lost person may not have died at all, but might be a lover or a parent who rejected or wounded the sufferer. The psychic wound may have occurred in the distant past, and may not even be consciously remembered. In both mourning and melancholia loss is experienced as injury, but the mourner will emerge from the grief work with the ego restored, and open to new relationships. While Freud acknowledged that melancholia has a physiological component, he saw it as a pathology to be addressed psychoanalytically: the treatment must help the patient uncover and let go of the buried, harmful attachment. In the years immediately after completing "Mourning and Melancholia," Freud conceptualized the superego, that internalized, punitive moral monitor, and it became clear to him that the overbearing superego was central to the melancholic's suffering.

Many years later I learned that Freud was developing these theories just as the psychoanalytic movement he created was undergoing a painful schism. The Swiss branch, led by Carl Jung, was breaking away from Freud's Viennese school. In early September of 1913, Freud traveled to Munich for the Fourth Congress of the International Psychoanalytic Association, where Jung's break with him was obvious. The Jungians sat apart from the Freudians, and Freud and Jung did not speak to each other that day, or ever again. The end of his fatherly relationship with Jung, whom he had called "my successor and crown prince," occurred just as Freud was working out his ideas about the impact of loss upon the psyche.

There was one high point during Freud's unhappy visit to Munich in 1913. Freud's friend and disciple Lou Andreas-Salomé attended the conference and invited along her former lover, the poet Rainer Maria Rilke. Before he met Freud in Munich, Rilke had considered undergoing psychoanalysis but decided against it. Despite his often fragile mental state and perennial writer's block, Rilke thought it best to continue on his own, for fear, he said, that if psychoanalysis caused his demons to leave him, his angels might leave too, and compromise his poetic gift. Valuing his literary vocation above all and hoping to resume work on his *Duino Elegies*, Rilke preferred not to illuminate the dark places of his psyche in case the process interfered with the unconscious sources of his writing. Andreas-Salomé declared the meeting between her two friends a success: "They liked each other, and we stayed together that evening until late at night." What they talked about is known only because Freud alluded to his conversation with Rilke two years later in an essay called

"On Transience," which can be considered a companion piece to "Mourning and Melancholia." Freud wrote this brief essay in 1915, when the war between Germany and the Allies made him continually anxious for news of his sons Martin and Ernst, who were serving at the front. Home and family, landscapes and cities, literature, libraries, civilization itself—all felt threatened and precious. The war made mourning a subject of personal and cultural urgency.

For the sake of the argument he wanted to make about transience and the sense of loss that attends it, Freud invented a new setting for his Munich conversation with Rilke, turning what had likely taken place in a city park into a summer walk in "a smiling countryside." Freud refers to Rilke only as "a young but already famous poet," who "admired the beauty of the scene around us but felt no joy in it. He was disturbed by the thought that all this beauty was fated to extinction, that it would vanish when winter came . . . All that he would otherwise have loved and admired seemed to him to be shorn of its worth by the transience which was its doom."

Puzzled by the poet's dejection, Freud saw his attitude as a "revolt . . . against mourning," a generalized, anticipatory sorrow for all that would vanish, which reduced his ability to take pleasure in the present. Whatever it was that Rilke actually said—and judging from his letters, Rilke was quite depressed at the time—Freud introduced the poet's feelings in order to contrast them with his own therapeutic views on mourning. For Freud, Rilke was fixated on loss, and therefore unable to contemplate future gratification. His example underscored for Freud how "libido clings to its objects and will not renounce those that are lost even when a substitute lies ready at hand. Such then is mourning." The substitute that the poet refuses is the knowledge that the turning of the year will bring back the landscape's beauties: in nature, at least, time provides compensation for what it steals from us.

But the argument is a puzzling one, for Freud never concedes that nature doesn't provide an accurate analogy for *human* life and death. Nature's losses are replenished in the springtime, as new generations of leaf and bud, flower and seed come into being. An individual human life comes into being only once. Freud's theory of substitution justifies his analogy to some degree: before too long, another loved person may be found to fill the void left by the first. Today, this process of adaptation and the openness to new relationships might be called resilience, a word that has become a touchstone for psychological health. So the Freud of "On Transience" espoused the pragmatic response—resilience in the face of loss—while the despondent poet looks to our eyes more like a depressed person, for whom loss blocks the view of future pleasures.

In January of 1920, three years after "Mourning and Melancholia" appeared in print, Freud's daughter Sophie Halberstadt fell victim to the worldwide influenza epidemic. The mother of two children and pregnant with a third, she died at twenty-six within days of becoming ill. He was relieved to be too deeply absorbed in work "to mourn my Sophie properly," but "way deep down I sense the feeling of a deep narcissistic injury I shall not get over." He wrote to his friend Sándor Ferenczi of the unexpectedness of this peacetime death: "For years I was prepared for the loss of my sons; now comes that of my daughter. Since I am the deepest of unbelievers, I have no one to accuse and know that there is no place where one can lodge an accusation." To his son-in-law, Freud lamented the "senseless, brutal act of fate, which has robbed us of our Sophie. . . . One must bow one's head under the blow, as a helpless, poor human being with whom higher powers are playing."

As "the deepest of unbelievers," did Freud really suspect that higher powers had robbed him and his son-in-law of their beloved Sophie? Perhaps the unexpected death of the young, those who are not supposed to die, calls up this primitive urge to blame the punitive tendencies of higher powers. In another letter he wrote, "Indeed, to outlive a child is not agreeable. Fate does not keep even to this order or precedence." All of Freud's letters in the aftermath of Sophie's death suggest that he received the blow, whether from fate or, more simply, from the plague of infectious disease that the war left behind, with an unprecedented degree of bewilderment and sadness.

As early as 1913, in *Totem and Taboo*, Freud had defined the crucial role that mourning plays in the eventual recovery of the bereaved person: "Mourning has a quite precise psychical task to perform: its function is to detach the survivor's memories and hopes from the dead." In 1933, when the poet Hilda Doolittle was in analysis with Freud, she mentioned having been very ill during the influenza epidemic, and Freud replied that his favorite daughter had died of the contagion. He opened a locket on his watch chain to show Doolittle a portrait of Sophie. "She is here," he said, as if the locket contained her actual presence. Like the letters he wrote in the wake of her death, the locket worn near his heart suggests that he was unwilling to detach himself from his bond with her.

Just three years after Sophie's death, misfortune struck a double blow. Freud developed a progressive cancer of the mouth and underwent the first of many oral surgeries. Then, in June of 1923, Sophie's four-year-old son, Heinele, died of tuberculosis. Freud, whom his biographer Peter Gay calls "the man without tears," wept at the death of the beloved grandson he called *mein Kind*. At the time of Sophie's death he had been more prepared for disaster, he later explained to a friend, because the war had increased his "resignation to fate." But now he was profoundly unsettled as death stole a still younger child from him. "I am taking this loss so badly, I believe that I have never experienced anything harder. . . . Fundamentally everything has lost its value." By July, he remarked on his "present distaste for life": "I have never had a depression before, but this now must be one." In August, he wrote to a friend that he was "obsessed by impotent longing for the dear child"; to another he said that the boy "meant the future to me and thus has taken the future away with him." A depressed Freud proved unable to follow his own prescription for successful mourning; his increasing age, his illness, and the mounting weight of his losses made it impossible for him to recover his energies and optimism. After the death of Heinele, the aging Freud felt indifferent to his remaining grandchildren and lost his pleasure in life.

When the eight-year-old son of his friend Ludwig Binswanger died in 1926, Freud sent a letter of condolence in which he recalled the deaths of Sophie and Heinele: "Although we know that after such a loss the acute state of mourning will subside, we also know we shall remain inconsolable and will never find a substitute. No matter what may fill the gap, even if it be filled completely, it nevertheless remains something else." Perhaps no substitute is possible for a child taken by death or for anyone truly beloved. Someone or something else may occupy the gap but the gap remains, in the shape of the absent one. Today, a large body of evidence shows that the death of a child makes mourning a difficult, prolonged, and possibly interminable project. *We shall remain inconsolable and will never find a substitute*, Freud writes, bereft of the optimism he espoused in "On Transience." In the face of transience in its most painful manifestation, the death of children, Freud abandoned the principle that mourning frees us "to replace the lost objects by fresh ones equally or still more precious." Ironically, a decade after meeting with Rilke, even as his theories were beginning to take hold and would powerfully influence psychiatric treatment in America and elsewhere, Freud had moved close to the poet's mournful position, which he had argued against. But he didn't revise his mourning theory, and his private reversal went unacknowledged in psychoanalytic practice, which would base its therapeutic model on Freud's wartime essay, "Mourning and Melancholia."

~~~

AND WHAT OF RILKE? He continued to work intermittently on the *Duino Elegies* begun in 1912, and completed the series a decade later. By then, he had increasingly resolved "to hold life open toward death." The poems assume a continuity between life and death, which together are "a great Whole." Instead of preserving a defensive boundary in the psyche between life and death, Rilke wanted to keep the door to the underworld open. In his perspective on death, Rilke sought what lies beyond material reality and rational perception. Death is the realm of the invisible, not an erasure but a metamorphosis.

What I found useful in reading Rilke's elegies was the idea that the state of mourning is inevitable, given a human being's finite life in time. Life and death are dual presences, equally valid and equally real. To a bereaved friend, Rilke suggested that mourning opens a path to a necessary kind of knowledge: "Our instinct should not be to desire consolation over a loss but rather to develop a deep and painful curiosity to explore this loss completely, to experience the peculiarity, the singularity, and the effects of particularly *this* loss in our life."

As early as the first elegy, completed in 1912, Rilke referred to "those who died young" and insisted that grief is not a negative condition, because our unbroken connection with those who have died is elemental and necessary. "In the end, those who were carried off early no longer need us," he writes,

> But we, who do need
> such great mysteries, we for whom grief is so often
> the source of our spirit's growth——: could we exist without *them?*

The ninth elegy includes a passage close to what Freud wrote in 1926 to Ludwig Binswanger upon the death of his son: because each person, each loss, is unique, there can be no substitute.

> Us, the most fleeting of all.
> *Once* for each thing. Just once; no more. And we too,
> Just once. And never again.

The double mystery of our uniqueness and our transient passage on earth is one that Rilke felt restlessly compelled to pursue and, ultimately, to celebrate. Through the process of writing the elegies, Rilke could arrive at the statement "Being here is magnificent," even as he approached his death from leukemia in 1926. He pushed his thinking about death right up against the edge of the knowable and the sayable. In doing so Rilke assured, as great poets do, his own immortality.

I'm drawn to Rilke's conviction that the dead remain with us in some way; I've come to believe that. They are what Virginia Woolf called "invisible presences." This might be seen as a defense against loss, but it's also a bridge—one that does not depend upon belief in an afterlife—between the present, where the mourner is bereft, and the past, where the loved one was still alive. Writing about this many years later, I see that for a long time I couldn't accept the fact that Anna was dead. I wanted to see her. I wanted her back.

This mode of thinking—which is essentially a refusal to mourn—isn't so unusual. I've come across it in the work of many writers across long periods of time. Joan Didion, in her acutely observed memoir *The Year of Magical Thinking*, writes about her unspoken and perhaps unconscious agenda in the weeks and months following the sudden death of her husband John Gregory Dunne. After she had seen his ashes interred in the wall of the Cathedral of St. John the Divine, after she had held a memorial service for him, led by an Episcopal priest and a Catholic priest, with hundreds of people in attendance, she acknowledges her disappointment at the outcome:

> *But I did the ritual. I did it all. . . . And it still didn't bring him back.*
> "Bringing him back" had been through those months my hidden focus, a magic trick. By late summer I was beginning to see this clearly. "Seeing it clearly" did not yet allow me to give away the clothes he would need.

I understood Didion's magical thinking very well: if wishing had the power to return the dead to life, her husband would be needing those clothes. After Anna's death, Jake and I put away the tiny clothes, the unopened package of diapers, the quilt and crib bumpers and the little sweater I'd made. I assumed that they would all be put to use, and that the child who arrived to use them would be Anna, again.

Stories from the ancient past also bear witness to this refusal to accept death's permanence. The poet Orpheus takes the extraordinary action of going to the underworld to beg for his wife, Eurydice, who dies of a snake bite on their wedding day. I remember crying when I first read this story as a child, in D'Aulaire's book of Greek myths. Walking back, Orpheus turns to be sure she is following, although he has been ordered not to turn around until they reach the earth's surface. He loses her at that moment. Hermes, walking alongside Eurydice, stops her. They turn and head back down the path. Rilke wrote a poem about this too.

NO CLASSICAL STORY felt more relevant to my own loss than that of the goddess Demeter and her efforts to get her daughter, Persephone, back from the world of the dead. It was recorded in an ancient poem called the Homeric *Hymn to Demeter*, with which I was unfamiliar until I taught it in a first-year literature course at a women's college. At the time, I was still trying to understand why what had happened to Anna and to me had been so devastating. I was still having what are called anniversary reactions, feeling sadness and anxiety increase in the darkening days of December, around the time of her death. The anonymous *Hymn* is the literary remnant of a secretive religion called the Eleusinian Mysteries, which for centuries provided solace to people who sought consolation in the face of their mortality.

Composed by an unknown writer of the Homeric school in the early sixth century B.C.E., the hymn was sung at religious festivals in honor of Demeter, the goddess of grain. It conveys with great power the effect on a mother of having her child stolen by death, while speaking directly to the issues of transience, loss, and mourning that preoccupied Freud much later. The story is familiar in its general outlines: Hades comes up to Olympus from the underworld with a proposal for his brother Zeus. He wants to take Zeus's daughter Persephone as his wife and queen. Zeus is troubled by Hades's request, knowing that Demeter will never agree to give her daughter to the god of death. So the brothers agree on a kidnapping, to be carried out without Demeter's knowledge. Playing in a meadow of flowers with her girlfriends, Persephone reaches for an extraordinary flower, a hundred-blossomed narcissus that Gaia, the earth, has placed there as a lure. At the moment Persephone plucks it, Hades's chariot emerges from a chasm in the earth, he grabs the girl, and the chariot disappears underground again.

Because the bond connecting this mother and daughter is symbiotic, the moment of the kidnapping doesn't go unnoticed by Demeter. On Olympus, the home of the gods, she thinks she has heard Persephone scream. Distraught and tearing her hair she descends to earth, searching for nine days until she learns from Hecate, the moon, that Hades has stolen her daughter. She refuses to return to Olympus and, disguising herself as an old woman, she mingles with the women of Eleusis, where she becomes a nursemaid to the king's infant son. At night, Demeter secretly tries to make the baby immortal by dipping him in fire. Discovered in this act by the child's terrified mother, Demeter reveals herself in all her divine beauty and scolds the mother for her stupidity, for she has ruined her son's chance of living forever.

In her withdrawal from Olympus, Demeter has allowed the grain to die. When all of the crops on earth wither away and mortals are threatened with famine, Zeus sends Hermes to the underworld to bring Persephone back to her mother. Demeter is overjoyed—until she learns that Persephone has eaten some pomegranate seeds that Hades offered her. Because she has accepted food from her host, Persephone is bound to return. She will spend a third of the year there as Hades's queen, and two-thirds of the year with her mother. On the surface, the story is a simple nature allegory: Persephone, whose name means *spring*, is a girl with a flower's beauty. Demeter is the life-giving mother, identified with ears of corn and sheaves of grain. In the underworld, Persephone eats of the pomegranate, a fruit filled with seeds. In its metaphors as well as its settings, the *Hymn* aligns flower, fruit, and seed with the female reproductive cycle and also inevitably with death. The seed falls to earth. The cycle begins again. The Greek called their dead *demetrioi*, Demeter's people, and sowed grain on their graves.

I soon discovered that many contemporary poets had returned to the Demeter-Persephone story, and these recent versions worked well side by side with the ancient one. Eavan Boland's poem "The Pomegranate" focuses on the way that a woman can enter the story of Demeter and Persephone from either perspective: as a mother or as a daughter. Her poem expresses the anxiety that a mother feels for her daughter each time she leaves the house, each time she is ill or hungry. That protective impulse is at odds with the knowledge that the daughter must grow up and enter into her own sexual maturity; the cycle must begin again. Louise Glück's engagement with the myth can be seen in her collection *Averno*, and in her early poem "Pomegranate," where she portrays Hades as the

seductive young man for whom a young woman feels a powerful erotic attraction, in direct opposition to her mother's wishes
for her. I was aware, teaching the *Hymn* alongside these contemporary responses to the myth, that my students were at the
point in their lives when they had just separated from their
mothers' protection and were free to experiment, to rebel, and
to be wounded.

How odd it was, I thought, that this poem was on the
required syllabus *because* my students were all women, and yet
it was in tension with the feminist principle that women's roles
should not be bound by their bodies' reproductive capacity. The
Hymn, and the whole basis of the bond between Persephone
and Demeter, was about the uniquely female role of childbearing that mothers and daughters could share. For me, the poem
crystallized the realization that childbearing meant moving
forward in the line of the generations: Giving birth to Anna, I
had become a mother as well as a daughter: I was one generation closer to my own death. Generation, in both senses, only
happens in time, and time is the medium of mortality.

But in myth there is no time, and the two millennia that
stood between the composition of the *Hymn* and my own first
reading of it at a desk that looked out on brick walls and the
tarred rooftops of an urban scene didn't matter at all. I identified
with Demeter's determination to get her daughter back. Like
Orpheus, she refuses to accept that the underworld is a place
of no return. Demeter manages it successfully only because she
is a goddess, and as powerful as her brothers. In her rage and
withdrawal from her life-giving role, she forces Zeus and Hades
to compromise.

At first, in her effort to make the human child immortal
by dipping him in fire, she seems to be trying to replace her

lost daughter with a substitute. According to Freud's model of mourning, this would be a positive and adaptive use of her energies. (It's likely that this aspect of the story alludes to the promise of a better afterlife that the Eleusinian Mysteries held out to initiates.) So too, the flower and seed analogy of the female reproductive cycle, represented by Persephone and her mother, provides another model of life, death, and the substitution for loss by the coming generations. In these ways, the story supports Freud's optimistic vision of transience by offering both the return of the beloved *and* the substitution for loss that he argued for in "On Transience," with nature's promise that spring will arrive.

That promise was especially meaningful to me because I was finding winters so hard to get through. It was as if my body remembered the trauma of the long winter that began with Anna's birth and ended with my arrival at the psychiatric hospital. Anxious for spring to come, I would go for walks in early March to see whether any shoots of crocuses or daffodils might be pushing up through dead leaves. When Jake and I were still together, each spring I would cut some lily of the valley, which grew under the eaves of the house, to bring inside. These fragrant white bells, arrayed along narrow stems and sheathed in bright green leaves, brought Anna's delicate newness to mind. It was a way of summoning her, if only by association. It was the best I could do, because unlike Persephone, Anna did not come back.

AFTER TWO SEPARATIONS, two reunions, and a brief pregnancy that ended in miscarriage, Jake and I had decided to divorce. By then nearly five years had passed since Anna's death.

All that time, the container that held her ashes sat quietly in the bottom drawer of his bedroom dresser. Now that we would be apart, what should we do with her remains?

The summer after I moved out, I spent a few weeks in Vermont near where we had gone to college. It was a familiar and beautiful landscape, where after a blizzard one winter we had spent several sunny days skiing in the woods. In bright meadows, red-twig dogwoods glittered with ice. In the pine plantations, branches sprang upward as we passed, shedding their load of snow. Off to the side of one trail was a falling-down cabin with a swaybacked roof and a missing wall. Inside there was a wooden bed, painted blue. When I was in college, such nostalgic ruins appealed to a strong domestic instinct: I wanted to rescue old houses, cut back the saplings crowding the doorways, transplant the lilacs that had taken root in cellar holes.

Now that the marriage had ended, it made sense to find a home for Anna in the landscape where Jake and I had first been together. Old graveyards are a common feature in Vermont, sometimes found on remote backroads. Some were family plots or the burying ground of small settlements now abandoned, with trees and long grass growing up among the graves. Years earlier, out walking on a narrow dirt road a few miles from our house, we had come across a tiny plot with graves belonging to a single family. The deaths of five unnamed children were indicated only by a single word repeated on small bumps of granite: "Infant." There was a full-sized stone for a daughter who died at eighteen. Beside her were her mother and father who, unless others had survived and were buried elsewhere, appeared to have outlived all their children. There was no shortage of grief in these old cemeteries, where carved slate or granite headstones tell the tale in names and dates. The name of this family, uncannily enough, was Child. Jake and I had stood stunned before this tableau of misfortune, unaware that our own misfortune lay ahead of us.

The cemetery I returned to in the summer of my divorce was the resting place of people who had lived and died, for the most part, in the nineteenth century. The headstones were loosely laid out beneath the wide branches of some old maple trees, and someone had hung a small chime that faintly registered passing breezes. Beyond the adjoining field the river rushed downhill in its rocky bed; it too could be heard faintly. Walking among the headstones, I noticed that many of the parents buried there had outlived their children. In one family plot a stone marked the grave of a child named Abby who died in September of 1853, "Age 11 months 11 days." A brief verse on her stone began, "But again we hope to meet thee." In another plot a pair of stones touched side by side on a single plinth, marking the graves of twin boys Bertie ("Age 10 months, 11 days") and Allie ("Age 10 months, 20 days") who died in April of 1876. The precise counting of days struck the note of anguish. On an engraved family monument, I read of the loss of two sons within six months in 1894. At nineteen, one son was "killed by an overturning load of lumber." The other was sixteen when he died on the Fourth of July, "killed by the explosion of a cannon." Such gravestones were eloquent in their brief notations, and told of how many families in a small place were struck by the death of their young, which in our own time happens far less often. That this quiet roadside graveyard was a place of shared misfortune was moving and also strangely comforting.

I proposed to Jake that we bury Anna's ashes in this place, and he agreed. It was unlikely that either of us would ever live nearby, but it felt like the right choice. When I inquired about buying a plot, I learned that the town was now burying its dead in a newer and much larger cemetery. The town clerk told me they couldn't locate the site plan for the old cemetery, which was unofficially closed to new burials. But he felt certain that no one was buried along the edges or where the turnoff from the road was. He allowed me to buy a plot along one side, and I was grateful.

In a nearby town, I visited a stone yard and purchased a small, slanted granite marker. Below Anna's name and the dates of her birth and death, I wanted to include a line of poetry that would distill the experience of losing her. For a long time I'd known that the poem would be T. S. Eliot's "Marina." Simpler than choosing a single line would have been to have the entire poem carved onto the stone—but that was of course impossible. The line on the stone somehow had to gesture toward the whole poem while managing to express something, however concisely, itself.

"Marina" wasn't among the Eliot poems I'd been assigned in college. My boss, the editor of our publishing house's highly esteemed poetry list, often browsed at the nearby used book stores Gotham and Argosy, and one day he'd brought me an early edition of Eliot's complete poems and plays. I opened that volume after I'd returned to work, when I was terribly depressed and anxious, trying to fend off suicidal ruminations, returning to "Four Quartets" and "Ash Wednesday." When I first read "Marina," I was struck by its rhythmic music. It begins with halting, bewildered questioning, moves through verses ending insistently with the words "Death" and "my daughter," and arrives, after its passage through loss and grief and memory, at consolation.

"Marina" is a powerful poem even when a reader has no idea that it's named for the king's daughter in Shakespeare's late romance *Pericles*. I first read it without knowing anything about the strange play it's based on. By the time I returned to it I was in graduate school and had read the play, which centers on Pericles, a young Greek king who suffers a series of misfortunes. In the midst of a raging storm at sea, his wife, Thaisa, dies (or so it appears) just after giving birth to a daughter, Marina. At the sailors' insistence that the body is bringing bad luck to the ship, Pericles allows his wife's coffin to be pushed overboard. Unable to care for his infant daughter, he leaves her in the care of friends and returns to his kingdom, where he learns some years later that she has been murdered. He doesn't know that his daughter is still alive, or that his wife's coffin washed ashore and that she was revived. The play ends with the three restored to each other. Fortune and misfortune move events in this play with no relation to anyone's deserving or willed actions.

Eliot's poem is based on the climactic moment of the play, when Pericles, mute and withdrawn, having lost all interest in life, gradually realizes that he is in the presence of the daughter he has long thought dead. It opens with the king's disoriented questions and with sensory associations awakening his memory. Bewilderment continues as the vision becomes more than memory: an apparition has materialized before his eyes, and with a halting set of statements, he recognizes the young woman as his own child:

I made this, I have forgotten,
and remember.

. . .

Made this unknowing, half conscious, unknown, my own.

"Marina" spoke powerfully to my helpless wish that my own child might be restored—or that in the absence of that miraculous event, at least another, different child might one day be given to me. But which single line could I put on the stone that would gesture toward the poem as a whole? I wanted to use the final three lines:

What seas what shores what granite islands toward my timbers
And woodthrush calling through the fog
My daughter.

But those three lines wouldn't fit on Anna's small gravestone. I chose instead the final line from the movement where Pericles recognizes that Marina is the future he would give up his own life for: believed dead, she has returned to life. She is

The awakened, lips parted, the hope, the new ships.

These nine words encapsulate the hope and the wish that the play fulfills: that lost children can return. For me, now divorced and moving into an uncertain future in which I might well remain childless, it also expressed the irony that my hope was suspended; my new ships were not arriving, not yet.

My parents came up to Vermont and we held a little impromptu ceremony before the newly carved stone that had been set in place. I read "Marina," and then I read a letter I had written to Anna the night before, addressing her as a child now five years gone. I told her how I looked for her still, in the children who had come into the family since her death. I could imagine her there, playing with my nieces who were roughly the age she would have been. The letter ended,

Since we could give you nothing but a name, this place and
this stone will preserve your name. This piece of granite

proves that you were with us, and that you fought your brief struggle for life. "When it hurts we return to the banks of certain rivers," the poet Milosz wrote, and it seems fitting to place you near the banks of a river, where birds will sing, ferns and wildflowers will push themselves up in the spring, red and gold maple leaves will flame above and drift down to cover you, where deep snow will blanket you on winter nights. The grace of this place, this distance in time, have brought me closer to accepting what happened to you, what happened to me. Perhaps we who lost you are now as healed as we'll ever be, and so we leave you here in peace.

After that I knelt and dug a hole perhaps six inches deep in front of the stone. I pried off the top of the can holding the ashes and tipped the contents into the hole, then reached in and loosened with my fingers the gritty remains that clung to the bottom. I rapped the bottom of the can to release the fine ash. No shimmering of the air, no ghostly blurring escaped from the can. It was a purely material substance: here was the last of her unique embodied life, now mingling with the soil of this particular, beloved place. By our presence there we were insisting on giving a home to Anna's spirit. Then with a trowel I filled in soil on top of the ashes and smoothed it level again. And we left her there, with the trees and the sky, and the river and the birdsong.

6

Early Blues

Most people with mood disorders—and people with other kinds of psychiatric illness too, I imagine—find it hard to put their subjective experience into words. Colors, metaphors, and visual images come to mind more readily than a precise verbal description. I've come to visualize depression as a series of gray tones deepening from pure white to pure black. For me, this image conveys the way depression moves subtly between darker and lighter as I feel worse and better and worse again over the passage of time. Put another way: if the healthy mind is a glass of clear water, depression is what happens if you add successive drops of ink and stir. Each addition darkens the consciousness within the mind, and the vision looking out from it.

Given my tendency to think of depression in shades of gray, I became curious about how it came to be called the blues. Long ago, when melancholia was thought to be caused by demonic possession, early Christian monks struggled against *acedia*, a state of apathy and despondence that the fourth-century monk

Evagrius Ponticus called the noonday demon. By the eighteenth century, people were referring to their dark moods as the blue devils, or fits of the blues. And the descendants of slaves and sharecroppers in the Mississippi Delta who played and sang the blues transformed all kinds of trouble—drinking and gambling, heartbreak and sexual longing, poverty and racism, into one of the great musical art forms.

It's a strange coincidence, then, one owing to science and not to art, that the color blue—a blue dye synthesized in 1876—was the first in a series of steps that led to the creation of a truly effective antidepressant. At that time, asylum psychiatrists could do nothing to cure those they treated because they didn't understand what was causing the symptoms. Their task was to calm their anxious, agitated, or psychotic patients, to physically restrain those who were violent, to prevent suicides, and to confine patients whose families couldn't take care of them. In the century before effective drugs for psychosis and depression arrived in the 1950s—by way of that blue dye—doctors sedated their asylum patients with opiates, digitalis, chloral, barbiturates, and bromides.

In the quest for effective antidepressant drugs, the two great challenges facing scientists have been learning the causes of disorder and finding ways to target and reverse those causes. Although one might think that the two go hand in hand, they haven't. Instead, substances that affect the nervous system were discovered at a time when the nervous system was still poorly understood, and these substances then became the ground of further exploration and hypotheses. Since the mid-twentieth century we have had chemical agents that ease the symptoms of depression, but arriving at a clear understanding of what their effects mean within the complex neurophysiological disorder that seems to underlie the illness has been more difficult. Nevertheless, millions of Americans have come to rely on them.

The color that started it all, methylene blue, was created by a chemist called Herbert Caro at a time when chemists were creating dyes for the booming nineteenth-century textile industry. Trained as a calico printer in his native Germany, Caro later moved to Manchester, England, and worked in a chemical firm that made aniline-based dyes to meet the industry's demand for new colors. As it turned out, methylene blue wasn't well suited to the printing of cottons because it wasn't colorfast, but its core compound, a three-ringed molecule called phenothiazine, was synthesized a few years later by Heinrich Bernthsen. Phenothiazine would prove important in drug research and in medicine as an anesthetic, an antipsychotic, an antihistamine, and an antimalarial.

In the late 1880s another German chemist, Paul Ehrlich, discovered that he could use methylene blue to stain cells. Under the microscope, he saw that the dye could isolate and deactivate certain live organisms, including plasmodium, the malaria parasite. (It was given to soldiers serving in the Pacific in World War II to prevent malaria; they were unhappy when their urine and the whites of their eyes turned blue.) It was phenothiazine, Ehrlich realized, that determined methylene blue's affinity with nerve cells. When he injected a bit of the dye into a frog and then excised the tip of the frog's tongue, he saw "the most subtle dark-blue ramifications of the nervous system of the tongue become visible . . . in a picture of impressive beauty." In his address on winning 1908 Nobel Prize for his work on immune system antibodies, Ehrlich set out the hypotheses that there must be receptors in the nervous system, and that phenothiazine might be helpful in the treatment of psychoses.

Decades later, he was proven correct. Pietro Bodoni, an asylum doctor in Genoa, usually goes unmentioned in this story, but in 1899 he wrote of his success in calming agitated and psychotic patients with methylene blue.

When reading about drug discoveries, one will almost certainly come upon the odd word "serendipity." It comes from an ancient Persian fairy tale in which the three traveling princes of Serendip keep stumbling upon what they are not seeking. Penicillin for infections, warfarin for smallpox—these are two such fortunate accidents. The serendipitous discovery of a new chemical agent often sets off a process of finding what it might be useful for. This was the case with methylene blue and its active molecule, phenothiazine. Herbert Caro's dye wasn't useful in dyeing cottons, but Paul Ehrlich found it useful for staining cells. The road to relief from both psychosis and melancholic depression began with phenothiazine and Ehrlich's hypothesis about receptors in the nervous system. Then nothing much happened for several decades.

~~~~~

BY 1950, RESEARCHERS at the French pharmaceutical firm Rhône-Poulenc were focused on the antihistamine characteristics of phenothiazine—particularly its sedative effect on the central nervous system. Scientists had realized that giving an antihistamine along with an anesthetic could lower the chances of surgical shock, a sudden and often fatal drop in blood pressure sometimes caused by anesthesia. Henri Laborit, a French army surgeon and anesthesiologist at the Val-de-Grâce military hospital in Paris, had been looking for something that would prevent shock by stabilizing the autonomic nervous systems of patients during surgery. In 1952, he tried a phenothiazine compound from Rhône-Poulenc called chlorpromazine, and found that it was not only effective in preventing surgical shock, but that it rapidly induced a state of calm indifference without loss of consciousness. Here was another confirmation that phenothiazine did something—it was unclear precisely what or how—to the central nervous system. Laborit suggested to the psychiatrists at Val-de-Grâce that it might be useful in treating agitated patients, and soon psychiatrists in Paris and beyond were carrying out trials with chlorpromazine. In the days before randomized clinical trials came to be the standard protocol, psychiatrists tested agents in this small-scale, ad hoc way, closely observing effects on their own patients, and sometimes on themselves.

At Sainte-Anne hospital in Paris, Jean Delay and Pierre Deniker gave small doses of the drug to thirty-eight patients with mania, and the calming effect was striking. With their psychotic patients, the results were even more impressive. In 1955, after Delay held an international conference and presented his results to psychiatrists from fifteen countries, the use of chlorpromazine spread rapidly. Heinz Lehmann, the director of a psychiatric hospital in Montreal, found that in his agitated schizophrenic and manic patients, many of whom had been delusional for years, chlorpromazine's effects were extraordinary. "One has the impression that this drug promotes an attitude of sober resignation and of critical reflection, even in acutely disturbed patients," Lehmann wrote. For people who at times had to be held in physical restraints, and for their caregivers, a breakthrough moment had arrived. The pharmaceutical company Smith, Kline & French, which gave it the brand name Thorazine for the U.S. market, was richer by seventy-five million dollars just a year after doctors began using it in American psychiatric hospitals. Troublesome side effects caused by prolonged use of chlorpromazine—neurological tics and weight gain, among others—were rarely mentioned amid all the buzz.

~~~~

IN SWITZERLAND, before all the chlorpromazine excitement broke out, the Geigy Company had also been seeking to create an antihistamine useful for sedation. Geigy began as a dye manufacturer, and its chemists decided to look back through the warehoused company archive for molecules similar to phenothiazine. They chose a dye from 1898 called summer blue, with an active molecule called iminodibenzyl, in the hope of finding a useful sedative or hypnotic. After creating and testing several versions, in 1953 the researchers concentrated their efforts on the one whose structure was closest to that of chlorpromazine. Geigy labeled their chosen compound G22355, and sent it out to psychiatrists who had tested compounds for them in the past.

One of these doctors was Roland Kuhn, chief psychiatrist at the Münsterlingen Asylum on Lake Constance, which had about seven hundred inpatients. He was already dispensing chlorpromazine when Geigy asked him to test their new drug on the asylum's schizophrenic patients. The results were not encouraging. Some became agitated, others became hypomanic, and those who had been taking chlorpromazine deteriorated. One man escaped from the grounds and rode a bicycle to town in his nightshirt, singing loudly all the way. The residents of Münsterlingen were not pleased, and Geigy brought the trial to an end.

After a time, Geigy asked Kuhn to try G22355 again, this time with his depressive patients. Like other psychiatrists of his day, Kuhn was accustomed to thinking of depressive patients in two categories: those with the melancholic type that he called vital or endogenous depression (an illness), and those with psychoreactive depression (a response to life events). Of the treatments available in the early 1950s, Kuhn felt that only two were effective. He used electroshock therapy for the worst cases in the first category, and psychotherapy for those in the second. Neither treatment was ideal. Prolonged shock therapy caused cognitive side effects and had to be managed carefully, while psychotherapy could take a long time to produce results. Stimulants like amphetamines were also used to treat depression at the time, but they were transient in their effects and could lead to addiction. Although he was a trained psychoanalyst, Kuhn was no purist. He hoped that his patients with severe depression might one day be treated with a drug as effective as chlorpromazine.

Kuhn began his trial of G22355 with a depressed and delusional patient called Paula F. on the twelfth of January, 1956. Six days later, a nurse reported that when Paula awoke that morning she appeared to be entirely well. Her "facial expression, her behavior, and her total being" were transformed. By April, Kuhn had tested the drug among broader groups of patients and was convinced that the compound had "markedly anti-depressive properties" and an "immense potential." Kuhn wrote in his report for a Swiss medical journal that G22355 was most effective in patients with endogenous depression: "We mean by this a general retardation in thinking and action, associated with fatigue, heaviness, a feeling of oppression, and a melancholic or even despairing mood, all of these symptoms being aggravated in the morning and tending to improve in the afternoon and evening." Such patients presented with "frequent depressive delusions and suicidal urges." In the autumn of 1957, Kuhn presented his findings at the Second World Congress of Psychiatry in Geneva to an audience of only about a dozen psychiatrists. They were unimpressed, probably because of their psychoanalytic bias. Frank Ayd, an American who was present, later commented that those in the room were slow to realize "we were hearing the first announcement of a drug that was going to revolutionize the treatment of affective disorders."

Six months later, Kuhn brought the news of his revolutionary discovery to the United States. He reported to doctors at the Galesburg State Hospital in Illinois that imipramine could bring about an extraordinary change within a short time, as patients' tormenting fixed ideas, despondency, and despair all gave way to increased energy and renewed hope in the future. Such dramatic results, he said, would "not be achieved by intensive prolonged psychotherapy." Kuhn admitted that for the present, imipramine's mode of action remained "completely unknown." Nonetheless, the implication was undeniable: imipramine could make hospitalization and electrotherapy unnecessary, and could also make obsolete the expenditure of time and effort that psychotherapy required of the patient with endogenous depression. A rapid drug response verified the ancient belief that endogenous depression—melancholia—was a disorder in the body.

Despite the positive response of Kuhn's patients, Geigy was slow to follow through in making Kuhn's new antidepressant available to the public. They had set out to develop a rival to chlorpromazine, the powerful tranquilizer that was calming agitated and psychotic patients in asylums all through Europe and the United States. Geigy executives remained unconvinced that imipramine, so well suited to patients with melancholia, could result in anything like the profits that chlorpromazine was generating. There just weren't all that many sufferers of melancholia. But it was not only melancholic patients who could benefit: Kuhn also reported excellent results in "several cases of apparently purely reactive depression." In 1956, the company began consulting with outside experts to try and determine whether imipramine could command a wider market worth investing in. It wasn't until a Geigy board member witnessed its extraordinary effect upon a relative with severe depression that the company decided to launch the drug in Switzerland. G22355 was now called imipramine hydrochloride, with the brand name Tofranil. It was the first in the family of tricyclic antidepressants, named for the three-ringed molecular structure they shared with methylene blue and chlorpromazine.

A scholarly looking ad for Tofranil published in a Swiss medical journal in 1956 offers a glimpse of how Geigy imagined the market for imipramine. It features an image of the mandrake plant from a fifteenth-century book of herbal medicine, and in small print refers to the earlier dependence on herbal remedies and magic in curing mood disorders. The juice of the mandrake plant, believed to have magical properties, was given as a soporific to people suffering from mania, melancholia, and other ailments from ancient times. It was also poisonous, and the large caption points to imipramine as a great step forward. Translated to English, it reads, "Tofranil, a milestone in the treatment of melancholia."

Imipramine finally arrived on the U.S. market in 1959, also branded Tofranil, at a moment when lesser forms of depression and anxiety were already being addressed in a market saturated with stimulants and with minor tranquilizers like Miltown. It was marketed solely to doctors, with print ads appearing in medical journals like *Mental Hospitals* and the *American Journal of Psychiatry*. Compared with the bright optimism of antidepressant ads four decades later, which were targeted at the whole consumer market in *Time*, *Newsweek*, and other general interest magazines, these ads are somber and serious. Geigy didn't change the tone of its advertising for the U.S. market, where ads for Tofranil conveyed the darkness of the illness it was meant to treat. In 1963, an eerie, alien-like face with sunken eye sockets appeared in the *Archives of Internal Medicine*, the image seeming to fade away much as the vibrant self does in melancholic depression. Two columns of small text alongside the image provided information a physician would need, and emphasized how Tofranil could halt a depressive disorder "before it becomes deeply entrenched, and will save the patient from hospitalization and electroshock."

Today, when depression is a leading global cause of disability, it's hard to imagine Geigy's hesitation in bringing imipramine to the market. But at the time, far fewer people were hospitalized for depression than for mania and schizophrenia. People were brought to asylums only when they could no longer function, or when they were suicidal. Those who were less severely depressed, I assume, went without treatment and possibly without notice, since depression tends to make people feel ashamed and unwilling to talk about their state of mind. The creation of effective drugs brought the illness out of the shadows, but it was not until the late 1980s that this development really took hold.

Antidepressants and other psychiatric drugs were a major advance in treatment at a time when psychoanalytic theory remained the basis of training residents in psychiatry. At the time that I began taking imipramine, the treatment paradigm included both medication and psychotherapy, each representing different assumptions about depression's cause and cure. Biological psychiatry assumed that illness resulted from physiological disorder, and that medication could address that disorder. Psychodynamic psychiatry assumed that depression was rooted in life experience, and sought to resolve problems by examining memories and bringing unconscious, unresolved conflicts to light. In the decades after my hospitalization, easy access to a whole array of drugs made the expensive and lengthy process of psychotherapy seem unnecessary. The decline in the cultural influence of Freud's ideas was aided by drug makers who promised that simply by taking a pill, depressives could transform themselves into more cheerful, socially engaged, successful people.

EVEN AS BATTLE LINES were being drawn between psychodynamic and biological approaches to treatment, there was already a theory in place that supported both positions. According to the diathesis-stress model, some people inherit a genetic risk (the diathesis) that creates a predisposition, while stress or loss in early life experience can trigger the onset of the disorder. People in the same family may not share the same degree of genetic risk, but they do share the same environment. Some will become ill, and others will not; greater resilience and a happier disposition may provide protection. It has become increasingly clear to me that I not only inherited the risk, but that other factors—my gender, my temperament, my religious upbringing, and my parents' stress—increased the possibility that risk would become disorder. My own history is an example of how a combination of genetic risk and psychological stressors can create the matrix out of which depressive illness may grow, and how its physiological and psychological components are best treated with both medication and psychotherapy.

As Roland Kuhn's patient, Paula, was awaking one morning in January of 1956 to surprise her caretakers at the Münsterlingen asylum with her extraordinary recovery, I was in my mother's womb. In April, my parents brought me home to a rowhouse in northeast Philadelphia. I was their second child, arriving seventeen months after my brother. By January of 1964 four more babies would arrive, and when we turned six each of us would go to the same parish school that my mother had attended, three blocks away.

The houses on our street were built just after World War II, and the front entrance jutted out from the stone façade to create a stoop and, on the inside, a vestibule. The strange word "vestibule" rolled around in my mind when I passed through it. Directly ahead as you came through, the stairway led up to three bedrooms, and the living room was to the right. This part of our house sets the stage for a strong memory. I was walking down the stairs and about to go outside to play, when just as I was about to enter the vestibule, a wave of sadness passed through me. It was such an unfamiliar feeling that I can still recall it. It was like walking through a cold atmosphere, or through a cloudbank. By the time I stepped out the front door into the sunshine, it had passed. Nothing that had just taken place had given me any reason to feel sad. I was so puzzled that I tried to make it happen again. I thought deliberately of the saddest things I could imagine. The death of my parents. My own death. I envisioned myself lying in a coffin, my family weeping. These thoughts brought tears to my eyes, but they didn't bring back that unsettling feeling. I was perhaps seven or eight at the time. That sensation returned once or twice while we still lived in that house. I've sometimes wondered whether it was the shadow of the depressive illness that was coming for me, or that was perhaps already present.

Since I would eventually need the drug that Roland Kuhn discovered in the year of my birth, and for exactly the symptoms he described—the general retardation in thinking and action, the feeling of oppression, the melancholic, despairing mood, the depressive delusions and suicidal urges—it's worth asking how this came about. When did my depression first set in, and how? There are no straightforward answers to such questions, as there would be for a disease like cancer or diabetes.

Scientists studying the genetics of mood disorder have found that in families where depression is present from generation to generation, more severe forms of the illness arise. Episodes appear earlier in life, and with greater frequency of later recurrence. While major depression is less strongly heritable than either schizophrenia or bipolar disorder, one study estimates the risk to siblings and children of a person whose first episode occurs before age twenty to be five times the risk in the general population. The risk decreases greatly in relatives of a person whose first episode occurred in middle age or later. There is also a strong correlation between depressive illness and stress, loss, neglect, or abuse in early life.

When I was first admitted to the hospital and a family history was taken, my parents told Dr. Young that each of their fathers had obvious periods of depression, and neither ever saw a psychiatrist or took medication. In that same meeting my father told him that he was on a tapering dose of imipramine, recovering from a period of serious depression brought on by a stressful time at work two years earlier. I hadn't known about this at the time, though I was well aware that my sweet-natured father was always sensitive and often brooding. In his later years he took an antidepressant regularly. My mother's father nearly attempted suicide with a razor blade when he was in his seventies and hospitalized for diabetes and Parkinson's. I never heard about this until I read it in the family history taken from my parents. While it may seem odd that all of this went unmentioned, silence was my family's default mode. We didn't talk about how we were feeling; we simply made space for the moods and irritability of others. Feelings were private, and we kept them to ourselves while as far as possible pretending to be okay.

My family became the subject of a great deal of discussion in therapy sessions, although it felt like a betrayal to talk about them and to reflect critically on aspects of my upbringing. As I recalled scenes from my childhood, I realized that I had grown up in a household headed by young parents who were stressed to the edge of their endurance. My father went to work each day at an insurance company downtown, left at midday to attend courses at the University of Pennsylvania for his master's degree, and then went back to work. He didn't get home until ten on many evenings. The part-time coursework toward the master's degree took six years, and his days were so long that he nearly gave it up more than once. In pictures of his Penn graduation, just days after his fifth child was born, he is holding my newborn sister in his arms. Next, he began to study after work to become a certified financial analyst. He often went to his parents' house several blocks away for the evening, pacing with his book so as not to fall asleep, while my mother took charge of bath and bedtime duties as usual. All of this was necessary for him to earn enough money to send us all to college, as he was determined to do. On weekend nights he relaxed and listened to music. Lying in bed I would hear jazz and blues floating up the stairs: Billie Holiday, Art Pepper, Lee Wiley, Gerry Mulligan.

During these years my mother, often pregnant and often nursing, took care of everything else. She did all of the washing, including the cloth diapers, and everything was hung to dry on the clothesline until she was able to buy a dryer, around the time her fourth child was born. She did the cooking, the shopping, and the housecleaning. She did much of the ironing—which included my father's shirts for work and the white cotton shirts of our school uniforms. Her mother often came by in the afternoons to lend a hand with the ironing. I can remember the warmth of my blouse on cold mornings when my mother did them as we were going out the door to school. It all seems extraordinary to me now, how difficult life was for both of my parents. But the burden fell heaviest on my mother. It's easier to spend a day working in an office among adults than buried in housework, surrounded by demanding toddlers.

In my grandparents' time, the large number of children in Irish families and the expectation that several would have to emigrate led in many instances to emotional distancing on the part of mothers. In my Irish-American family a version of this occurred as well, because my mother encouraged her older children to be independent, to soothe conflicts, to take ourselves out of the way. I responded by trying not to ask anything of her, and never seeking solace or support. When I discovered the work of child psychiatrists John Bowlby and D. W. Winnicott, who were both working in England during the 1950s and '60s, I realized that they would have seen in my case a problem with attachment, and I would have to agree.

THE YEARS OF MY childhood coincided with the years in which Americans began to take drugs to help with the kinds of stresses my parents were under. My parents were exactly the sort of people—mothers stressed at home and fathers stressed at work—pictured in the ads for the mild tranquilizers that were popular in those years. Exhausted parents were also targeted in ads for uppers, like Dexedrine and Ritalin. Some of the images are scenes right out of my childhood. In an ad for Meprospan, a mother in skirt and blouse sits on the bathtub edge looking wearily at a naked little girl about to step into the tub, as if she can't wait for her day to be over. The caption reads, "Her kind of pressures last all day. Shouldn't her tranquilizer?" But in the early years of their marriage my parents would never have spoken to a doctor, much less a psychiatrist, about anxiety, depression, or exhaustion, and wouldn't have thought of taking pills for relief. Growing up as the children of parents whose early lives had been harsher than their own, they never expected to have an easy life handed to them.

A 1956 ad for Dexedrine addresses doctors who might think of prescribing it for weary patients like the young woman pictured, who stands in her bathrobe holding a dishtowel and leaning on a kitchen counter piled with dirty dishes. "Why is this woman tired?" the caption asks. If she is a housewife and physically overworked, a physician should prescribe rest. If she is mentally exhausted, however, "crushed under a load of dull, routine duties," the pill might renew "her energy and well-being," her "interest in life and living." The ad invites doctors to prescribe amphetamines for what sounds like depression, but it addresses the lack of fulfillment that Betty Friedan called "the problem that has no name"—a problem specific to women, and something neither amphetamines nor tranquilizers could cure.

My mother never moped in her bathrobe, but she was certainly tired. She was seventeen when she met my father at a New Year's Eve dance, and she looks radiantly happy in the photograph taken that night. They married nearly five years later, after waiting out his Army service. When I was born, she was twenty-five. By the time I turned eight, she was thirty-three and the mother of six. She was still very beautiful but, like the woman the ad describes, crushed under dull, repetitive tasks. Because I was named after my mother and had the same dark hair and hazel eyes, I couldn't help identifying with her. Her own mother had worked as a maid in the house of a wealthy family when she first came to this country. I hated the idea that this domestic servitude was the fate of women, and awaited me as well. I would have preferred to be a boy, since boys were clearly more valued and more privileged, and they didn't do housework.

Just as I couldn't help identifying with my mother, I couldn't help absorbing her emotional force field. I noticed when her nerves were strained and when she seemed exhausted or exasperated. I helped in small ways—I ran to the store for milk, changed diapers, looked after the younger ones. We knew that to fight among ourselves was to put more strain on our parents. To this day my mother recalls, "I just wanted you all to be good." But it wasn't so simple. That word was huge, as huge as God. Being good meant being quiet, not making messes, not getting our clothes dirty, not arguing, doing well in school, and behaving well in front of the neighbors so as not to shame the family. We were always failing to be good in one way or another. One day a woman across the back alley complained

to my mother about one of us, and she replied with great seri-
ousness, "I am the one who is responsible to God Almighty for
these children." My mother and I laughed about this when she
remembered it recently. It came up in the context of the fact
that none of us go to church anymore.

If my mother was often angry as well as overwhelmed, the
cultural perspective she inherited didn't allow her to see anger
as a justified response to her circumstances. She shared the
assumptions of her own parents, who carried them to this country from the west of Ireland of their formative years, before 1925
or so. Instead of rebelling, she kept trying to meet the ideal of
the self-sacrificing, subservient wife and mother, and she kept
on performing the tasks required of her—cleaning, cooking,
making sure her children were well dressed and polite—to the
limit of her endurance. She had no choice. She had to meet the
standards of my father's mother, who had been sent to board
at a convent school where she learned French and lace-making
and fine embroidery, and who alone among my grandparents
had attended school past the age of fourteen. She imposed her
perfectionism upon my mother, who never received a word of
praise or approval from her.

My own worries about not being good enough were present
from the time I could read, if not before. When I was six, my
mother gave me a book on the lives of the saints. I was aston-
ished by the story of Joan of Arc, and stunned at how bravely
the martyrs in Rome went to their deaths, first having to lie
on beds of nails, or have their eyes plucked out, or some other
unimaginable horror. I knew that if challenged to defend my
faith I would cower and fail, like Judas. I just hoped I wouldn't
ever have to. It was a strange thing to be concerned about, given
that in school we occasionally had to crouch under our desks for

nuclear explosion drills. The political fears of those years—the Cuban missile crisis or that often-mentioned thing called the Iron Curtain, for instance—didn't affect me at all. It was always the impossible challenges of faith that troubled me.

Another childhood memory: It was a summer night, and I was standing with a group of kids outside the house of a friend around the block. It was time to go home, and something in our conversation had started me thinking about time. The problem of Hell, introduced by the nun who taught my first-grade class, had provoked this bout of pondering. Eternity is time without end, and the suffering of hell has no limit in time. I kept trying to think further and further in time, the furthest out in time I could imagine, but I kept failing to grasp eternity. I walked home slowly, revolving these thoughts in my mind, feeling somehow pleased with the hard problem but also scared of its immensity, and trying not to imagine the pain of the fire that would burn me eternally.

On Palm Sunday in third grade I was kneeling next to my best friend Mary Kelly at Mass. We were following along in our missals as the priest read the story of Christ's passion and, for a moment, tears came to my eyes. Mary looked at me with surprise. Walking home, she told me that she was impressed by my holiness. But I wasn't holy. I was trying hard to overcome the distance between myself and Christ's suffering. I was just trying to feel what I thought I should be feeling.

Something in my character made me take all those teachings very seriously. They were presented, of course, as deadly serious. But why did I accept the weight when other children in my family and among my friends appeared to be relatively unconcerned? All of this would dovetail with the illness that was to come, in which guilt and shame and a sense of never

being good enough would sometimes expand to take up all
the space in my consciousness. Surely this connection between
childhood guilt and shame and depression is not a coincidence.

In a box of old photographs that included my third-grade
class photo, I came across a little red booklet called "Stations
of the Cross for Children" that might have been the source of
my fervent wish to empathize with Jesus. Inside the cover, in
shaky Palmer method script, I had written my name, address,
and phone number. On the back, too, I had written my name.
I'm amused now, but also horrified, to see this child's thorough-
going possession of the little book. Perhaps we were given these
booklets in school, or perhaps I picked it up at church during
Lent, when it was customary to meditate on Christ's ordeal from
his triumphant arrival in Jerusalem, through his trial and cruci-
fixion, to his resurrection. Inside it, each station of the cross has a
picture and a prayer, ending in a plea to "Teach me." Here is the
one for the second station, "Jesus Is Made to Carry His Cross":

Dear Jesus, the cross which they are laying on Your shoulders
is so heavy.
How it must hurt!
And You are all wounded and bleeding
how will You be able
to carry it up that steep hill?
Teach me to remember
That when I sin
It hurts You
Even more than that heavy cross.

The logic of all this was that children had to accept responsibility, just as adults did, for the death by torture of the son of God,

because he died to redeem our sins. There was no such thing as an innocent child.

From my present perspective, this all seems a bizarre and certainly harmful approach to educating children. Since the Church's priority in those days seems to have been indoctrination and discipline rather than education, children in themselves were unimportant and were not treated as individuals. Catholic homes and schools alike were places of surveillance and self-surveillance. We memorized the catechism, confessed our childish sins to the priest, and were told that God sees all. One pathetic memory proves just how pointedly I had taken this to heart. When a relative gave me a little red diary as a gift, I wrote on the first page, "To God, the only one who really understands me." The very few entries that followed were addressed, "Dear God." I was uncomfortable writing in it because despite its tiny lock and key, I felt sure that anyone in the house would read it if they could. In a house full of people, I enlisted God to be my friend and confidant.

I've wondered whether the aloneness I felt in the midst of my large family was an early manifestation of depression, although perhaps it's a common thing for children to feel. I was conscious of things that were troubling and couldn't be spoken of to any reassuring adult. The solitude of one's own consciousness can be liberating, and reading was a joyful way—often the only way—for me to be alone. But there's no doubt that an uncomfortable gap opened up around me early in life. I see myself standing apart, silent and observing, aware that I wasn't as happy as I was expected to be. My trouble was invisible, and I sensed that I should keep it that way.

Despite my inwardly troubled state, I wasn't outwardly a shy or anxious child. I felt more free when I was out of the house, playing games with the gang of kids who lived on our block. I liked bike races, stickball, climbing trees, and walking along the tops of fences. I was physically fearless, and found that being a tomboy was the best way of dealing with the problem of being a girl. I knew how to get along with people, so my inward separateness and my outward sociability ran parallel. I developed a double self, and was accomplished at appearing to be just fine.

When I was twelve my father took a new job in Manhattan, and we moved north to a larger house on rolling Pennsylvania farmland that was giving way to suburbs. I had my own room for the first time, and I started seventh grade in the brave new world of public school. My Catholic childhood had instilled the hyperactive conscience and the cruel self-critic, qualities that Dr. Young would later call "the most powerful superego he had ever seen," and Dr. Waters would call a "lack of empathy" for myself. My attention to detail, my sense of orderliness, my desire to be as good, and as good *at* everything as I could be, came out of that particular home and school life. Along with a deeply internalized sense of shame—including the shame instilled about sex and the body—it all dovetailed perfectly with an incipient depressive disorder. There is a niche in me where shame will always live, no matter how far I've moved from the world of my parents and grandparents, and no matter what I've managed to achieve.

As time passed, the feeling of oppression became intolerable. Occasionally I rebelled. I was about sixteen when, one Sunday morning as we were all leaving for Mass, I announced that I wasn't going. The sameness week after week—the priest's droning of the liturgy, the congregation's lifeless responses, the self-conscious parade to communion, the sermon of empty platitudes—it all drove me mad. I declared that I would walk to the nearby Quaker meetinghouse instead. My parents were livid, but I refused to get into the car, and we went our separate ways. Another weekend, I refused to clean the bathroom—something that my sisters and I were assigned in weekly rotation. It infuriated me to get down on my knees and scrub the floor around the toilet when my brothers didn't have to. It was a beautiful day, and I went off on my bicycle to meet my friends. When I got home I learned that my mother had cleaned the bathroom. Rebellion inevitably boomeranged in this way, returning full force as guilt.

I began to realize that I was "sensitive" when I wanted to spend more and more time alone in my room, reading or listening to music. I assumed that being sensitive was a good thing, connected with my interest in poetry and books. In my junior year I dropped the mask of sociability, that part of my double self that appeared to be happy, popular, even enviable. I stopped seeing my friends and stopped going out with boys. High school—all of it—was stupid and boring and meaningless, and I couldn't get away to college soon enough. This, I later recognized, was my first definite and prolonged depressive episode. I remember lying awake in the middle of the night as surges of anxiety tightened my chest and made it hard to breathe. I was intensely irritable, but also aware that I couldn't feel anything—no love, no enthusiasm, no pleasure. I refused to go to the senior prom or even to my graduation. I took a road trip with my sister instead, down through the Blue Ridge mountains and east to the beaches of the Outer Banks. Outdoors, I could always breathe more easily. During these long stretches of gloom, I never thought of confiding in my parents. And it wouldn't have occurred to them that they could have me see a psychiatrist, or that medication was available for what must have looked to them like a period of ordinary teenage angst.

I've sketched the early period of my life and its particular familial and cultural setting to show how I responded to my family's stressful circumstances. There was nothing unusual about our situation, with parents too overwhelmed to focus on nurturing and bolstering the confidence of each of their children. "Emotional intelligence" was not yet a thing; "parenting" was not yet a word. We had two parents who were assuring that their six children would go to college, and they didn't spare themselves. In this we were truly fortunate. My father had lived at home and worked in a supermarket during his college years, and my mother, having taken the business track in high school, had gone to work as a bookkeeper when she graduated from high school.

It's clear at this point that challenging circumstances leave physiological marks upon children, changing the developing neural pathways. Over the past few decades, so many persuasive studies have linked early stress and early loss with depression that we can accept that relationship as a reality. Recent research also indicates that prenatal exposure to prolonged maternal stress can cause lifelong hyperactivation of the hypothalamic-pituitary-adrenal (HPA) axis in the developing child, resulting in greater vulnerability to depression and other disorders. The HPA axis is the part of the neuroendocrine system activated in response to stress, and the source of uncontrolled surges of cortisol in melancholia. Given how permeable and defenseless children are, their parents' emotions pass through them like lightning through water. Any sort of early loss—the loss of a parent or of a parent's love—is felt by a child as a nearly unbearable stress. If depression is an illness closely associated with something as pervasive and universal as stress, it's no wonder that depressive disorders are so common.

Guilt and shame are also felt as stress by a child, and my longstanding hunch that my childhood experience was linked more than coincidentally to my later illness was justified recently with the publication of new research. A team at Washington University found that the anterior insula, a part of the brain involved in emotion and perception, was smaller in depressed children who expressed excessive guilt than in children who were not depressed. These children were more likely to have chronic and relapsing depression as they got older. Andrew Belden, the lead author of the study, said that while excessive guilt has long been recognized as a predictor of depression, "our findings would suggest that guilt early in life predicts insula shrinkage," and that depression in early life may predict changes in the brain. MRI scans increasingly point to evidence that locates depression in several areas of the brain's anatomy. Whether these anatomical features are the causes or effects of the illness is not always clear, but, as in this study, they can help to identify children who need early treatment.

⌇

WHEN I LEFT THE HOSPITAL, both of my doctors seemed to believe that my immediate problems were psychological ones. Dr. Waters, my new outpatient psychiatrist, met me in the aftermath of a single episode of melancholic depression that had apparently been triggered by a postpartum bereavement. The prominent psychoanalyst who was the director of the hospital sent her a copy of my discharge report, which included Dr. Young's notes on the family history taken from Jake and my parents the morning after I was admitted. I wasn't present in that meeting, so when I first read through the report years later, it was strange to see myself through their eyes.

PERSONAL HISTORY:

The patient's past history is most remarkable for the apparent lack of significant problems at any time in the past. She has consistently maintained a very good level of function and has demonstrated a quite stable ego-resourcefulness over time. She is a magna cum laude, Phi Beta Kappa graduate of a prestigious New England college and has worked as a book designer in Manhattan since graduation.

PREMORBID PERSONALITY:

The patient seems to have always had a constricted range of interpersonal relatedness, maintaining a small group of personal friends and relying predominantly on family. Her capacity to relate to others is in fact quite good but a shy, quiet complacency has kept her quite constricted.

PREVIOUS ILLNESS:

The patient has no prior formal psychiatric contacts nor history of sustained alterations of mood and affect beyond what may properly fall in a normal/neurotic spectrum. This current episode represents a first episode of psychological difficulty requiring professional attention.

RECOMMENDATIONS FOR FUTURE TREATMENT:

Long-term intensive individual treatment with an insight-oriented approach is essential for this patient. It is recommended that she continue on nortriptyline.

Given that Jake and my parents described me in the family meeting as a person who had always seemed well-adjusted and performed well in school and at work, not only my suicidal depression but my later admission of deep unhappiness came as a complete surprise to them. This suggests, again, the presence of a double self: I presented to others the person they expected to see—going along, doing fine—while acquiescing to my circumstances and trying to manage my misery privately. But under "premorbid personality," they've also described me as a shy, complacent, constricted person—a person who sounds to me like she is already at least mildly depressed. If this was the façade of happiness I was presenting, I wasn't doing it very well. Nonetheless, it seems that this muted, placid, "constricted" affect was what they were used to in me.

Dr. Young strongly recommended long-term psychotherapy; the continuation of nortriptyline seemed less important by comparison. He offered in the report his insight into my object relations (the unequal power dynamics of the marriage), but we hadn't explored the question of whether I remembered having previous depressive episodes, whose presence would suggest that an endogenous disorder was already present and recurrent. My prognosis appeared to depend on how I resolved my marital troubles, and the discharge report underscores the psychodynamic emphasis of the hospital's approach to treatment.

My own impression at the time was that therapy was the more critical element of my post-hospital treatment, and that the medication would serve to keep relapse at bay in my transition back to the world. Like Dr. Young, Dr. Waters was trained psychoanalytically, and we never talked about what a melancholic episode with psychosis might portend. Dr. Waters continued to prescribe my antidepressant medication as our work together moved beyond my marriage and into my earlier life, to dredge up what had prepared the ground for my current situation. I began to recognize that the sadness and feeling of separateness I experienced as a child had returned at intervals through my teenage years and into my young adulthood. When I wanted to know whether someday I would no longer need to take medication, she would reply that she really couldn't say, but that it was certainly possible.

Over the next few years, as episodes kept recurring, it became more and more obvious that what I had begun to voice to myself in high school—*there's something wrong with me*—was true, and not just the common malaise of being a teenager. The *something wrong* was a mood disorder I had lived with unawares for a long time, and which was indistinguishable from the inward, pessimistic, and self-critical aspects of my character. Elements of my upbringing—the silence and self-suppression, the habit of yielding to others that looks like complacency but is driven by guilt—certainly led to some of my difficulties. Given the power of inheritance and conditioning, it's a lot to ask of either psychotherapy or medication to change what is so deeply marked in habits of thinking and feeling by the time someone reaches adulthood, and it was very late for me when I began to try to change those habits.

The slow awakening to the knowledge that one has been living with a depressive disorder, which allows one's past experience to click into focus through this new lens, is something that countless sufferers have commented upon. David Karp, a sociologist who has interviewed hundreds of people with depression, offers the framework of the "career" for this dawning recognition, which in turn requires accepting the necessity of medication and adjusting one's expectations to the limits imposed by the illness. When I read his book *Speaking of Sadness*, I recognized my experience in all four stages of this awakening. He writes, "Every person I interviewed moved through these identity turning points in their view of themselves and their problem with depression":

1. A period of *inchoate feelings* during which they lacked the vocabulary to label their experience as depression.
2. A phase during which they conclude that *something is really wrong with me*.
3. A *crisis stage* that thrusts them into a world of therapeutic experts.
4. A stage of *coming to grips with an illness identity* during which they theorize about the cause(s) for their difficulty and evaluate the prospects for getting beyond depression.

"Each of these career moments," Karp writes, "assumes and requires redefinitions of self." The slowness of this process may explain why so many people don't get professional help until their illness is well established. The first two steps above align with my vague awareness of sadness in childhood and my deepening malaise in high school; the third aligns with the crisis that followed Anna's death. But step four—coming to grips with an illness identity, which meant acknowledging the necessity of medication—took a very long time.

Imipramine, the drug that Roland Kuhn discovered the year I was born, was the first medication prescribed for me. It didn't save me from hospitalization and electroshock, as the ads claimed it would, but I'm fairly confident that it would have if I had started taking it a month or two earlier. The tricyclics can take several weeks to reach a therapeutic level in the blood, and

I was already desperately ill and suicidal when I began to take it just two weeks before my first suicide attempt. Suicidal patients need to be closely watched in the first few weeks on antidepressants because as the medication begins to take effect, people who had been immobilized by illness begin to be capable of taking action. If energy increases before mood improves, this renewed energy may provide just enough motivation to attempt the act of suicide. This is what seems to have happened with me. And this was why, once I was in the supposed safety of the hospital, they decided to continue the imipramine and give it more time to take effect. This plan ended with my second suicide attempt.

The second drug I was given, a couple of weeks after ECT was over, was nortriptyline, another tricyclic, and like imipramine, it wasn't trouble free. Once out of the hospital, I tried to go running several times a week in an effort to regain some energy and to lose the weight I had gained since beginning to take it. But even at a slow easy pace, my heart pounded at an alarming speed, over 180 beats per minute. Given my youth and relative fitness, I should only have reached this heart rate at a much higher level of exertion. I would stop and walk, then jog again slowly. In bed in the morning, my resting heart rate was also much higher than normal. Dr. Waters sent me for an EKG, which confirmed the tachycardia, a common effect of the tricyclics. Since my mood was just getting stabilized, she didn't want to change my meds. She suggested I forget about running and walk for exercise instead.

In addition to increasing levels of norepinephrine and serotonin, the tricyclics affect other neurotransmitters as well. Two of these, histamine and acetylcholine, account for the sedation and the drying of mucus membranes. The side effects reminded me daily that I was a person with a psychiatric disorder, and I would stop taking them as soon as I was feeling better for a month or two. Then I would slide gradually into a trough of despair, start the meds again, feel better for several months, stop again, get depressed, go back on. Because I was seeing a psychiatrist regularly, this was safer than it might have been otherwise. Therapy provided support and insight, but it couldn't reverse the underlying physiological disorder. It would take another suicidal phase, eight years after the first, to make me realize that medication was absolutely necessary to arrest the freefall of my moods.

7

The Promise of Prozac

In 1985, I was at a friend's wedding reception when a woman I'd known in college told me that she was so sorry about my baby, and that she'd heard I'd had a nervous breakdown. Embarrassed, I replied no, it was *clinical depression.* She was a medical student at the time, and I figured she would know what that meant. It was a term I'd begun to rely on since my discharge a year earlier, though it didn't seem to express the extremity of what I had been through. In saying that I hadn't had a nervous breakdown, I was pushing back against the idea that a failure of nerves had been my problem.

It may be hard to believe, but as recently as the mid-1980s, depression as an illness hadn't made much of a mark on the public consciousness. The catchall term "nervous breakdown" was a remnant of earlier decades, when it served as a euphemism for any sort of collapse that might necessitate a period of social withdrawal, absence from work, or even a timeout in a psychiatric facility. Nervous exhaustion, mental illness, alcoholism—all huddled with a blush of shame under the word "breakdown."

Barely a decade later, "depression" was everywhere. And as the century came to a close, the sheer numbers of people taking antidepressants made it look like an epidemic. The timing of my diagnosis, in the mid-eighties, meant that I belonged to a generation of depressive patients who would become the subjects of a mass experiment. We would shift from the most commonly used older medications—the tricyclics, which were well-known and proven effective—to a new type of drug whose qualities, dangers, and long-term effects were as yet unclear. These were the SSRIs, selective serotonin re-uptake inhibitors, of which Prozac was the first. And we would be joined in taking these new drugs by many people who had never seen a psychiatrist; the majority of antidepressant prescriptions would soon be written by general practitioners. To understand the scale of this revolution, consider that in 1975 only 4 percent of Americans had ever taken an antidepressant, and total sales for the year amounted to no more than around three hundred million dollars. In 1995, just seven years after its introduction, sales of Prozac *alone* reached two billion dollars. Within twenty years of Prozac's arrival, by 2008, the number of Americans using antidepressants had risen by 400 percent. Now, depression is "the common cold of mental illness." What could account for so dramatic a change, and in so short a time?

In retrospect, it's clear that a single drug—Prozac—looms large, and so does the third edition of the so-called bible of psychiatry, the *DSM-III*, which arrived in 1980 with a totally reconceived approach to naming and diagnosing disorders. Between the two, the result was a broader definition of depression and far greater public attention, with an assist from pharmaceutical marketing, to identifying and treating the disorder. If, like me, you have a diagnosis and you take medication, you're probably aware that while doctors provide diagnoses and write prescriptions, they may not have the time to explain why your old medication has become outmoded and why something new is worth a try. Does the new drug represent real progress, or is it merely a marvel of successful marketing, channeled through your doctor? Rather than ask questions, you fill the prescription and hope for the best. While to summarize what has changed since 1980 it is necessary to oversimplify, I'll share some of what I've found useful to know, along with the account of my own struggle to come to terms with the benefits and limitations of medication.

THE SEARCH FOR effective ways to treat psychiatric disorders has historically been rooted in two central questions. The first—*Is the cause of symptoms to be found in the patient's body?*—points to a quest for the physiological processes that underlie dysfunction, and is the focus of the biomedical approach. The second—*Is the cause of symptoms in the patient's life?*—points to an effort to locate the sources of conflict or stress in the patient's experience, past or present, and is the focus of the psychodynamic approach. The first seeks to treat the body; the second, to treat the person. In the twentieth century, a power struggle between these two modes of thinking shaped the profession's models for diagnosing and classifying illness and, in turn, the lives of the innumerable patients they treated.

The historian Edward Shorter comes down firmly on the side of the biomedical camp when he writes, "It is Kraepelin, not Freud, who is the central figure in the history of psychiatry."

In America, the pendulum swing of twentieth-century psychiatry moved from Kraepelin to Freud and then, with *DSM-III*, back again. Emil Kraepelin, who was born in Germany in 1856, just three months before Sigmund Freud was born in Moravia, began his career working in asylums and tending to patients with the most serious forms of mental illness. He made a systematic study of his patients' courses of illness over as many years as he could follow them, creating a card for each patient and listing an initial diagnosis, then revising the diagnosis over time. If the patient was discharged and later returned, Kraepelin would again note changes on the card. His notecards, over the years, began to suggest a taxonomy of illnesses and their probable course and outcome. He was able to see that a psychosis in young people, which he called dementia praecox, was a distinct disease, probably biological in origin. Kraepelin then divided the known mental illnesses into two groups: those without and those with an affective—emotional—component. These, in today's parlance, are the mood disorders. He developed and modified his thinking in the nine successive editions of his textbook, the *Compendium der Psychiatrie*, from 1883 to 1927.

Kraepelin brought three major mental illnesses into clearer view: schizophrenia, and what we now know as bipolar and unipolar depression (he saw these as two different manifestations of a single disease, which he called manic depressive insanity). Melancholia was present in both, but Kraepelin had seen manic states develop in some depressed patients and not in others. In both types he recognized periods when the illness seemed to resolve itself, only to return. Today, major depression and bipolar disorder are categorized separately in the *DSM* and require different treatment, but since their genetics and biological underpinnings appear to be closely related, Kraepelin may have been correct in seeing them as different expressions of the same disorder.

Kraepelin set in place the medical model of psychiatric diagnosis, emphasizing that "it is disturbances in the *physical foundations* of mental life which should occupy most of our attention . . . disturbances of comprehension, memory and judgment, illusions, hallucinations, depression, and morbid changes in the activity of the will." He founded the department of psychiatry at the University of Munich, and his efforts led to the opening in 1917 of the German Institute for Psychiatric Research, where scientists gathered to work on brain anatomy, genetics, and metabolism, hoping to discover the physiological underpinnings of mental disturbance. And he refused to take into account Freud's theories about the causes of those disturbances, because he saw in psychoanalysis no basis in science.

In America, Kraepelin's medical model proved influential at the critical moment when the association of asylum psychiatrists—the forerunner of the American Psychiatric Association—created a handbook of psychopathological conditions in 1918. It was called the *Statistical Manual for the Use of Institutions for the Insane* and listed twenty-two diagnostic categories, nearly all of which presumed, as Kraepelin had, the presence of organic brain dysfunction. But over the next few decades, with hard evidence of brain disease still elusive, the perspective from the asylum receded. Psychiatrists increasingly turned to Freud's psychogenic theories to explain disturbances of thought and behavior.

In America, this shift was largely the work of the two influential psychiatrists, Adolf Meyer and Karl Menninger, who shared Freud's belief that mental illness and health existed on a continuum. The Swiss-born Meyer, who became a professor of psychiatry at Cornell and later headed the Scripps Clinic at Johns Hopkins, was for several decades a figure of tremendous authority. In 1921 he was asked to speak at the centennial celebration for the Bloomingdale Hospital in White Plains, where I would eventually be treated, and where Meyer's influence could still be felt. In that speech, he emphasized his belief that the "life problems" of individuals put "their mind and the entire organism and its activity in jeopardy." Mental disorder was a maladaptive reaction of the mind, body, and personality to life situations. One harmful extension of this approach, the "refrigerator mother" theory of the 1950s and '60s, proposed that autistic children were socially withdrawn because their mothers were emotionally cold. Autism, in other words, was a reaction type, psychological rather than neurological.

One of the first American psychiatrists to receive psychoanalytic training, Karl Menninger called himself "more Freudian than Freud." Along with his father and brother he founded the Menninger Foundation and Clinic in Topeka, where thousands of students were trained in the principle that psychiatric illness resulted from the failure to adapt to one's environment. Environmental stress—war, an unloving family, poverty, social oppression—could cause psychoneurosis and, in more severe cases, psychosis. Instead of focusing on the clinical differences between types of illness, he wrote, "we propose to think of all forms of mental illness as being essentially the same in quality, and differing quantitatively." A case of melancholia, for instance, differed from mild depression in degree, not in kind. The psychiatrist's task, Menninger stated, was to reveal "how the observed maladjustment came about and what the meaning of this sudden eccentricity or desperate or aggressive outburst is. What is behind the symptom?"

The American Psychiatric Association officially enshrined the lineage of Freud, Meyer, and Menninger in the first two editions of its *Diagnostic and Statistical Manual*—*DSM-I* appeared in 1952 and *DSM-II* in 1968—where categories of disorder included various types of reaction and neurosis. The APA also recommended that all psychiatrists should be trained in Freudian and psychodynamic concepts, and psychoanalytic training institutes began to spring up in major cities. Psychoanalysts chaired the psychiatry departments at most universities and held the medical directorships of most psychiatric hospitals, including the one where I would be treated. Research into the physiological basis of mental illnesses had languished for decades, as had any real interest in refining and clarifying the task of diagnosis. Most psychiatrists chose to treat patients with relatively mild emotional disturbance in private practice, rather than the more desperately ill patients found in psychiatric hospital wards. For those who did attempt to treat psychotic patients with psychoanalysis, things could go very badly.

So matters basically stood until the 1970s, when psychiatry found itself facing a crisis of legitimacy. Thomas Szasz, a leader of the growing antipsychiatry movement, cast doubt on the validity of diagnostic categories. In a debate on the question "Is Depression a Disease?" Szasz pointed out that depression is not included in pathology textbooks. "Show me the pathology," he demanded, disregarding the reality that, at the time, pathology in the brain was difficult to confirm without an autopsy. Sociologist Erving Goffman, psychiatrist R. D. Laing, and others pressed the case against psychiatry as well, arguing that diagnoses were more often labels of social deviance than of real illness. In 1973, gay activists proved that to be true when they won their campaign to have homosexuality removed from the *DSM-II*, where it had been listed among the socio-pathic personality disorders. In that same year, Stanford professor David Rosenhan further exposed the arbitrary nature of psychiatric diagnosis when, under the title "On Being Sane in Insane Places," he published the results of an experiment: he and seven others participants presented themselves at eight different hospitals, reporting that they heard a voice saying "thud," or "empty," or "hollow." All were admitted, diagnosed with schizophrenia, and given antipsychotic drugs, even though they behaved normally once they were admitted. None of this was good for psychiatry's public image.

In response to these challenges, the American Psychiatric Association convened a task force in 1974 to revise the *DSM* in a way that would redraw the lines of diagnostic categories. The goal was to create a uniformity of diagnosis: any patient should, on the basis of an interview, receive the same diagnosis from any doctor using the manual. One member of the task force expressed what many in the profession felt: "There is a terrible sense of shame among psychiatrists, always wanting to show that our diagnoses are as good as the scientific ones used in real medicine." Psychiatrist Robert Spitzer, who led the task force and was himself frustrated with the indefinite results of the psychodynamic approach, proposed that *DSM-III* would be "a defense of the medical model as applied to psychiatric problems." Committees assembled criteria sets for each category of illness, debated them, and agreed upon the number of symptoms within each set that would become the threshold for making a diagnosis.

As Spitzer recalled, the process of developing the new manual was anything but harmonious. Those committed to psychodynamic treatment felt marginalized, and were unhappy about Spitzer's insistence that diagnoses of neurosis would not be included. Insurance companies would not pay to treat neurosis: "disorder" must be the preferred term. Going forward, biological dysfunction would be the presumed foundation of psychiatric illness, with the new diagnostic categories intended to catalyze research. A century on from Kraepelin, psychiatry was returning to its roots in science, demanding to be taken seriously once again as a field of medicine.

The newly created major depressive disorder provides an example of how difficult it was for the creators of *DSM-III* to set a sharp dividing line between mental health and illness. The threshold for the diagnosis required, for a period of at least two weeks, one of the disorder's two core symptoms:

☐ a depressed mood
☐ a loss of interest or pleasure in one's usual activities

And at least four of the following symptoms had to be present as well, for at least two weeks:

☐ poor appetite or significant change in weight
☐ insomnia or hypersomnia
☐ psychomotor agitation or retardation
☐ decreased sexual drive
☐ fatigue or loss of energy
☐ feelings of worthlessness, self-reproach, or excessive or inappropriate guilt
☐ diminished ability to think or concentrate or indecisiveness
☐ recurrent thoughts of death or suicidal ideation or suicide attempt

If you have one of the core symptoms and four of the others, you have the disorder. If you have one of the core symptoms but only three of the others, you don't. The symptoms of melancholia—the illness that put Roland Kuhn's patients in the hospital, the illness that responded unmistakably to imipramine and ECT—are here, and so are non-melancholic symptoms. Below the checklist are several specifiers, including "With melancholia," with its own menu for a finer-grained diagnosis, and "With psychotic features." But looking at the symptom menu for major depressive disorder one can't help but ask: Do people with insomnia and hypersomnia have the same illness? Do these various symptoms, in various degrees, all derive from the same underlying physiological dysfunction? Perhaps. Or perhaps not. It didn't matter how you had become depressed or why; what mattered was whether you met the necessary number of criteria, which could be determined (more or less) by a short interview.

As an effort to draw a clean line between disorder and non-disorder, the construct called "major depression" created yet another controversy. Psychiatrists using the new manual reported a newly "high prevalence" of major depressive episodes (MDEs) in their patient populations. A doctor at the VA Medical Center in the Bronx, for instance, noticed that "a large number of very mild depressives who would, appropriately, never be considered for a trial of medication or even psychotherapy, meet the criteria for MDE." For authors Allan Horwitz and Jerome Wakefield, major depressive disorder was too inclusive, containing "all of the heterogeneous categories of endogenous, exogenous, neurotic, and even psychotic forms of depression that existed before 1980." The *DSM-III* created the conditions in which people in all of these categories—as well as people with

normal sadness who nonetheless met the criteria—could now
be encouraged to take medication to ease their symptoms.

GIVEN THE CIRCUMSTANCES, the arrival of Prozac eight
years later could not have been better timed. Had there been
no *DSM-III*, no new and expansive definition of depression, it is
hard to imagine any new drug commanding such a large share
of the market. In another stroke of fortunate timing, in May of
1988 the National Institute of Mental Health launched Depression Awareness, Recognition, and Treatment (DART), an ambitious public/private program aimed at drawing attention to the
dangers of untreated depression. Among the NIMH's many
partners in this project were pharmaceutical companies, who
were invited to supply educational materials to health-care
providers. Eli Lilly distributed eight million pamphlets about
depression and the value of serotonin-enhancing medication to
doctors' offices just months after Prozac arrived on pharmacy
shelves all over the country. While there is no doubt that ini-
tiatives like DART did help many people in whom depression
went unrecognized, and that false positives are in the long run
a far less serious problem than untreated depression, Lilly's contribution to the DART public awareness program was a master-
stroke of strategic marketing. To make prescribing as simple as
possible for general practitioners, Lilly also brought out Prozac
in one dosage only, the 20-milligram capsule.

An early ad in *The American Journal of Psychiatry* provided
a schematic illustration to help potential prescribers visualize
Prozac at work. It shows a balloon-like nerve ending filled with
bright balls of serotonin, a neurotransmitter associated with positive mood. The text alongside describes what is special about

the product: "Unique . . . Specific. Prozac (fluoxetine hydro-chloride) is the first highly specific, highly potent blocker of serotonin uptake. Prozac. The most frequently prescribed anti-depressant by psychiatrists in the United States." In promoting the notion that their antidepressant could correct an imbalance in brain chemistry, Lilly also sold a new and readily understood explanation of depressive disorder and encouraged people to believe that depression is common, curable, and nobody's fault. In doing so, they made it easier for people to ask for medica-tion. If depression was a widespread dysfunction, there was no need to feel stigmatized. Social chatter about depression, long unmentionable by sufferers, was soon heard everywhere, and anyone who wasn't on Prozac knew someone who was. What was so shrewd about this approach was that it quietly dodged those basic and inescapable questions of psychodynamic psychi-atry: What experience lies behind these symptoms? And what is the meaning, or interpretation, of these symptoms? Who cares? Prozac helped. It had something to do with brain chem-istry. Did anyone really need to know more than that?

Prozac's selling point—the idea of making serotonin more available in the synapses—was made possible because psychoac-tive drugs like chlorpromazine and imipramine had become the basis of advancing neurobiological research. By the mid-1950s, scientists had identified neurotransmitters in brain tissue, and had also begun to understand the process of chemical signal-ing in the nervous system. Biochemist Julius Axelrod found that imipramine blocked the reuptake of norepinephrine at the site of the synapse between neurons, increasing its availability for transmission in brain circuits. Here was proof that imip-ramine interacted with a substance necessary for efficient sig-naling. When Joseph Schildkraut, a psychoanalytically trained psychiatrist, saw how imipramine improved the condition of his hospitalized patients, he was suddenly aware "that there was a new world out there, a world of psychiatry informed by pharmacology." Convinced by the claims of Axelrod and others that depression was associated with an insufficiency of norepinephrine, Schildkraut published a paper in 1965 that was cited more often than any other in psychiatry's journals—"The Catecholamine Hypothesis of Affective Disorders"—where he laid out the chemical imbalance theory of depression that would later be crucial in selling antidepressants to the public.

By the end of the 1960s, the Swedish pharmacologist Arvid Carlsson had discovered that some of the tricyclic antidepressants blocked the reuptake of serotonin, and an additional hypothesis, associating depression with an insufficiency of serotonin, was set in place. Working with antihistamines, Carlsson and his team discovered a serotonin-reuptake-inhibiting molecule called zimelidine, which promised to be as effective as imipramine and the other tricyclics. Taking their cue from Carlsson, in 1972 a team at Eli Lilly tested a large group of antihistamine-based compounds and found one that appeared to inhibit the reuptake of serotonin. This was LY-110140, later called fluoxetine hydrochloride, and later still, Prozac.

Carlsson's antidepressant launched in Europe in 1981 and was about to be released in the United States when scattered reports of Guillain-Barré syndrome, a neurological disorder, caused it to be withdrawn. This left the American market open to Lilly's entry, but it wasn't until 1985 that fluoxetine showed evidence of antidepressant effects in randomized clinical trials. In all, it took sixteen years for LY-110140 to move from discovery through research, development, trials, and licensing to reach the market. Lilly hired Interbrand, the firm that branded giants like Nike, to give their drug a name that would send the right message. The team behind the launch said "We created the name Prozac, intentionally distancing it from everything typically associated with anti-depressants: strong chemicals, side effects and mood swings." The two syllables, *pro* and *zac*, were meant to sound professional and energetic.

Prozac was a cultural touchstone of the 1990s right from the start. As the decade began, the now iconic green and ivory capsule appeared much enlarged on the cover of *Newsweek* with the headline, "The Promise of Prozac: A Breakthrough Drug for Depression." The article proclaimed it "a wonder drug." *The New York Times* described it as "one of the best antidepressants ever designed." In his best-selling book *Listening to Prozac*, psychiatrist Peter Kramer speculated on the implications of a drug that could transform personality, making people less timid, more confident, more successful. Kramer was widely criticized for seeming to embrace a future in which people could choose to better themselves through what he called "cosmetic psychopharmacology." But he wasn't the only person speculating on such a future. Neuroscience promised to reveal a new understanding of mind and brain, as well as new solutions for the treatment of mental disorders. Journalists and scientists alike projected a near future in which pills would boost personality and performance. These would be created not so much for "patients," a news article reported, as for "people who are already functioning on a high level . . . enriching their memory, enhancing intelligence, heightening concentration, and altering for the good people's internal moods." Released on the brink of what President George W. Bush designated the Decade of the Brain, Prozac dovetailed with this ambitious and optimistic outlook.

What is clear from the extraordinary early success of the

second-generation Prozac-style antidepressants is not that they
were uniquely effective medications, but rather that the power
of their appeal consisted in the yearning for transformation
invested in them by so many. People hoped, and were led to
believe, that the SSRIs could aid them in becoming more asser-
tive, more likeable, more cheerful, more the kind of person
deemed successful in those years. That so many users failed
to experience the transformation they wanted was only to be
expected—these were chemical substances, not magical ones.
Initial excitement was followed by widespread disenchantment,
which was followed in turn by a normalization of expectations.

During its many years in development, the molecular formula (fluoxetine hydrochloride) that Lilly eventually marketed
as Prozac didn't impress anyone as a wonder drug. In 1981, a
French neuroscientist noted that drugs like fluoxetine had not
yet been released for clinical use "because of their not inconsiderable side effects." These were effects on the central nervous system, like anxiety, insomnia, and nausea. Reactions of
the digestive system result from the fact that 90 percent of the
body's serotonin is synthesized in the gut, where its function
is to control digestion and to communicate hunger and satiety
to the brain. The intestinal symptoms are unavoidable consequences of the drug's global effect on serotonin, and they tend
to subside as the body adjusts to the medication.

Today, these side effects and many more are listed as possible with the SSRI antidepressants, but they weren't adequately
acknowledged at the beginning. Mild to severe sexual dysfunction, including difficulty reaching orgasm, turned up in the
majority of patients—as many as 70 percent rather than the
5 percent that Lilly listed at the outset. According to a 2014
issue of the Harvard Health Letter, "For many patients, SSRIs

diminish sexual interest, desire, performance, satisfaction, or all four." The big difference between Prozac and the tricyclics was that the so-called anticholinergic symptoms were gone: no dry mouth, no lethargy, greater physical energy.

While the tricyclic antidepressants affected several neurotransmitters, and the MAOIs inhibited the action of an enzyme that broke down neurotransmitters, Prozac targeted serotonin alone. This, Lilly argued, was what made it "clean," or relatively free of side effects. When Prozac arrived, the earlier tricyclic and MAOI antidepressants were no longer under patent protection, and their makers had little incentive to advertise them. Compared to the tricyclics, Prozac was safer in overdose situations. The tricyclics required a physician's oversight and the monitoring of the patient's blood levels to determine the most effective dose. The MAOIs required careful attention to diet, because certain foods interacted with them to create life-threatening hypertension. Prozac seemed to present no such dangers or difficulties, and though it cost as much as twenty times more per capsule than these older, less exciting drugs, it seemed to be worth the price.

Other drug companies soon followed Lilly's Prozac with similar offerings. The acronym SSRI, which refers to the entire class of drugs, was invented by SmithKlineBeecham for the launch of Paxil in 1993. Pfizer's Zoloft came out in 1992, Forrest's Celexa in 1998. The competition for customers raised the stakes. At first, Lilly advertised in the psychiatric journals, and then in general-interest magazines. The great advance for pharmaceutical companies came in 1997, when the FDA allowed drug makers to advertise directly to television audiences. With that, the triumph of drug advertising was complete: the industry's directive—"Ask your doctor!"—penetrated the private home.

By 2001, three of the ten best-selling drugs *of any kind* in the United States were SSRI antidepressants. That same year, Lilly's patent on Prozac expired. In its thirteen years under patent protection, Prozac made twenty-one billion dollars in sales for Eli Lilly—roughly 30 percent of the company's revenue during that period—and American doctors had written twenty-seven million prescriptions for it.

For Lilly and the other makers of SSRIs, the chemical imbalance theory was the key to success. In an increasingly competitive society, a drug that could top up an inadequate supply of a neurotransmitter, a lack that might be keeping you from becoming all you could be, was irresistible. Psychiatrist Jonathan Metzl writes of patients coming into his clinic saying, "I have a chemical imbalance that keeps me from getting married" and "I saw the Prozac ad in *Self* magazine and realized, 'This is *me.*'" The theory was so widely embraced, and featured in so many ads for antidepressants, that in the public mind it took on the authority of fact. In Zoloft's popular television commercials, molecules passing between "Nerve A" and "Nerve B" illustrated the chemical imbalance, while a sad, sighing blob suffers from depression or social anxiety. Many people found the animated creature adorable, and were able to ignore the long list of possible side effects in quiet voiceover as the blob emerged from his cave and became joyful. Forgotten was Schildkraut's emphasis on the *hypothetical* nature of his paper, and his statement that his proposal was "at best a reductionistic oversimplification of a very complex biological state" involving brain metabolism and endocrine disturbances as well as other physiological and psychological factors.

In the absence of better explanations, psychiatrists might be forgiven for falling back on the simplicity of the chemical imbalance theory. Daniel Carlat describes his conversation with a depressed patient about an SSRI antidepressant introduced in 2002: "I explained that Lexapro worked by increasing the amount of serotonin in the brain, and it seemed to have fewer side effects than other anti-depressants." But the process is not so easily understood, he writes, because "while Lexapro increases levels of serotonin in the nerve synapses, there is no direct evidence that depression is a disorder of reduced serotonin." For Carlat, the chemical imbalance explanation was especially useful for patients who were reluctant to take medication: "Using these words makes their illness seem more biological, taking some of the stigma away from having a mental illness. The implicit message I deliver in using such language is 'Your illness is biological, it is not your fault, and you are not going to be able to cure it by thinking it away.'"

⟿

"YOUR ILLNESS IS BIOLOGICAL, it is not your fault": these are words that a depressive person longs to hear. Many patients would be told that depressives need antidepressants in the same way that diabetics need insulin. I heard this diabetes analogy for the first time from my own psychiatrist, when she suggested that I try Prozac. For several years I had been trying not to need antidepressants, taking them in bad times, stopping in better times, but resisting continuous use. It was getting to be obvious that I *was* inescapably a depressive person, as opposed to—well, in addition to—a person who was just going through a tough time in life. Separation and divorce, uncertainty about my career and my future employment, all of this kept me in a state of stress that increased my vulnerability to recurrent episodes.

Although it would become my medication too, I was

unaware of Prozac's existence when it first launched. Those were quieter days; there was no Internet, there were no television ads for antidepressants. By the end of 1987, when Lilly received approval from the Food and Drug Administration to sell Prozac for the treatment of depression, I had completed a part-time master's degree in literature while working in book design, first freelance and then full-time for a publisher of glossy coffee-table books, putting in long hours for low pay. Then I quit the publishing world and worked for a friend who had a gardening business in Manhattan while I tried to figure out what to do next. I was in a state where decisions become impossible to make because *everything* feels wrong, because the self feels so damaged, helpless, and paralyzed.

As the days darkened and the anniversary of Anna's birth and death approached, I began to have trouble sleeping. I wasn't sure if I felt hopeless about the future because I needed to find more satisfying work, or because I was just a lost soul. I kept coming disconnected from my life, and could easily imagine myself homeless, jobless, and alone. I remembered the letter Paul had written me after I was discharged from the hospital, while he was still there and awaiting release. He said, "It's funny, Mary; I still get sort of sad and feel alone and look off into space. Sometimes there seems to be no happiness left in me. I'm just hoping the lithium holds me up." He was going to be placed in a supported living situation, which he said was "the best that could be arranged, I guess." I had been assuming all this time that I was getting better, and that I was luckier than my friends in the hospital who were more disabled than I, and less able to have a normal life. And I *was* luckier. But I was finding myself again falling into the state Paul was describing, feeling existentially alone and afraid.

In an old folder, I found some passages that express my terror of the sick self that kept returning. I wrote them on a typewriter on a sunny January morning in 1988—coincidentally, just after Prozac was launched—as snow melted from the tips of hemlock branches outside the window and huddled in clumps on the neighbor's roof. I was alone in the silent house, giving words to a waking nightmare.

I see a big house with no one in it, with paint peeling from all the shingles and a thick layer of dust covering the floors. The inhabitants have departed. In the last room at the end of the wide hall, there is a closet door slightly ajar. I walk across the room, my footsteps sounding impossibly loud in the stillness, and begin to feel apprehensive, even fearful, as I approach it and grasp the glass doorknob. A strange thrill enters my body, almost pleasurable until I recognize the feeling. It is terror. I pull the door open, quickly, before I can change my mind. Light floods the closet, which is under the eaves where the ceiling angles downward. I see—a woman. Her face is turned away. Her whole body is hunched, crouched on the floor. Her expression is first of surprise, then her eyes take on a look of recognition and cruelty. She makes no sound. We stare at each other. Then, like a wolf, she throws her head back and from her cloth-muffled body there emerges a howl that shatters the silence. The sound pierces my ears, pain fills my head and sends me staggering backwards, out of the room, out of the house, running. Because I know who that woman was. If my face were stripped of the nice and normal expressions that I use to fool people into thinking I'm like them, I would look just like her. I've been near there again, that place where time stops and I have to be shut away, because I can't take care of myself anymore.

This fear—that something in me was making me unfit for love, for domestic life, for being a part of the human community—had to be suppressed as I tried to keep moving forward. I kept pushing it down, this fear that I might really be *mentally ill.* (Reading the passage above for the first time decades later, I recognized something I doubt I was conscious of as I wrote it: the woman's crouched position is the position in which, in the shower at the hospital, I made that nearly lethal suicide attempt.) I didn't usually think of myself that way, but each time this thing returned I was afraid that I might have to. And certainly my capacity for engaging fully in my life was stricken, and my confidence shaken, with each recurring episode. Each time the wave swept through, it washed away what little progress I'd made. Each time, I had to rebuild the little hut of myself, with ever smaller scraps and twigs of strength, willpower, and hope.

I recently asked Dr. Waters to share the list of drugs that she prescribed for me over the years. That January, just as Prozac went on the market, she again prescribed nortriptyline, the tricyclic antidepressant that I'd first taken while in the hospital. She didn't mention Prozac at the time: given my quickly deteriorating condition, it would have made sense to work with a drug that she knew would help, rather than try something new and untested. That same month, I went back to graduate school, having been offered a fellowship to Columbia's PhD program. On medication I soon felt hopeful again, excited by my work, able to breathe. During the summer, energized by my new freedom, I stopped taking medication once again. This was my life, so far as I can recall, while the Prozac revolution was quietly beginning.

I usually felt better during the summer, and when I felt

better I tended to stop taking medication. I did this because being on nortriptyline was uncomfortable, and also because I had trouble coming to terms with the fact that I had a serious problem that kept returning. All that summer and fall I got by without medication, and by winter, not surprisingly, I was very depressed once again. Looking back on these years, it is clear to me—as it must be to any reader—that I wasn't seeing the pattern. But if you're feeling good, if you hate the side effects, if you want to get pregnant, you will want to stop taking meds. And until you hit a crisis, that seems to work okay.

In response to this decline—it was now the beginning of 1989—Dr. Waters suggested that I try Prozac. She recommended it enthusiastically, and I was more than happy to try it. Most doctors were impressed with Prozac's relatively mild side effects, because side effects were what most often caused patients like me to stop taking their medication. In this regard, Prozac seemed like the breakthrough drug that psychiatrists and their depressive patients had been waiting for. I had high hopes that, if Prozac didn't cause the heart palpitations and the dry mouth, the sluggishness and the heightened appetite that came with nortriptyline, I could stay on it.

Because I was immersed in graduate studies over the next few years, I wasn't paying attention as the Prozac-taking population exploded. From conversations with my psychiatrist, I knew that Prozac was supposed to be a game-changer, but I wasn't finding it so wonderful. At first, it seemed to be a great improvement. Its effect on my mood was similar to that of nortriptyline: I definitely felt better, although it was slower at delivering relief. There was no dry mouth, no racing heartbeat, and no weight gain, but orgasms could be elusive. It didn't take long for people to begin to complain that their sexual lives were compromised on Prozac. While it's true that during a major depressive episode one is far from feeling any desire, Prozac's sexual side effects meant that many people, including me, stopped taking it as soon as they started to feel better. In and out of new relationships after my divorce, good sex was important, and sharing my mental health status with lovers wasn't something I wanted to do.

Then I met someone whom, slowly and somewhat reluctantly, I came to love. Reluctantly, because I felt incapable of loving someone without also being ambivalent (if not downright negative, critical, and irritable—in other words, without acting like a depressed person) and without jeopardizing that person's happiness as well as my own safety. I suspected that in any committed relationship I would again feel restless and claustrophobic. I was afraid of being alone forever, but I was equally afraid of risking marriage and its compromises.

When I was feeling low I was raw and sensitive and inhibited, and Jim's outsized personality was hard to handle. He was in many ways my opposite: hyperenergetic, hyperproductive, hypertalkative. He was also generous, funny, and smart. He mirrored none of my own paralysis, self-deprecation, and despondence. I trusted in his essential goodness. Before long, I told him about Anna, my hospitalization, the whole grim tale. Eventually, we decided to marry and try to have a child. Because its effects on a fetus were still unknown, I stopped taking Prozac.

After our wedding we traveled through the southwest of England, then up to the Hebrides and the north of Scotland. We visited a friend in Italy and went hiking in Switzerland. So far, so happy. Then we settled down to work in a rented house in Cambridge, spending our days in the library and taking walks across the meadows in the evenings. Jim, an academic on a tenure track, was writing his second book; I was finishing my dissertation.

By the end of the summer I was irritable and negative, certain that I had made a terrible mistake in getting married. I would never be contented with anyone, I thought, and I would make anyone who loved me miserable. I kept these thoughts to myself, but I was panicking. It was crushing that the happiness and optimism of just a few months earlier had been so fleeting. The worries that anyone might have at the beginning of a marriage were amplified and distorted so much by the nihilism of depressive thinking that I really couldn't tell what was true anymore.

We returned to New York at the end of the summer, and I checked in with my psychiatrist to let her know how I was doing. Because I couldn't go back on Prozac while trying to get pregnant—or if I did become pregnant—we agreed to continue meeting weekly during this difficult period without medication. Toward the end of September, a legendary teacher of Columbia's Literature Humanities course became terminally ill, and I was asked to take over his class. I wanted to say no, but I worried that if I didn't say yes I might not be asked again. Had I known that I would be teaching that most daunting of courses, I would have spent a good part of the summer preparing. Imagine having only a few days to read and plan four hours of classes on Herodotus's *Histories* and then, in a fragile psychological condition, walk into a seminar room to meet twenty or so first-year students who, having enrolled in a section with a star professor, could only be disappointed to see you. Imagine a week later having to teach Thucydides's *History of the Peloponnesian War*, followed by the tragedies of Aeschylus, Sophocles, and Euripides, Virgil's *Aeneid*, and other classics. Two students dropped the class immediately.

I tried to take that in stride. I needed to be engaging enough to win them over while also appearing authoritative and confident—a performance that, given my deepening depression, was difficult to pull off. One particularly tough morning, I realized I was shaking as I passed through the campus gates on my way to class. The shameful feeling that I was failing to teach well enough made me work all the harder. This stress only added to my other worries: I was thirty-six, trying to get pregnant, and had been without medication for months. I was also trying to make a life with Jim, while again doubting my ability to make a life with anyone.

As the weeks went by my anxiety rose to a near-unbearable level. I kept doing what needed to be done, and trying to meet my own high standards. I recently asked Jim what he remembered from that time, and he told me that for the first and only time in our years together, he feared that I might be suicidal. He was especially anxious when I was in the bathroom for what seemed like far too long a time, and once or twice, he said, he stood outside the door listening for signs of trouble. He was right to be worried. Down and down my mood was plummeting, so much so that one afternoon in November I opened the window of our fifteenth-floor apartment to have a look at the landing place below, a narrow airshaft between two buildings. I could see my body down there, smashed on the empty concrete alleyway between the sad ailanthus tree and the fence topped with razor wire. I wasn't ready to do it, but I was checking out the possibilities.

It's strange to say, but I had been so focused on pressing forward, resisting the despair, that only in that moment did I realize how much danger I was in. I called Dr. Waters immediately to tell her I needed to get back on Prozac. Because I had been trying to conceive, she said I should have a pregnancy test and based on the results, we would decide how to proceed. The pregnancy test, to my great surprise, was positive. Under the circumstances, this was unwelcome news.

Two weeks later, an ultrasound showed that I had again miscarried. The pregnancy, which the technician called a blighted ovum, had never been viable. I took a Prozac capsule as soon as I got home from the D&C. It took a little over two weeks, and then there was a loosening of the tightness in my chest, a quieting of the fear and the obsessive self-castigation, a greater sense of ease and possibility. When antidepressants begin to work, the relief feels almost like joy.

Earlier that year I had considered ending my psychotherapy, thinking I had learned enough to be able to go it alone. Therapy was expensive, and my insurance was limited. Now it was all too obvious that I shouldn't do that. Dr. Waters suggested that we bolster the Prozac with lithium for a while until my mood began to stabilize. Despite years of work, I was unable to escape these periods of paralysis and hopelessness, and going without medication was clearly too risky. Dr. Waters suggested that what I couldn't overcome was "hard-wired," by which she seemed to mean that it was biological, and of such an archaic psychological formation—childhood habits of thought, childhood feelings—that it formed a bedrock layer of my character. She also suggested that I try to remember that this susceptibility to despair was *a part* of me—not the whole. I needed to keep that part as small as possible, even if I couldn't eradicate it. The trouble was that once it was activated, as this last episode demonstrated, it was immensely powerful. Severe depression feels monolithic, but you can train yourself to remember that the mind thinking such terrible thoughts isn't *all* of your mind, and doesn't define you.

It took a long time to work all of this out, because it's very hard to see yourself clearly when depressed. The problem is that you think with your mind, but your mind is ill and untrustworthy. Your mind is your enemy. Once you've lived through several terrible episodes, you begin to get a feeling for how the thing will go. (In a story he wrote while still in college, David Foster Wallace called it "The Bad Thing," which nicely captures both the abstraction and the horror.) Eventually you realize that you can and do end up splitting yourself: a part of you can remain detached, watching the thing that is squeezing out any light and vitality within you. If a little space remains for the observing, rational consciousness, you can hold on. If not, you can get swept away in the delusion that you can never get better. Trying to kill yourself, for instance, is getting swept away. When the situation is critical, you need to have someone who knows how bad things are for you, someone to watch over you.

This person needs to be experienced and professional, and someone you completely trust, because he or she will hold the lifeline as the waves crash over you. This person should be your psychiatrist, not your spouse, your lover, your sister, or your best friend—none of whom should be exposed to the full force of your despair, or feel responsible for keeping you alive. Your psychiatrist is deeply invested, far more than you are yourself, in your survival, and knows that even a person in your wretched condition can survive. When I first tried to kill myself, I didn't yet know this, and I didn't yet have this kind of relationship with a psychiatrist. This is why the therapeutic bond between therapist and patient is such a crucial partnership. Severe, even suicidal depression can be managed. Surviving it teaches you that it is survivable. You take your meds. You keep in touch with your psychiatrist. You wait it out.

The moment when I opened the window and looked down led me, at last, to a reckoning. I was vulnerable, over and over, to this thing that just wouldn't leave me. That feral madwoman in my brain kept trying to emerge. Nine years after my first suicidal episode, it was time to accept that this was what my life would be like. The severity fluctuated, but depression was always with me at some level. If I were going to try to get pregnant, it would have to be a pregnancy on medication.

Other decisions followed. Soon I would be finishing my dissertation and entering a ruthless job market where anyone lacking in confidence, anyone not having cultivated relationships with the right mentors, anyone without the ability to excite people about her ideas, was unlikely to be hired. I didn't see how I could do well in an interview when just imagining an interview filled me with panic. Could someone with chronic low self-esteem and unpredictable but frequent depressive episodes succeed in the academic profession? It may be possible, but at the time I didn't believe it would be possible for me.

Graduate school was competitive and stressful. During the three years of course work, I never got through all the pages assigned for my classes because I had a hard time concentrating. I realize now that it's unlikely anyone got through them— maybe skimming and triage were all anyone could do to manage the reading load. Eventually I realized it was better to take a break than to sit at my desk reading the same sentence again and again, so I went running, or swimming. Exercise became a necessary daily stress reliever. Still, in seminars I looked around at my peers and felt like an outsider. I couldn't find in myself their confidence or their obvious drive to succeed. Writing, so necessary for survival in a publication-driven profession, was for me extremely slow and dread-inducing. Somehow I won two writing prizes in graduate school, but a cruel internal critic continued to judge me a failure with every sentence.

In *A Room of One's Own*, Virginia Woolf identifies the problem I was facing: "Life for both sexes . . . is arduous, difficult, a perpetual struggle. It calls for gigantic courage and strength. More than anything, perhaps, creatures of illusion that we are, it calls for confidence in oneself." Is it true, as studies have suggested, that depressive people lack the self-inflating illusion that keeps so many people going? And that our less rosy outlook is just another name for realism? Perhaps—during our better times. But during a bad episode, the pessimism and self-disdain are delusional.

~~~~~

WATCHING JIM GO THROUGH a brutal tenure battle, I knew that I lacked the ego strength and the resilience to survive what he had just experienced. I needed to have a child, and I was running out of time. To try to heal the bitter trauma of the past was more necessary than having a tenure-track position. If I were going to try to get pregnant, I couldn't extend my job search to a wide area and possibly end up living far away from my partner (as happens to many academic couples). After failing to get an interview for two positions at nearby colleges that year, I decided to take the more flexible path of staying in New York, teaching as an adjunct, and supplementing my low pay with freelance writing. Although in retrospect this choice of the less ambitious path sometimes looks cowardly to me, I know that at the time it was a pragmatic acknowledgment of my reality. Given that stress makes depression worse, this was a sensible, self-protective choice.

To step back and lower expectations for myself was to acknowledge that I was unsuited for a level of professional engagement that other people could manage. I had fought hard to return to "normal"; now I would simply stop hoping that "normal" was out there ahead of me. Life didn't become much less stressful with this decision—Jim and I were both teaching full-time and we would, in the next few years, be undergoing infertility treatment as well. But at least I had laid down one part of my burden, the search for a tenure-track job.

I still didn't fully accept an illness identity—I didn't think of myself as "mentally ill" or disabled from day to day. I didn't talk about my diagnosis or my troubles with anyone but the people closest to me. I went on trying to be like the other competent, professional adults I knew. But I made space for the depressive episodes that, it now seemed fairly certain, would continue to accompany me through life, and for the inevitable feelings of dejection, failure, and despondence. There was no making peace with this situation, but I tried not to enter into the feelings overmuch, and I tried to keep moving. My attitude shifted: instead of trying to outrun this fate, I would try to understand it.

From 1989 until 1992, I took Prozac for months at a time, and when I was feeling better I stopped for months at a time. Then, realizing I was suicidal once again, I took it faithfully, pretty much, for ten years. In 2002, while we were living for several months of a London winter in a mildewed garden-level flat near Hampstead Heath, I sank again into a state of blank inner deadness. Antidepressants, psychiatrists say, "put a floor under" patients who take them, and it's an accurate metaphor.

If a mood disorder is like a malfunctioning elevator, antide-pressants stop the elevator at, let's say, the basement level. This low and no lower, they command. Without meds, the elevator plunges ever lower, down to where suicide becomes a possibil-ity. This time, Prozac was failing to put a floor under me. This common problem is usually addressed by increasing the dose, adding an additional medication, or switching medications.

When we returned to New York I switched to Lexapro (the brand name of escitalopram), a new SSRI just out that year. Gradually, I began to feel better than I had felt in many years. The sense of buoyant well-being was so unaccustomed that I began to wonder, "Is this how normal people feel?" The heavy wall of resistance that I'd had to push away in order to get anything done was simply gone. I began to feel pleasure in my days—more confidence and ambition, a greater ease and socia-bility and, as time went on, sustained relief from the oppression that had accompanied me for so long. Eventually Lexapro also stopped being quite so great, but on the whole it was better than anything I'd taken before. Because it had no noticeable side effects, it also allowed me to forget that I was on medication.

Like Prozac, Lexapro is an SSRI. So why, I wondered, did it provide greater relief than Prozac did? Escitalopram is a mirror molecule (an enantiomer) of citalopram, which had been on the market as Celexa since 1998. Patenting the mirror-molecule of an existing drug is one way that drug makers keep the money coming in when the earlier one goes off patent, since profits decrease drastically once a drug can be prescribed in generic form. But escitalopram—the "S" enantiomer of the citalopram molecule—is more potent and more specific in its effects on the serotonin transporter. Escitalopram, says its manufacturer, Lundbeck, is the "most selective" of the SSRI antidepressants.

If escitalopram is so effective because of its ability to bind to the serotonin transporter, then serotonin *is* clearly a piece of the puzzle of depressive illness, at least in my case. Scientists have long known that depleting serotonin in people who don't have a depressive disorder does not make them depressed, but that serotonin is very low in the cerebral spinal fluid of people who have died by suicide. In the years since the chemical imbalance hypothesis was so widely adopted, more refined studies suggest that whatever the complicated causation of symptoms, increasing serotonin concentration contributes to repairing the brain's neural networks. Serotonin is necessary for the body to make BDNF—brain-derived neurotrophic factor, which is in turn necessary to build neural connections. The loss of BDNF may be what accounts for the shrinkage of the hippocampus in the brains of people with severe depression. It is possible that I noticed such an improvement on Lexapro because my brain was functioning better than it had been in a long time.

So I lived my life, taking Lexapro every day and doing pretty well, until a growing controversy became impossible to ignore: Were the SSRIs truly effective over the long term? Was it possible that they were doing more harm than good? By 2010 or so, anyone taking an SSRI regularly and following coverage of the debate was pitched into a state of uncertainty. The book that caught everyone's attention was *The Emperor's New Drugs* by the psychologist Irving Kirsch, who had been researching placebo effects for years. It was based on a study he'd coauthored and published in 2008 in the journal *PLoS Medicine*, in which his team reviewed the trial data of the six most widely prescribed SSRIs. These were all of the double-blind, placebo-controlled trials completed before those drugs were approved by the FDA, and included unpublished trials with negative results.

Kirsch and his colleagues concluded that these antidepressants were barely more effective than placebo for the majority of people who take them, and they are most effective for patients "at the upper end of the very severely depressed category." Eli Lilly pushed back, declaring that Lilly was proud "of the difference Prozac had made to millions of people living with depression." A rash of news reports and publications followed, questioning the ethics of drug marketing as well as the fact that so many psychiatrists had been willingly seduced by drug reps who offered free lunches, paid junkets, even actual payments, in return for talking up the benefits of a particular drug at a conference or prescribing it readily to patients.

Then, in the summer of 2011, Marcia Angell's article, "The Epidemic of Mental Illness: Why?," appeared in *The New York Review of Books.* She discussed Kirsch's book along with two others that criticize the overdiagnosing, overmedicating, and overselling of mental illness—Daniel Carlat's *Unhinged: The Trouble with Psychiatry* and Robert Whitaker's *Anatomy of an Epidemic.* This article and the one that followed it in a two-part series, "The Illusions of Psychiatry," caused a great deal of consternation: accusations of bias and defenses of psychiatric practice appeared in the many impassioned letters of response.

While many details of Angell's article were troubling— including the increasing prescription of antipsychotic medications for children as young as two—the most unsettling as it related to my own situation was Whitaker's assertion that psychoactive drugs create dependency by altering the brain's neurochemistry. If a person stops taking the drug, the brain is no longer used to performing without it. Relapse awaits, with the inevitable return to the medication. This was a possibility I had never heard about. Whitaker is an award-winning investigative reporter and author of a book called *Mad in America*, which is also the name of the website he runs. He is considered an antipsychiatry fringe figure by many in the profession, but his argument about dependency and relapse was based on reputable sources. One part of it comes from a 1996 paper by the neuroscientist Steven Hyman, a former director of the National Institute of Mental Health and now the head of the Stanley Center for Psychiatric Research at Harvard and MIT's Broad Institute. The long-term use of psychiatric drugs, Hyman wrote, results in "substantial and long-lasting alterations in neural function," so that the brain begins to function in a manner "qualitatively as well as quantitatively different from the normal state."

The Italian psychiatrist Giovanni Fava had published a paper in 1994, also cited by Whitaker, arguing that psychiatric drugs "perturb" the pathways in the brain of the neurotransmitters they target. The brain adapts to this perturbation by trying to restore "homeostatic equilibrium." In the case of the SSRIs, which produce an extra supply of serotonin, the brain may shut down some portion of its own production of serotonin or its serotonin transport mechanism. "Oppositional tolerance" is Fava's term for this process. This may explain why, for so many people, antidepressants are less and less effective over time.

My reading of Angell's articles, and my subsequent reading of many other writers on the controversies she raised, left me with so much confusion and unease that I decided to begin my own investigation. Amid the lack of scientific clarity about the functioning of neural networks in mental illnesses, the muddle of diagnostic criteria, the uncertainty about what *exactly* psychiatric medications are doing to the brain, and debate about their long-term effects, where is the truth? What is the state of my brain, and is it worse than it would have been had I not taken antidepressants continually for the past twenty-five years? My investigation has involved looking closely at my past, and has brought me to this conclusion: I am someone who should not stop taking medication.

—✦—

I SWITCHED MEDICATIONS AGAIN when after thirteen years on Lexapro I believed that it was no longer doing much for me. I began taking Wellbutrin, a non-SSRI that affects the norepinephrine and dopamine systems. As with the tricyclics, I had trouble with an elevated heart rate, as well as lots of discomfort caused by dry sinuses. I had to reduce the dose to the point where it didn't have much effect, and then I gave up and began taking a recently developed SSRI-style drug called vortioxetine.

Daily use of these medications has meant that I haven't had a dangerous episode for many years. It's clear that the maintenance approach—taking medication every day—prevents those deep depressions from happening as frequently as they used to. Still, I would love to stop taking medication and get by with lots of exercise, a healthy diet, and the support of my family and friends. I would then be my full and "true" self, open to a whole range of emotion. So the fantasy goes. But it's just not worth the risk. Evidence from numerous studies shows very clearly what I've recounted from my own experience. For people like me, depressive illness is progressive and unrelenting: only the steady use of medication protects against it. Readers who take antidepressants will recognize this trial-and-error process of trying to live without medication, as well as its less than ideal results. Whatever their drawbacks, the drugs have provided what's called "neuroprotection" against the physiological processes underlying my depression.

The antidote to outraged polemics against medicalized psychiatry like Angell's and Whitaker's, I've found, is in the calmer voices of clinicians who write about seeing patients day after day, and know through this ongoing work that despite arguments to the contrary, antidepressants certainly do help people. Richard Friedman, a clinical psychiatrist and a frequent contributor to *The New York Times*, offered his skeptical and pragmatic point of view: "The hypothetical risk of long-term SSRI treatment is dwarfed by the very real risk of untreated depression, which carries a 2 to 12 percent risk of suicide."

Psychiatrist Peter Kramer, the author of *Listening to Prozac* and *Against Depression*, wrote a *New York Times* editorial arguing that Kirsch's study was weakened both by his choice of data and his statistical analysis of that data. Like Friedman, Kramer believes that despite undoubted overprescription, too many people with severe depression still go untreated. Kramer recently weighed in on the "antidepressants don't work" controversy with a full-length book called *Ordinarily Well*, an exhaustive and persuasive refutation of Kirsch's conclusion that antidepressants are merely expensive placebos. He writes, "I have seen antidepressants pull patients from the brink and hold them steady."

Since I'm one of the people for whom antidepressants clearly do something, I gratefully attest to their positive effect. They're not perfect by any means, but I'm lucky that they work for me. They have the power that Kramer claims they do, to pull me back from the brink, and hold me steady. And yet, after a period of time, the incredible sense of relief and well-being that they produce when I begin taking them in the midst of a grim episode—this fades, and feeling flattens out. Enthusiasm and true pleasure are more difficult to access. The "holding steady" becomes a steady, detached, and flattened state. I have heard and read that many people on SSRIs complain about this flattening of emotion, which is ironic because it's just what depression produces. I first recognized it at the age of sixteen or so: the inability to feel.

The default on meds is neither high nor low, and "feeling" feels more like thought. I don't know whether this lack of feeling (or excitement, or enthusiasm) could be defined as anhedonia, but it is something like that. Maybe this is the problem with the new neural baseline that the meds have created: you won't go lower, but neither will you go higher. When I'm tempted to stop taking my medication, it's because I want to feel all that I'm capable of feeling. Not the very low lows, but the emotions of a person who is fully alive to the moments and days of her life, and not at a slight remove. Surely, between episodes, there should be a return to a full emotional range? If so, that is what I don't experience on continuous medication. Is the flattening a medication effect, or a lingering aspect of the illness that medication leaves untouched? Or both?

I have enormous respect for Peter Kramer, Richard Friedman, and other clinicians like my own psychiatrist who continue to work intensively with patients using a combination of talk therapy and medication. But unless psychiatrists themselves have lived for decades on antidepressants, they can't know how it feels to be hostage to medications whose long-term effects upon the brain and body—how responsiveness might be dulled, how neural networks might be altered, what effects are transmitted to a child during pregnancy or in breast milk—are still not entirely clear. This is a situation that didn't exist before the 1950s, when the first psychoactive drugs came into being. While it appears that they are safe in long-term use, there has been no systematic study of SSRI effects that lasted longer than ten years. We who take these medications regularly, whether we like it or not, remain the subjects of an experiment whose outcome may not be known in our lifetime.

The so-called "pipeline" for new antidepressants is nearly empty now, and most pharmaceutical companies have transferred energies and investment away from trying to produce new remedies. There's little profit in it. They have no new paradigms for treating depression; all of the drugs since imipramine and Prozac have been variations on a type: they modify neurotransmitters. They are a blunt instrument, modifying neural pathways in ways not understood, creating change but not cure. While we await a more thorough understanding of the processes that result in severe depression, and until the next treatment innovations arrive, these drugs—imperfect, uncomfortable, but life-saving nonetheless—are what we have.

8

No Feeling Is Final

This book is the result of an investigation that began soon after that day in 1992, when the mental image of my body falling toward the pavement far below made me realize, eight years out from the hospital, that I was still broken in some fundamental way. I could accept the need for continual medication, but I was far from accepting that each time I pushed the boulder of myself to the top of the hill, it would roll back down again. I was disappointed that after years of psychotherapy I hadn't been able to escape recurring periods of low mood, energy, and motivation. I began to read widely, in the hope that a better understanding of my disorder would make me feel less frustrated and powerless.

My reading led me to more questions, and eventually to the decision to write a book that would help me come to terms with my experience. I wanted to confront the mystery of how depressive illness permeates and disables the self. But there was a serious problem with this project: I wasn't comfortable writing about myself. A new journal had taken the place of the one I destroyed on that day in 1984 when I intended to end my life, and I used it in similar ways: to reflect on what I was thinking about or reading, and to worry about what was wrong with me. In college, I was aware that people were taking courses in creative writing, but I never considered doing so myself. I remained under the influence of my family's taboo on self-expression—their unspoken rule that it was inadvisable to draw attention to yourself, and that self-exposure could only be cause for embarrassment. If, as Phillip Lopate asserted, "To be a writer is a monstrously arrogant act," one that "presumes that you should be listened to for pages on end," it was a presumption I had never dreamed of. But the need to write this book never left me because I sensed that writing about depression—and not just for myself—was the only way to wrestle with a subject so difficult to grasp, and an inner experience so continually, unrelentingly frustrating.

At the time that I began my investigation, popular books on depression were only beginning to appear in bookstores. The most prominent and acclaimed among them was William Styron's memoir *Darkness Visible*. It recounts the suicidal depression that enveloped Styron at sixty, after poor health had forced him to give up his lifelong habit of heavy drinking. By then the well-connected and successful author of *Sophie's Choice* and several other novels, Styron was in Paris to accept an international literary prize when he became certain that he was losing his mind. From there he deteriorated even further, although he never actually attempted suicide. He spent some time in a hospital and recovered. The book appeared at a time when, although the Prozac phenomenon was beginning to make it easier for sufferers to identify themselves, no one of Styron's stature had given expression to the peculiar, surreal suffering of a person besieged by melancholia.

I was stunned by the beauty of his book's conclusion, which borrows the end of Dante's *Inferno* to compare the recovery from depression to a passage out of hell:

> For those who have dwelt in depression's dark wood, and known its inexplicable agony, their return from the abyss is not unlike the ascent of the poet, trudging upward and upward out of hell's black depths and at last emerging into what he saw as "the shining world." There, whoever has been restored to health has almost always been restored to the capacity for serenity and joy, and this may be indemnity enough for having endured the despair beyond despair.

> *E quindi uscimmo a riveder le stele.*
> *And so we came forth, and once again beheld the stars.*

To end on a note of such beauty, offering the counsel of patience and hope—and even joy—to fellow sufferers, was Styron's gift to the many readers who had no words to describe what they had been through. His title comes from a passage in John Milton's epic poem *Paradise Lost*, in which Satan describes Hell, his new home, as a place where "no light, but rather darkness visible, served only to discover sights of woe," "where hope never comes that comes to all." In borrowing the language and imagery of not one but two great poets, Styron elevates the horror of suicidal depression and makes its sufferers and survivors, by inclusion in these metaphors, feel heroic.

This poetry was very close to me at the time: I was teaching a course at Columbia that included *The Inferno* and *Paradise Lost* the year that I read *Darkness Visible*. Because it hadn't been long since I had recovered from my second suicidal episode, nothing Styron wrote or borrowed seemed too dramatic. I was aware, too, that Styron had gotten off relatively lightly when it came to the severity of the episode that put him in the hospital. Mine had gone further, darker, and was more damaging to me as a young woman just starting out in life. Severe depression came to me early enough to seep thoroughly into my sense of self. Other lines in *Paradise Lost*—Satan's words, "which way I fly is Hell, myself am Hell"—expressed what it had been like for me, and this feeling returned at intervals to remind me that my ordeal was not over. Nonetheless, at the time Styron's book was clearly *the* book on the subject. It seemed to render unnecessary anything that I, someone with no literary connections, no status, and no confidence, might offer. I went to hear Styron speak at a conference on American writers and suicide in November of 1994, just as another serious matter was claiming my attention. It had been two years since I had last miscarried, and I had not become pregnant again.

Jim and I visited a series of specialists. They looked inside my body with ultrasound and a tiny scope, saw nothing out of order, and prescribed monthly supplies of reproductive hormones. They tested Jim as well, and found nothing problematic. Another year passed, and nothing happened. I suspected that my trouble conceiving, my miscarriages, and my depression were all somehow related, but no doctor was willing to enter into that question when I asked. Facing yet another unexplained disorder, I entered a state that felt more like a spiritual crisis than a depressive one. Seeking solace in the face of all this frustration I joined a chorus, and over the next couple of years I joined fifty other people rehearsing and performing works of Bach, Vivaldi, Duruflé, and others. Singing sacred music is a physical experience, and feels exactly like what it is: a powerful, embodied form of communal prayer. I pursued other spiritual remedies as well: I began taking yoga classes in an effort to release pent-up tension from my body. I read books on Buddhism and joined a meditation group, convinced that these practices offered a way of gaining distance from intolerable feelings, only to find that I didn't have the patience or the discipline to keep up a daily meditation practice.

By then I was thirty-nine, and had been told by each doctor I had seen that my chances of pregnancy were drastically decreasing. The resentful, vestigial Catholic in me still believed that God owed me a child, and all this time I had been set on reversing what had happened over a decade earlier. I believed that if I didn't have a child, I would never fully recover from that loss. Having tried less invasive and less expensive methods without success, we turned at last to in vitro fertilization. Couples who have gone through IVF know what a commitment of time and money it is, and how awkward, unnatural, and emotionally difficult. Jim and I chose a hospital in New Jersey with the highest IVF success rates, and the procedures began. They shut down my irregular menstrual cycle and started it again so that it would run precisely on schedule, hypercharged for egg production. Several times a week we drove to New Jersey at five in the morning for my ultrasound and bloodwork, making sure we beat the rush-hour traffic coming back so as not to be late to teach our morning classes.

In early November we had four eight-celled embryos. On the day of the transfer, I lay on a table and watched the embryos appear and disappear on the technician's screen beside me, as one by one an embryologist in the adjoining room drew them from a petri dish into a pipette. As these were transferred into my body moments later, I prayed I would have the chance to give birth again and raise a healthy child. As we were leaving they gave us a picture of our four embryos, each a collection of round blobs. Jim said, "They look just like me." His sense of humor kept us sane.

Ten days later there was a phone message from the hospital with the results of bloodwork. It began, "You're pregnant but . . ." One of the hormone levels was lower than they liked, so they were treating the pregnancy "cautiously." It seemed like a bad sign. I barely slept that night. In the morning we went to the hospital to have blood drawn again. We took a number; there were eighty-eight people in line ahead of us. We waited two hours. Was that a bad sign? We were in the hands of powers whose signs we couldn't read at all. Was it a good sign when, trying to escape bad fusion jazz on the speaker in the hospital waiting room, I went into another room across the hall where a woman called out to a little girl in pink fuzzy pajamas with feet, "Anna, come here"—and the little girl replied, "Go away, Mama, you stand over there"?

Later that day, to cheer ourselves up, Jim and I went to look at the paintings of Howard Hodgkin. In one of the galleries, a wealthy-looking young woman with a giant stroller-throne was feeding a baby from a jar of baby food. I went into the bathroom a bit later and there was the same woman, changing the baby's diaper. As she did so, she called the baby Anna. It's become a popular name, I thought. A beautiful name, a palindrome. A mirror in which, Anna having disappeared, I'm left seeing only myself.

The great question of the weeks that followed was, Good sign or bad sign? Cramping, a little bleeding, nausea? Good or bad? We waited and worried. Will tomorrow be the day of miscarriage, we wondered? Will it be tonight? Will we have to call our doctor's emergency number? Will we ever stop asking these questions?

I was teaching the Bible at the time, as it happens, and we were reading the Book of Job. After losing all his children, his house, his oxen, sheep, and servants, after being tormented by boils, after listening to his friends argue that he must have done something to deserve all this punishment, Job confronts God himself. God speaks to him from the whirlwind: Where were you when I created everything? I am God. I do what I want. Job says, okay. Once Job attests to the insane, unreasonable power of God, God gives him back all that he has lost. He gives Job ten children. Different children—new ones. It's a happy ending.

We went for a sonogram on the twelfth of December. Twelve years earlier on that day, Anna was dying. A bad sign. It took the doctor a few beats to find "the pregnancy" in my uterus, and for a few anxious seconds Jim and I stared at darkness, remembering the blighted ovum we had stared at on a similar screen exactly three years earlier—a circle, dark inside. Another bad sign. Then we saw our little creature, the sole survivor of four embryos. A rough outline, not human-looking yet—head, heart, rump, attached to the yolk sac. We saw and heard its robust heartbeat, pounding away. Our spirits lifted as the doctor said, "All looks good." He told us we could now choose an obstetrician close to home.

On the day of amniocentesis, we waited a long, anxious time in the hallway of the hospital before we were finally admitted into the room for the sonogram. We had decided to have amnio so that if there were some congenital problem we would know what we were facing, and not be taken by surprise when I gave birth. The technician said she was aware that ours was a high-risk pregnancy—my history and IVF both made it so—and was so calm and kind that I felt more relaxed. She proceeded carefully and thoroughly, measuring the baby's head and femur bones, looking at the spine and ribs, the stomach, liver, heart, brain, bladder. She told us everything looked just fine.

On the monitor the baby was moving its arms and legs, putting one arm over its head, arching its back. Jim asked, "Can you tell if it's a boy or a girl?" and the woman pointed to the penis, not plain as day exactly, but clearly there. I was a little shocked because I had expected a girl. I was glad to know the baby's sex, so I could get used to the idea of a boy. This was a good thing, I realized: I would not have another Anna. No repetition, no replacement. He would be himself. We would move into the future together.

I hadn't taken Prozac during the IVF period—the protocols forbade all medications not absolutely necessary—and I waited as long as possible before I began again, sometime during the third trimester. The sonogram had been so reassuring that until I went into labor and the doctor hooked me up to a fetal heart monitor, I refused to let myself worry about the baby. That would have ruined the pleasure I had in anticipating his arrival. Jim, on the other hand, not usually a worrier, worried a lot. Two friends of his had recently lost babies to cord strangulation, and he feared the terrible things that could take place in the delivery room. Our son arrived a few months after my fortieth birthday, with two knots in his umbilical cord. Our obstetrician marveled at this medical rarity, and kept the cord to show her students. What could have been another devastating situation had not turned into one. Just a little joke. God, chuckling: I do what I want. With the blessed relief of this baby's good health, the pain of Anna's death could begin to fade. We named him Luke, from the Latin *lux*, light.

⌒⌁⌒

WE SPENT TIME in Vermont that fall, and on our way home one day we stopped at Anna's grave. Luke, three months old, was asleep in his car seat. It was dusk when I got out of the car. As I walked through the gate, past the maples and the other graves, I had the sensation of being a moving camera, moving back in time. I knelt and touched the granite stone and brushed my fingers over the incised letters of her name and the words below. "The awakened, lips parted, the hope, the new ships." Jake and Anna felt so near, yet so far away in the past, as Jim walked up and handed Luke to me. "I wanted Luke to see his sister," he said, and there were tears in his voice. I stood holding the precious body of my living child—the hope, the new ships—remembering the precious body of my dead one.

At some point in those painful years between Anna's death and Luke's birth, I taped a picture to the wall above my desk: a photograph of the statue called "The Angel of the Waters," seen through a light snowfall. The statue, together with the fountain and pool below it, make up the centerpiece of Central Park's Bethesda Terrace. In the photograph, only the angel and the snow are visible. I love the angel's attitude of arrival, its hand lifted in a gesture that seems to say: *Be comforted. Be blessed.* Sitting at my desk, it made me feel better in those days to gaze at the angel, the blue winter light, and the haze of snow. At its dedication in 1873, its sculptor Emma Stebbins revealed that this was a healing angel, inspired by a passage from the Gospel of John, chapter 5, verses 2–4: "For an angel went down at a certain season into the pool, and troubled the water: whosoever then first after the troubling of the water stepped in was made whole of whatsoever disease he had." In that expansive, elegant public space completed not long after the end of the Civil War, it conveys to all who see it a message that the pain we endure can be healed. With Luke's arrival, I was blessed and comforted.

Luke in childhood—the extraordinary, tensile aliveness of his restless little body, his intense brown-eyed gaze, his murmured narration of stories for his menagerie of plastic animals, his desire to be read to every night, his deep capacity for pleasure, his love for his mommy and daddy—all this made being his mother a joyful everyday event. The joy is palpable in our family photographs. I can see it in pictures of the three of us together, and in pictures I've taken of Luke. In a series taken on a beach in Ireland, for instance—the beach in my grandfather's village, when we were visiting with my parents—Luke is running toward me from a long distance with the wide curve of shore behind him, arms waving, the wind pushing at his shirt and hair. I can see him planning mischief as he runs: is he going to stop, or is he going to run right into me? As he gets closer and closer I keep pressing the shutter until his laughing eyes and broad, toothy smile fill the frame.

In second grade, Luke made an abstract painting and called it "Hyper Happy." When he was in fifth grade his class was studying China and making ink drawing scrolls, and the teacher asked each child to make a name chop, the artist's signature seal found on ancient Chinese prints. Choosing from among the Chinese characters they had learned, Luke combined the *hànzì* for sun, mother, and child, and named himself *Really Happy Child*. Luke was just what I needed: a boy bursting with life, in temperament more like his irrepressible father than his moody mother. He's in college now, and no less a wonder. To my great

relief, he has never shown the slightest sign of the family vulnerability to depression.

The gift of this child, this heartening ascent from darkness,
would be a satisfying place to end my story. Raising Luke has
given me a more secure stake in the world, but his presence
hasn't magically put an end to my troubles with depression.
When he was diagnosed with ADHD at seven I told him that
I take medication too, for depression, and that lots of people
have conditions that they need some help with. Otherwise I
didn't talk about my depression with him, and it wasn't a big
deal in our family life. So it took me off guard when one day
the two of us were eating lunch at the kitchen table and he said
"Hey, what's that scar on your neck?" He was now sixteen, and
had never asked me this before. I had begun working on this
book, but I was unprepared for the question. Trying to sound
nonchalant, I said, "Oh, I don't remember." He looked at me,
puzzled, and then we talked of something else. I hadn't ever
wanted to tell him about that until he was old enough not to
feel threatened that he might lose me to suicide or to a long
bout of depression. I've always wanted him to see me as strong
and capable and reliable. As books have piled up on my desk in
the last few years—books on suicide, depression, drugs, shock
treatment—I've told him what I'm writing about. He knows
now that I attempted suicide after Anna's death. But until he
reads this book, he won't know the details of what happened.

Every day in the bathroom mirror I see the scar that most
people never notice, a constant reminder of what, irreversibly,
has happened. It's the sign of a story I've kept mostly to myself for
over thirty years. But visible scars do tend to provoke the question, "What happened?" Usually, we know how people close
to us have come by theirs. There's the one my sister Kathleen

got when her roller-skates went out from under her and the wire points of the cyclone fence she was leaning on pierced the inside of her elbow. I was there, and it was awful. Or the ones my brother Tom has from the time when, airborne in an ultimate Frisbee tournament, a collision left him with a compound fracture of his upper arm and a whole set of plates and screws to put it back together. If we survive the injuries that make them, scars remember dangerous events in our histories. They mark cancer surgeries, car accidents, war trauma, bizarre mishaps, the birth of children.

Perhaps the most famous story of a scar is found in Homer's epic poem *The Odyssey*, when the hero Odysseus arrives home as an unrecognizable stranger, planning to attack the men who have occupied his palace in his absence. In twenty years, he's survived a war, he's lost his ships and his men, he's had countless other adventures and misfortunes. An old woman who was his nurse in boyhood is washing his feet when suddenly she recognizes him by the scar on his thigh. The poet leaps back in time to tell the whole complicated tale of how Odysseus was named by his grandfather, and on a visit to this same grandfather, was wounded in a boar hunt. But he also killed the boar, an act that marked his initiation into manhood. The scar is as much a sign of his identity as his name is. He is a hero and a survivor, about to survive the battle for his homecoming.

My scar is not the sign of my identity—I can't identify with the mind that compelled that action—but it stands for a defining double trauma: the loss of my child, the loss of myself. It's the sign of an illness that has shaped my history. It hasn't allowed me to forget the most harrowing days of my life. It has reinforced my sense of shame at being a person who attempted suicide, and it reminds me of my residual anger at those in the hospital who let that happen. The story of my scar isn't heroic, but, no less than the hero Odysseus, I am a survivor. In the much older body of the desperate young woman who tried to end her life with a piece of broken glass, I am still here.

After bearing this mark in silence for so long, I've given myself permission to say what happened. My silence, I now see, has been more than a matter of trauma and shame. I've been complicit with all those who don't want to look squarely at what happens to people under the influence of a depressive disorder. My story is a way of bearing witness, as a person whose illness was diagnosed only after it had already done enormous damage, to the suffering of so many people whose depression goes unrecognized and untreated, and to those who have died by suicide, unable to live another day in a torment they believed would never end. Most importantly, I want to encourage people in the depths of hopelessness to believe that they can come through, and to find help from a compassionate, responsible professional who will care for them until they do. People in the grip of severe depression might take as their mantra a line from Rilke so relevant to all kinds of human trouble that it has become an Internet meme: "Just keep going. No feeling is final."

As I began this final chapter, I thought again of the closing paragraph of *Darkness Visible*. Even when I read it the first time, I knew that however beautifully shaped the story of *Darkness Visible* was, its ending was too good to be true. While the return to mental balance after a suicidal episode can feel, both metaphorically and literally, like you have emerged from the underworld to see the starry sky, it's quite possible that you'll be plunged into it again. It's just not fully within your control.

Styron himself had to face the underworld once more. He had fifteen good years until, at seventy-five, he entered a depression even more severe and longer lasting than the first. He was hospitalized and given shock treatment, but never fully regained his health. He prepared a suicide note, and he asked his biographer Jim West to make sure, in the event that he killed himself, which he feared he would do, that the following message to readers would appear in all future editions of *Darkness Visible*:

> I hope the readers of *Darkness Visible*—past, present and future—will not be discouraged by the manner of my dying. The battle I waged against this vile disease in 1985 was a successful one that brought me 15 years of contented life, but the illness finally won the war.

Rose Styron says that her husband worried that in ending his book on an optimistic note, "he had misled people." Styron did not end his own life; six years later, he died of pneumonia at age eighty-one.

I can't rule out the possibility of a dangerous relapse in my future, but I haven't had a suicidal thought since that day I looked down from the fifteenth floor in 1992. While the loss or illness of someone close to me, a possibility I don't wish to contemplate, could put me back in danger, I like to think that I'll never again be as desperately ill as I was at twenty-seven. My sense of safety has grown with time, but I have no choice but to accept the presence of this disorder, and to remain wary of it. Perhaps living with this challenge has in the long run made me stronger and taught me greater patience and resilience. But I would have given—and would still give—almost anything to be free of it.

Writing this book has made me recognize how thoroughly depression has shadowed my life. Over the years, in periods of great difficulty, feeling the paralysis of ambition and the absence of vitality, I've called myself a failure—a boring, vacant, uncreative person—instead of recognizing that depression had taken over once again. I've had too little compassion for myself, and my self-condemnation has only made things worse. Serious depression causes useless, prolonged suffering, and—given how common it is—a wasting of human potential on an enormous scale. The World Health Organization figures that among illnesses, depression ranks highest in disability-adjusted life years, which it defines as one lost year of healthy life.

I would love to have some of those years back, but I understand, having lost them, that there's a reason I haven't accomplished as much as the people I so admire and envy. People like my husband—a cultural historian who has written six books in the time I've known him—or like friends who are novelists, poets, journalists, and artists. I realize that yearning for a more fully lived, fully accomplished life is itself a provocation to sadness. It's not unlike the mourning of the melancholic, this refusal to lay to rest the imaginary, ideal person you might have been. To harbor the wish that things could have been otherwise prevents me from seeing how undeniably fortunate is the life I do have, and how generously I've been blessed and comforted.

The late Leonard Cohen, one of the great songwriters of our time, knew that just about everyone feels broken in some way—not only those of us who have actually cracked up. Rather than obsess about our flaws and failings, we could acknowledge imperfection as the natural and shared condition of being human. He offered us these four lines, the chorus of his song "Anthem":

> Ring the bells that still can ring
> Forget your perfect offering

There is a crack in everything
That's how the light gets in.

I plan on taking his good counsel as I move into the rest of my
life, remembering to let the light in.

Acknowledgments

In the years since the events with which this book begins, my friends and family have provided invaluable support. I'm especially grateful for the love and generosity of my parents, John Barry Cregan and Mary DeCourcey Cregan. The loss of my father two years ago made writing about matters of life and death all the more poignant.

Heartfelt thanks to Tom Jacobson for his help with remembering events that were as painful for him as they were for me; to Julie Campoli, Susan Chira, Monica Cohen, Nora Cregan, Hannah Cregan, Jane Ezersky, Sam Swope, Clare Connell, Fintan O'Toole, Marsha Wagner, and Richard McCoy, whose intelligent, empathic responses to whole or partial drafts helped me to write a better book; and to Karen Hopenwasser, for her unwavering support through the years. I'm also indebted to my friend and agent Anne Edelstein, to my editor Jill Bialosky, and to Drew Weitman, Ingsu Liu, Chin-Yee Lai, Laura Starrett,

Becky Homiski, Erin Lovett, Steve Colca, and everyone else involved at Norton for their care and expertise in bringing this book into the world. Barnard College has provided a professional home for many years, and I've learned a great deal from my wonderful students and colleagues there.

Thanks also to the Columbia University Libraries and to the New York-Presbyterian/Weill Cornell Medical Center archives.

Finally, boundless love and gratitude to James Shapiro and our son Luke. With them, I always know how extraordinarily lucky I have been.

Notes

The notes that follow identify the published sources on which I draw. For books, place of publication is New York unless otherwise stated.

Preface

xi *In 2016, nearly 11 percent:* National Institute of Mental Health, "Prevalence of Major Depressive Episode Among Adults" (Nov. 2017).

xi *correlation between depression and suicide:* Erkki Iometsaä, "Suicide Behavior in Mood Disorders—Who, When, and Why?" *Canadian Journal of Psychiatry* 59 (2014): 120–30; John Michael Bostwick and V. Shane Pankratz, "Affective Disorders and Suicide Risk: A Reexamination," *American Journal of Psychiatry* 157:12 (2000): 1925-32.

Chapter 1: What Happened

4 *genetic vulnerability:* Johns Hopkins Medical Institutions, "Chronic Form of Depression Runs in Families, Study Finds," *Science Daily* (11 Sept. 2006); F. M. Mondimore et al., "Familial Aggregation of Illness Chronicity in Recurrent, Early-Onset Major Depression Pedigrees," *American Journal of Psychiatry* 163 (2006): 1554–60.

4 *five disorders:* Cross-Disorder Group of the Psychiatric Genomics Consortium, "Identification of Risk Loci with Shared Effects on Five

Major Psychiatric Disorders: A Genome-Wide Analysis," *The Lancet* 381 (2013): 1371–79. See also NIH Research Matters, "Common Genetic Factors Found in Five Mental Disorders," 18 Mar. 2013.

5 *party drugs and psychedelics:* Tony Kirby, "Ketamine for Depression: The Highs and Lows," *The Lancet Psychiatry* 9:2 (2015): 783–84; "Highlight. Ketamine: A New (and Faster) Path to Treating Depression," NIMH Strategic Plan for Research (2015); Michael Pollan, *How to Change Your Mind: What the New Science of Psychedelics Teaches Us About Consciousness, Dying, Addiction, Depression, and Transcendence* (Penguin, 2018); Lauren Slater, *Blue Dreams: The Science and the Story of the Drugs that Changed Our Minds* (Boston: Little, Brown, 2018).

5 *we don't know enough:* Joshua Kendall, "Joshua Gordon Wants to Remake Mental Health Care, on a Budget," *Undark,* 16 June 2017.

6 *apparent epidemic:* Marcia Angell, "The Epidemic of Mental Illness: Why?," *The New York Review of Books,* 23 June 2011, and "The Illusions of Psychiatry," *The New York Review of Books,* 14 July 2011.

7 *He had stopped taking Nardil:* See David Lipsky, "Afterword," *Although of Course You End Up Becoming Yourself* (Broadway Books, 2010), xvii–xix, and D. T. Max, *Every Love Story Is a Ghost Story* (Viking, 2012), 297–301, for the details of Wallace's decisions about medication in the last year of his life.

7 *forgiveness machine:* Tim Adams, "Karen Green: David Foster Wallace's Suicide Turned Him into a 'Celebrity Writer Dude,' Which Would Have Made Him Wince," *Guardian,* 9 Apr. 2011.

8 *his friend's ashes:* Jonathan Franzen, "Farther Away: 'Robinson Crusoe,' David Foster Wallace, and the Island of Solitude," *New Yorker,* 18 Apr. 2011.

8 *goalkeeper Robert Enke:* Rob Bagche, "Eloquent and Sensitive Story Does Justice to Robert Enke and His Illness," *Daily Telegraph,* 28 Nov. 2011.

11 *the best chance for survival:* Centers for Disease Control, "Facts about Hypoplastic Left Heart Syndrome," and Department of Surgery, UCSF, "Pediatric Cardiothoracic Surgery: Hypoplastic Left Heart Syndrome."

14 *"This is the Hour of Lead":* Emily Dickinson, "After great pain, a formal feeling comes—," *The Complete Poems of Emily Dickinson,* ed. Thomas H. Johnson (Boston: Little, Brown, 1960).

15 *bereaved mothers:* F. M. Boyle et al., "The Mental Health Impact of Stillbirth, Neonatal Death or SIDS: Prevalence and Patterns of Distress among Mothers," *Social Science & Medicine* 43 (1996): 1273–82.

15 *Vancouver study:* Sydney Segal, Margaret Fletcher, and William G.

Meekison, "Survey of Bereaved Parents," *Canadian Medical Association Journal* 134 (1986): 38.

27 *"suicides have a special language":* Anne Sexton, "Wanting to Die," *The Complete Poems of Anne Sexton* (Houghton Mifflin Harcourt, 1981), 142.

Chapter 2: What Happened Next

30 *the night-side of life:* Susan Sontag, *Illness as Metaphor* (Farrar, Straus & Giroux, 1977), 3.

31 *the body's circadian clock:* A. M. Leventhal and L. P. Rehm, "The Empirical Status of Melancholia: Implications for Psychology," *Clinical Psychology Review* 25 (2005): 25–44.

32 *first page of my chart:* For a discussion of the methods and rituals involved in compiling a psychiatric inpatient's chart, see Tanya Luhrmann, *Of Two Minds: The Growing Disorder in American Psychiatry* (Knopf, 2000), 30–31.

32 *Dr. Reed:* I have changed the names of all doctors involved in my treatment, as well as those of patients and staff.

32 *"endogenous":* The term was first used by Kurt Schneider in 1920 (by way of Emil Kraepelin) to mean a biological disorder. Jin Mizushima et al., "Melancholic and Reactive Depression: A Reappraisal of Old Categories," *BMC Psychiatry* 13 (2013): 311.

33 *"The distinguishing mental features":* Sigmund Freud, "Mourning and Melancholia," trans. James Strachey, *The Standard Edition of the Complete Psychological Works of Sigmund Freud,* vol. 14 (London: Hogarth, 1957), 243.

33 *"a recurrent, debilitating, pervasive":* Michael Alan Taylor and Max Fink, *Melancholia: The Diagnosis, Pathophysiology and Treatment of Depressive Illness* (Cambridge University Press, 2006), 15.

34 *Some biological psychiatrists:* At a 2006 conference in Copenhagen, a group of psychiatrists recommended that melancholia, "a time-tested diagnostic concept, should be reinstated as a defined mood disorder in psychiatric classification." See Max Fink et al., "Melancholia: Restoration in Psychiatric Classification Recommended," *Acta Psychiatrica Scandinavica* 115.2 (2007): 89–92.

34 *A search in* The New York Times *archives:* "A Fatal Leap," *New York Times,* 6 May 1874; "Suicide in Central Park," *New York Times,* 30 July 1880; "Brooklyn," *New York Times,* 10 July 1880.

35 *"remarkable consistency":* Stanley W. Jackson, *Melancholia and Depression: From Hippocratic Times to Modern Times* (New Haven: Yale University Press, 1986), ix.

36 *Hippocrates:* Jackson, *Melancholia and Depression,* 30–31; Allan V. Horwitz and Jerome C. Wakefield, *The Loss of Sadness* (Oxford University Press, 2007) 57.

36 *black bile:* Jackson, *Melancholia and Depression,* 4–5.

36 *Galen:* From *On the Affected Parts,* quoted in Jackson, *Melancholia and Depression,* 42.

36 *Samuel Butler:* "A Melancholy Man," in *Characters* (1659), quoted in Jennifer Radden Keefe, ed., *The Nature of Melancholy* (Oxford University Press, 2000), 58.

36 *Hannah Allen:* Allan Ingram, ed. *Patterns of Madness in the 18th Century: A Reader* (Liverpool: Liverpool University Press, 1998), 29, and Hannah Allen, *A Narrative of God's Gracious Dealings with that Choice Christian Mrs. Hannah Allen* (London, 1683), 13, 42–44, 72–73.

37 *Timothy Rogers:* Timothy Rogers, *A Discourse Concerning Trouble of Mind, and the Disease of Melancholy* (London, 1691), i–iii, v, xi.

38 *Cotton Mather:* Quoted in Jeremy Schmidt, *Melancholy and the Care of the Soul: Religion, Moral Philosophy and Madness in Early Modern England* (Burlington, VT: Ashgate, 2007), 118.

39 *Robert Burton's:* Robert Burton, *The Anatomy of Melancholy,* ed. Holbrook Jackson (New York Review Books, 2001), 1:434, 431–32.

45 *"Were suicidal patients able":* Kay Jamison, *Night Falls Fast: Understanding Suicide* (Knopf, 1999), 150–51.

45 *Emil Kraepelin:* Quoted in Jamison, *Night Falls Fast,* 151.

45 *"the most suicidal of all lunatics":* Åsa Janson, "From Statistics to Diagnostics: Medical Certificates, Melancholia, and 'Suicidal Propensities' in Victorian Psychiatry," *Journal of Social History* 46.3 (2013): 722. See also Anne Shepherd and David Wright, "Madness, Suicide and the Victorian Asylum: Attempted Self-Murder in the Age of Non-Restraint," *Medical History* 46.2 (2002): 188.

45 *the risk of a patient becoming suicidal:* T. S. Clouston, *Clinical Lectures on Mental Diseases* (Philadelphia: Henry C. Lea's Son & Co., 1884), 104.

47 *"Tools used to assess risk":* Geetha Jayaram, Hilary Sporney, and Pamela Perticone, "The Utility and Effectiveness of 15-Minute Checks in Inpatient Settings," *Psychiatry* (Edgmont) 7.8 (2010): 46–49.

47 *"the risk of suicide is highest":* Jamison, *Night Falls Fast,* 110.

48 *The practice of heightened observation:* Luhrmann, *Of Two Minds,* 121; Nafees Aidroos, "Nurses' Response to Doctors' Orders for Close Observation," *Canadian Journal of Psychiatry* 31.9 (1986): 831–33.

54 *ECT as a first line treatment:* M. Bauer et al., "World Federation of Societies of Biological Psychiatry (WFSBP) Guidelines for Biological

Treatment of Unipolar Depressive Disorders, Part 1: Update 2013 on the Acute and Continuation Treatment of Unipolar Depressive Disorders," *World Journal of Biological Psychiatry* 14 (2013): 358.

60 *his very first patient:* Daniel J. Carlat, *Unhinged: The Trouble with Psychiatry* (Free Press, 2010), 21–24.

63 *first cause of the illness:* Burton, *The Anatomy of Melancholy,* 177, 130–37.

Chapter 3: How to Save a Life

64 *"what* Jaws *did for sharks":* Rupert Hawksley, "One Flew Over the Cuckoo's Nest: 10 Things You Didn't Know About the Film," *Daily Telegraph,* 28 Feb 2014.

64 *"to keep you from biting your tongue":* One Flew over the Cuckoo's Nest. Milos Forman. United Artists. 1975. Film.

65 *Kesey's 1962 novel:* Ken Kesey, *One Flew Over the Cuckoo's Nest* (Penguin, 2002), 179, 250, 164.

67 *MK Ultra:* "The Fresh Air Interview: Ken Kesey," in Scott F. Parker, ed., *Conversations with Ken Kesey* (Jackson: University Press of Mississippi, 2014), 104.

67 Madness Network News: Leonard Roy Frank et al., *Madness Network News: A Journal of the Psychiatric Survival Movement,* vol. 1(2): 23 and vol 1(3): 29.

68 *"therapeutic state":* Thomas Szasz, *The Therapeutic State: Psychiatry in the Mirror of Current Events* (Buffalo: Prometheus Books, 1984); Anthony Stadlen, "Thomas Szasz," Obituary, *Guardian,* 4 Oct. 2012.

68 *"Georgia Power cocktail":* Edward Shorter and David Healy, *Shock Therapy: A History of Electroconvulsive Treatment in Mental Illness* (New Brunswick: Rutgers University Press, 2007), 93–94.

69 *"ECT stands practically alone":* David J. Rothman, "ECT: The Historical, Social, and Professional Sources of the Controversy," *Psychopharmacology Bulletin* 22.2 (1986): 455–502.

69 *Kesey replied:* See their correspondence and Kesey's letter of February 28, 1963 on the official Szasz website, *The Thomas S. Szasz M.D. Cybercenter for Liberty and Responsibility,* http://www.szasz.com/kesey.pdf.

69 *"Peyote . . . inspired my chief narrator":* Quoted in John Clark Pratt's introduction to Ken Kesey, *One Flew Over the Cuckoo's Nest,* ed. John Clark Pratt (Viking Critical Library, 1996).

70 *"If I could go back in time":* Christopher Reed, "Ken Kesey," Obituary, *Guardian,* 12 Nov. 2001.

70 *compression fractures:* Kitty Dukakis and Larry Tye, *Shock: The Healing Power of Electroconvulsive Therapy* (Penguin, 2006), 96–98.

70 *"I wondered what terrible thing"*: Sylvia Plath, *The Bell Jar* (Harper Perennial, 1999), 143.

71 *without her informed consent*: Linda Wagner-Martin, *Sylvia Plath: A Biography* (Simon & Schuster, 1987), 103; Anne Stevenson, *Bitter Fame: A Life of Sylvia Plath* (Houghton Mifflin, 1989), 44–47.

71 *"as if she were being electrocuted"*: Quoted in excerpt from Elizabeth Winder, *Sylvia Plath in New York: Pain, Parties, and Work* (Harper Perennial, 2014), published in *Guardian Observer*, 2 Feb 2013. See also Alex Beam, *Gracefully Insane: Life and Death inside America's Premier Mental Hospital* (Public Affairs Books, 2001), 153ff.

71 *"It was a queer, sultry summer"*: Plath, *The Bell Jar*, 1.

71 *"All the heat and fear had purged itself"*: Plath, *The Bell Jar*, 215.

72 *"in other words—a seizure"*: Carlat, *Unhinged*, 164.

72 *"as boring as possible"*: Michael Henry, M.D., of McLean Hospital, quoted in Daniel Fisher, "Shock and Disbelief," *Atlantic Monthly*, Feb. 2001, 88–89.

72 *"It is a nonentity"*: Quoted in Max Fink, *Electroconvulsive Therapy: A Guide for Professionals and Their Patients* (Oxford University Press, 2009), 4.

72 *undramatic nature of present-day ECT*: "Peter's ECT Session 2009," published on YouTube, September 6, 2012, by Peter Cornish, shows an ECT treatment at a Utah hospital that allowed family members to be present. See also the BBC *Newsnight* video, "Why are we still using electroconvulsive therapy?" YouTube, published 21 Dec. 2013.

72 *Carrie Mathison*: "Marine One," *Homeland*, Season One, episode 12. Directed by Michael Cuesta. Written by Alex Gansa and Howard Gordon. Showtime Networks, aired 18 Dec. 2011. See also Lucy Tallon, "What Is Having ECT Like?" *Guardian*, 13 May 2012.

73 *one of the show's producers*: Jamie Stiehm, "My So-Called Bipolar Life," *New York Times*, 18 Jan. 2012.

73 *Shelley's novel reflects popular interest*: Sharon Ruston, "The Science of Life and Death in Mary Shelley's *Frankenstein*," British Library Online.

73 *"infuse a spark of being"*: Mary Shelley, *Frankenstein or The Modern Prometheus*, ed. Maurice Hindle (Penguin, 1992), 58.

73 *Aldini, who carried out experiments*: Iwan Rhys Morus, "Galvanic Cultures: Electricity and Life in the Early Nineteenth Century," *Endeavour* 22.1 (1998): 7–11, and André Parent, "Giovanni Aldini: From Animal Electricity to Human Brain Stimulation," *Canadian Journal of Neurological Sciences* 31.4 (2004): 583.

74 *the head of a farmer*: S. A. Boudreau and S. Finger, "Medical Electricity and Madness in the Eighteenth Century," *Perspectives in Biology and Medicine* 49.3 (2006): 337–38.

74 *"Look who's back"*: Dick Cavett, "Goodbye, Darkness," *People*, 3 Aug, 1992.

75 *"saved the life of a pretty Chicago nurse"*: Laura Hirschbein and Sharmalie Sarvananda, "History, Power, and Electricity: American Popular Magazine Accounts of Electro-Convulsive Therapy, 1940–2005," *Journal of the History of the Behavioral Sciences* 44.1 (2008): 5.

75 *an imbalance of connectivity*: Jennifer S. Perrin et al., "Electroconvulsive Therapy Reduces Frontal Cortical Connectivity in Severe Depressive Disorder," *PNAS* 109.14 (2012): 5464–68.

75 *neurogenesis*: Tom Bolwig, "How Does Electroconvulsive Therapy Work? Theories on Its Mechanism," *Canadian Journal of Psychiatry* 56.1 (2011): 13–18.

76 *killed 15 percent of his patients*: Gretchen Vogel, "Malaria as Lifesaving Therapy," *Science* 342.6159 (2013): 686.

76 *"With all these people"*: Deborah Blythe Doroshow, "Performing a Cure for Schizophrenia: Insulin Coma Therapy on the Wards," *Journal of the History of Medicine and Allied Sciences* 62.2 (2007): 214.

77 *"half a century of nihilistic hopelessness"*: Edward Shorter, *A History of Psychiatry* (John Wiley & Sons, 1977), 208.

77 *Working from the antagonism hypothesis*: David Healy, *The Creation of Psychopharmacology* (Cambridge: Harvard University Press, 2004) 71; Lothar Kalinowsky, "History of Convulsive Therapy," *Annals of the New York Academy of Sciences* 462 (1986): 1–4.

78 *Neither approach had the desired effect*: B. Baran et. al., "The Beginnings of Modern Psychiatric Treatment in Europe: Lessons from an Early Account of Convulsive Therapy," *European Archives of Psychiatry and Clinical Neuroscience* 258 (2008): 435.

78 *"after forty-five minutes"*: Quoted in Fink, *Electroconvulsive Therapy*, 88.

78 *"My body began to tremble"*: Quoted in Edward Shorter and David Healy, *Shock Therapy: A History of Electroconvulsive Treatment in Mental Illness* (New Brunswick: Rutgers University Press, 2007), 26–27.

79 *"He spontaneously arises from bed"*: Quoted in Shorter, *A History of Psychiatry*, 215.

79 *Meduna's autobiography*: "Autobiography of L. J. Meduna" (Part 2), *Convulsive Therapy* 1.2 (1985): 122.

79 *Medical historians have accepted*: Shorter and Healy, *Shock Therapy*, 28.

79 *When he published the results*: Fink, *Electroconvulsive Therapy*, 33.

80 *intense fear of imminent death*: Solomon Katzenelbogen, "A Critical Appraisal of the 'Shock Therapies' in the Major Psychoses and Psychoneuroses III—Convulsive Therapy," *Psychiatry* 3:3 (1940): 412.

80 *He died in the Institute:* B. Baran, I. Bitter, et. al., "The Birth of Biological Therapy in Hungary: The Story of László Meduna's First Patient Receiving Convulsive Therapy," *Psychiatrica Hungarica* 23.5 (2008): 366–75. Abstract.

81 *In the early 1930s:* Sherwin B. Nuland, "The Uncertain Art: Lightening on My Mind." *The American Scholar* 71.2 (2002): 128.

81 *"the specter of the electric chair":* Quoted in Bruce Wright, "An Historical Review of Electroconvulsive Therapy," *Jefferson Journal of Psychiatry* 8.2 (1990): 70.

81 *"He expressed himself exclusively":* Ugo Cerletti, "Old and New Information about Electroshock," *American Journal of Psychiatry* 107.87 (1950): 90.

82 *mind "had completely unraveled":* F. Accornero, "An Eyewitness Discovery of Electroshock," *Convulsive Therapy* 4.1 (1988): 44.

82 *he cried out:* Shorter and Healy, *Shock Therapy,* 42–43.

82 *bawdy popular song:* Accornero, "An Eyewitness Discovery," 46.

82 *perfectly clear Italian:* Nuland, "The Uncertain Art," 128.

82 *a more dramatic story:* Shorter and Healy, *Shock Therapy,* 43.

82 *"perhaps I have been asleep":* Cerletti, "Old and New Information," 91; Shorter, *A History of Psychiatry,* 220.

83 *Cerletti never responded:* Shorter and Healy, *Shock Therapy,* 43.

83 *Cerletti's method now superseded:* Shorter, *A History of Psychiatry,* 221.

84 *succinylcholine began to be used:* S. Mukherjee et al., "Electroconvulsive Therapy of Acute Manic Episodes: A Review of 50 Years' Experience," *American Journal of Psychiatry* 151.2 (1994): 169–76.

84 *annually for each subscriber:* Shorter and Healy, *Shock Therapy,* 144; Jan Otto Ottosson and Max Fink, *Ethics in Electroconvulsive Therapy* (Routledge, 2004), 7.

84 *"all that was brutal and inhumane":* Shorter and Healy, *Shock Therapy,* 144; see also Ottosson and Fink, *Ethics in Electroconvulsive Therapy,* 7.

84 *"What to me is inexplicable":* L. Rose, "Fear of ECT," *BMJ* 2.6038 (1976): 757.

84 *a remarkable 46 percent:* Shorter and Healy, *Shock Therapy,* 145.

85 *"Everybody who does electroshock":* Quoted in Daniel Smith, "Shock and Disbelief," *Atlantic,* February 2001.

85 *downward trend:* James W. Thompson et al., "Use of ECT in the United States in 1975, 1980, and 1986," *American Journal of Psychiatry* 151.11 (1994): 1657–61; Max Fink, "Electroshock Revisited," *American Scientist* 88.2 (2000): 162–67.

85 *roughly 100,000:* Nancy Payne and Joan Prudic, "Electroconvulsive Therapy Part II: A Biopsychosocial Perspective," *Journal of Psychiatric Practice* 15.5 (2009): 371; Max Fink, *Electroshock: Restoring the Mind* (Oxford University Press, 1999), 103.

85 *lack of treatment centers:* Fink, "Electroshock Revisited," 164.

87 *greater temporary cognitive deficits:* Nancy Payne and Joan Prudic, "Electroconvulsive Therapy Part I: A Perspective on the Evolution and Current Practice," *Journal of Psychiatric Practice* 15.5 (2009): 356.

87 *inability to actively take in oxygen:* J. Lew et al., "Oxygenation During Electroconvulsive Therapy," *Anesthesia* 41.11 (1986): 1092–97.

87 *seizure thresholds:* Richard D. Weiner, "Clinical Applications," in M. Mankal et al., *Clinical Manual of Electroconvulsive Therapy* (Arlington, VA: American Psychiatric Publishing, 2010), 59–79.

88 *I consulted ECT expert:* Max Fink kindly answered my questions via email in November of 2014.

88 *sine-wave current of earlier machines:* Payne and Prudic, "Electroconvulsive Therapy Part I," 356.

93 *current in wall outlets:* Richard D. Weiner, "Basics," in Mankal et al., *Clinical Manual of Electroconvulsive Therapy* (Arlington, VA: American Psychiatric Publishing, 2010), 48.

93 *"most persistent long-term deficits":* Payne and Prudic, "Electroconvulsive Therapy Part I," 356. See also Joan Prudic, "Strategies to Minimize Cognitive Side Effects with ECT: Aspects of ECT Technique," *Journal of ECT* 24.1 (2008): 46–47.

94 *Ernest Hemingway protested:* Quoted in Smith, "Shock and Disbelief."

94 *"You'll be all right":* Quoted in John Jeremiah Sullivan, "Donald Antrim and the Art of Anxiety," *New York Times Magazine,* 21 Sept. 2014.

94 *a small and vocal group:* Anti-ECT activist Linda Andre sets out this position in her book *Doctors of Deception: What They Don't Want You to Know about Shock Treatment* (New Brunswick: Rutgers University Press, 2009).

95 *American Psychiatric Association claims:* APA Task Force on Electroconvulsive Therapy, "The Practice of Electroconvulsive Therapy: Treatment, Training, and Privileging." (Washington, DC: American Psychiatric Association, 1990).

96 *Lithium could have been given:* Andrea Cipriani et al., "Lithium in the Prevention of Suicide in Mood Disorders," *BMJ* 346: f3646 (2013); M. Bauer et al., "Role of Lithium Augmentation in the Management of Major Depressive Disorder," *CNS Drugs* 28.4 (2014): 331–42.

Chapter 4: The Paradise of Bedlams

97 *On the morning of August 8, 1894:* Source for the move to White Plains is *The New York Herald,* 9 Aug. 1894, 5 Aug. 1894, and 22 July 1894.

99 *"New Home for the Insane": New York Times,* 18 Oct. 1894.

99 *accommodate over four hundred patients: New York Herald,* 22 July 1894.

101 *the mentally ill were kept apart:* See Deanna Pan, "Timeline: Deinstitutionalization and Its Consequences," *Mother Jones,* 29 Apr. 2013.

103 *"relieve the melancholy mind":* Quoted in Andrew Dolkart, *Morningside Heights: A History of Its Architecture and Development* (Columbia University Press, 2001), 18.

103 *Under the headline:* "Remove Bloomingdale!" *New York Herald,* 18 Apr. 1888.

103 *Real estate brokers complained:* "Must Bloomingdale Asylum Go?" *New York Herald,* 14 Mar. 1886.

103 *"no neighborhood, no development":* "Remove Bloomingdale!" *New York Herald,* 18 Apr. 1888.

104 *"most magnificent park and residence district": New York Times,* 19 May 1888.

104 *"we will not be driven": New York Herald,* 15 Aug. 1887.

104 *White Plains farm:* Betsy Brown, "Scope of Proposal for Hospital Land Is Focus of Debate," *New York Times,* 8 Jan. 1984. See also "The Bloomingdale Insane Asylum" on the website of the Bloomingdale Neighborhood History Group.

105 *"cells for the reception of lunatics":* Gerald Grob, *The Mad Among Us: A History of the Care of America's Mentally Ill* (Free Press, 1994), 23.

105 *northern edge of the city:* Dolkart, *Morningside Heights,* 14.

105 *By 1792: The New York Hospital Annual Report,* 1941, 9. Internet Archive.

105 *Lunatic Asylum, opened in 1808:* Henry M. Hurd et al., *The Institutional Care of the Insane in the United States and Canada,* vol. 3 (Baltimore: Johns Hopkins University Press, 1916) 135; *The New York Hospital Annual Report 1971,* 42.

106 *chains being used:* Hurd et al., *The Institutional Care of the Insane,* 133.

106 *Philadelphia's hospital:* Shorter, *History of Psychiatry,* 16.

106 *Going to gaze:* Lynn Gamwell and Nancy Tomes, *Madness in America: Cultural and Medical Perceptions of Mental Illness before 1914* (Ithaca: Cornell University Press, 1995), 35.

106 *social order:* Andrew Scull, *Social Order/Mental Disorder: Anglo-American Psychiatry in Historical Perspective* (Berkeley: University of California Press, 1989), 98–99.

107 *Two strands:* Gamwell and Tomes, *Madness in America,* 37.

107 *wave of asylum building:* Shorter, *History of Psychiatry,* 8.

107 *Philippe Pinel:* Dora B. Weiner, *"Le Geste de Pinel"* in Mark S. Micale and Roy Porter, eds., *Discovering the History of Psychiatry* (Oxford University Press, 1994), 238, and Dora B. Weiner, "Philippe Pinel's 'Memoir on Madness' of December 11, 1794: A Fundamental Text of Modern Psychiatry," *American Journal of Psychiatry* 149.6 (1992): 725–32; James C. Harris, "Pinel Orders the Chains Removed from the Insane at Bîcetre," *Archives of General Psychiatry* 60.5 (2003): 442.

108 *death of Hannah Mills:* Roy Porter, *Mind-Forg'd Manacles: A History of Madness in England* (Harvard University Press, 1987), 134–35.

109 *"fatal neglect," rape, and whippings:* Anne Digby, "Changes in the Asylum: The Case of York, 1777–1815," *Economic History Review* 36.2 (1983): 225.

109 *"a quiet haven":* Quoted in Richard Hunter and Ida Macalpine, "Introduction," in Samuel Tuke, *Description of The Retreat* [1813] (London: Dawsons, 1964), 1.

109 *under investigation:* Digby, "Changes in the Asylum," 225.

109 *atmosphere was domestic:* Porter, *Mind-Forg'd Manacles,* 223.

109 *results at The Retreat:* Porter, *Mind-Forg'd Manacles,* 223.

110 *a small book:* Tuke, *Description of The Retreat*; Shorter, *A History of Psychiatry,* 21.

110 *Eddy urged his fellow board members:* Thomas Eddy, "Hints for Introducing an Improved Mode of Treating the Insane in the Asylum," Communication to the Board of Governors, April 1815. Reprinted in *A Psychiatric Milestone: Bloomingdale Hospital Centenary 1821–1921* (The Society of New York Hospital, 1921), Appendix III.

110 *fresh air, exercise, and useful work:* Dolkart, *Morningside Heights,* 14.

110 *the aspect of a prison:* Quoted in Hurd, *The Institutional Care of the Insane,* 142.

111 *"dependent unmarried females":* Quoted in Grob, *The Mad Among Us,* 37.

111 *"a lounging, listless, madhouse air":* Charles Dickens, *American Notes for General Circulation* [1842] (Penguin, 2000), 104.

112 *"If insanity is to be diminished":* Quoted in Charles Pilgrim, "Treatment of the Insane in New York," *American Journal of Insanity,* 68.1 (1911): 8.

112 *"there are scarcely two physicians":* Pliny Earle, *History, Description and Statistics of the Bloomingdale Asylum for the Insane* (Egbert, Hovey and King, 1848), 102.

113 *"a paradise no longer":* Julius Chambers, *A Mad World and Its Inhabitants* (D. Appleton and Co., 1876), 145.

113 *in his report of 1887:* The *117th Annual Report of the State of the New York Hospital and Bloomingdale Asylum for the year 1887* (New York Hospital Society, 1888), 202.

114 *the period immediately after discharge:* Taylor and Fink, *Melancholia: A Clinician's Guide,* 134.

115 *nearly 45,000 suicides:* National Center for Injury Prevention and Control, "Suicide Rising Across the U.S." Centers for Disease Control and Prevention, 2018.

115 *perhaps 6 percent:* Yad M. Jabbarpour and Geetha Jayaram, "Suicide Risk: Navigating the Failure Modes," *Focus* 9.2 (2011): 186.

115 *a psychiatric nurse will be confronted with a suicide:* This study took place in London, and is cited in James L. Knoll IV, "Inpatient Suicide: Identifying Vulnerability in the Hospital Setting," *Psychiatric Times,* 23 May 2012.

115 *"inadequate monitoring":* Cited in Knoll, "Inpatient Suicide." See also Isaac Sakinofsky, "Preventing Suicide Among Inpatients," *Canadian Journal of Psychiatry* 59.3 (2014): 131–40.

115 *In 1880, while in a storeroom:* "Suicide of a Brooklyn Lady," *New York Times,* 11 Nov. 1880.

115 *In 1914, a thirty-nine-year-old patient:* "Fled Bloomingdale to Drown," *New York Times,* 7 Aug. 1914.

115 *In 1916, a wealthy woman:* "Mrs. Ticer Killed by Train," *New York Times,* 5 Nov. 1916.

121 *Stevie Smith captures:* "Not Waving but Drowning," *Collected Poems of Stevie Smith* (New Directions, 1972).

122 *"Be not far from me":* Psalm 22: King James Bible.

123 *"God is never really absent":* Anthony Bloom, *Learning to Pray* (Mahwah, NJ: Paulist Press, 1970), 26.

124 *"biopsychosocial" illness:* This multifaceted view of mental illness stands against the position of those who advocate a purely biological approach to psychiatry. See George Makari, "Psychiatry's Mind-Brain Problem," *New York Times,* 11 Nov. 2015, and Tanya Luhrmann, *Of Two Minds: The Growing Disorder in American Psychiatry* (Knopf, 2000).

127 *shift in identity:* Erving Goffman, *Asylums: Essays on the Social Situation of Mental Patients and Other Inmates* (Anchor, 1961).

127 *permanent reminder of that identity:* In *Stigma: Notes on the Management of Spoiled Identity* (Simon & Schuster, 1963), Goffman distinguishes between *discredited* and *discreditable* status: "Does the stigmatized individual assume his differentness is known about already or is evident on the spot, or does he assume it is neither known about by those present nor immediately perceivable by them? In the first case one

deals with the plight of the discredited, in the second with that of the discreditable. This is an important difference" (4).

Chapter 5: Where Do the Dead Go?

133 *Imagine 2 percent of the world's population:* "Pilot," *The Leftovers,* HBO, 29 June 2014. The first season is based on Tom Perrotta's novel, *The Leftovers* (St. Martin's, 2011).

135 *"In mourning, we grieve the dead":* Darian Leader, *The New Black: Mourning, Melancholia and Depression* (Minneapolis: Graywolf Press, 2009), 8.

136 *people who have suffered more terrible losses:* In the time I've been thinking about this book, my experience has been placed in microscopic perspective by innumerable large- and small-scale events like the genocides in Bosnia and Rwanda, the Syrian civil war, and the mass murder of twenty children in Newtown, Connecticut. I've read Aleksandar Hemon's story about his daughter's death from brain cancer at the age of two ("In the Aquarium") and Sonali Deraniyagala's account of losing her entire family in the tsunami of 2004 (*Wave*). I've met writers who lost grown children and whose grief is expressed in their books, like David Grossman (*Falling Out of Time*) and Edward Hirsch (*Gabriel*), and a couple who lost their teenage son to suicide.

136 *losing a child you've never known:* In "When a Grieving Mother Talks, Listen" (*New York Times* 21 Dec. 2017), Jen Gunter writes about women whose babies were stillborn or died in the first week of life.

136 *"They give birth astride of a grave":* Samuel Beckett, *Waiting for Godot* (Grove Press, 2011).

136 *the concept of limbo:* International Theological Commission, "The Hope of Salvation for Infants Who Die Without Being Baptized," 2007.

137 *Judaism's approach to neonatal death:* Maimonides, *Mishneh Torah,* Laws of Mourning 1:6. Ron Wolfson, "Jewish Stillbirth and Neonatal Death." Excerpt from Wolfson, *A Time to Mourn, A Time to Comfort* (Woodstock, VT: Jewish Lights Publishing, 2008).

137 *New ritual observance:* Rabbi Stephanie Dickstein, "Jewish Ritual Practice Following a Stillbirth," YD 340:30.1996a.

137 *"Stonecutters, hone / the chisels":* Jan Kochanowski, *Laments,* trans. Stanislaw Baranczak and Seamus Heaney (Farrar, Straus & Giroux, 1995). See also Jonathan Aaron, "Across Four Centuries: Jan Kochanowski's *Laments," Harvard Review* 10 (1996): 60–62.

143 *necessity of working through:* George A. Bonanno, "Loss, Trauma, and Human Resilience," *American Psychologist* (Jan. 2004): 21.

144 *Jung's break with him was obvious:* Florian Illies, *1913: The Year before the Storm* (Public Affairs, 2013), 192–93.

144 *"my successor and crown prince":* Sigmund Freud, Letter from Sigmund Freud to C. G. Jung, 16 April 1909, *The Freud/Jung Letters: The Correspondence Between Sigmund Freud and C. G. Jung,* ed. William McGuire, trans. Ralph Manheim and R. F. C. Hull (Princeton, N.J.: Princeton University Press, 1974), 218–220.

144 *"They liked each other":* Lou Andreas-Salomé, *The Freud Journal of Lou Andreas-Salomé* (Basic Books, 1964), 169.

145 *"the transience which was its doom":* Sigmund Freud, "On Transience," *The Standard Edition of the Complete Psychological Works of Sigmund Freud,* Volume XIV (1914–1916), trans. James Strachey (London: Hogarth Press, 1957), 304. See also Herbert Lehmann, "A Conversation between Freud and Rilke," *The Psychoanalytic Quarterly* XXXV (1966): 423–27. In this essay Lehmann identifies Rilke as the unnamed poet of "On Transience." I believe that Lehmann is correct not only because the two men did meet that day, but also because of the correlation between Rilke's work and what Freud reports about the conversation. See also Matthew von Unwerth, "On Transience: Freud, Rilke, and Creativity," *Issues in Psychoanalytic Psychology* 32 (2010): 133–46.

146 *"to mourn my Sophie properly":* For Freud's response to the deaths of his daughter and grandson, including quotations from letters, see Peter Gay, *Freud: A Life for Our Time* (Norton, 1988), 392–93 and 421–22.

147 *"Mourning has a quite precise":* Sigmund Freud, *Totem and Taboo* (1913), *The Standard Edition of the Complete Psychological Works of Sigmund Freud,* Volume XIII (1914–1916), trans. James Strachey, (London: Hogarth Press; 1955), 64.

148 *"we shall remain inconsolable":* For a discussion of how Freud's thinking on mourning became more complex over time, see Tammy Clewell, "Mourning Beyond Melancholia: Freud's Psychoanalysis of Loss," *Journal of the American Psychoanalytic Association* 52.1 (2004): 43–67.

149 *"to replace the lost objects":* Freud, "On Transience," 304.

149 *"to hold life open toward death":* Letter to Nanny von Escher (22 Dec. 1923) in Rainer Maria Rilke, *Letters of Rainer Maria Rilke, 1910–1926,* trans. Jane Bannard Greene and M. D. Herter Norton (Norton, 1948), 330.

149 *"Our instinct should not be":* Letter to Countess Margot Sizzo (6 Jan.1923) in Rainer Maria Rilke, *Letters on Life,* ed. and trans. Ulrich Baer (Random House, 2005), 108–9.

150 *"could we exist without them?":* The First Elegy, *Selected Poetry of Rainer Maria Rilke,* ed. and trans. Stephen Mitchell (Vintage, 1984), 155.

150   *"Just once. And never again"*: The Ninth Elegy, *Selected Poetry of Rainer Maria Rilke*, 199.

150   *"Being here is magnificent"*: The Seventh Elegy, Kathleen Komar's translation of *"hiersein ist herrlich."* Kathleen L. Komar, "Duisener Elegien," *Encyclopedia of German Literature*, ed. Matthias Konzett (Chicago: Fitzroy Dearborn, 2000), 823–24.

151   *"invisible presences"*: Virginia Woolf, "A Sketch of the Past," in *Moments of Being*, 2nd ed., ed. Jeanne Schulkind (Harvest, 1985), 80.

151   "But I did the ritual": Joan Didion, *The Year of Magical Thinking* (Vintage, 2005), 43–44.

152   *Rilke wrote a poem about this:* "Orpheus. Eurydice. Hermes." *Selected Poetry of Rainer Maria Rilke*, 49–53.

153   *without Demeter's knowledge:* My discussion of the myth is indebted to Walter Burkert's *Greek Religion* (Cambridge: Harvard University Press, 1985), 159–61, and Helene P. Foley, ed. *The Homeric Hymn to Demeter* (Princeton: Princeton University Press, 1994).

154   *Eavan Boland's poem:* Eavan Boland, "The Pomegranate," *In a Time of Violence* (Norton, 1994), 26.

154   *Louise Glück's engagement:* Louise Glück, *Averno* (Farrar, Straus & Giroux, 2006) and "Pomegranate," *Salmagundi* 22 (Spring–Summer 1973).

160   *"I made this"*: T. S. Eliot, "Marina," in *The Complete Poems and Plays 1909–1950* (Harcourt, Brace & World, 1971), 72–73.

162   *"When it hurts"*: Czesław Miłosz, "I Sleep a Lot," in *The Collected Poems 1931–1987* (Hopewell NJ: Ecco Press, 1988), 177–78.

Chapter 6: Early Blues

163   *series of gray tones:* My mental image comes from "the zone system," created for black and white photography by Ansel Adams and Fred Archer. See https://en.wikipedia.org/wiki/Zone_System.

164   *the noonday demon:* See Andrew Solomon's *The Noonday Demon: An Atlas of Depression* (Simon & Schuster, 2001).

164   For the origin of "the blues" and "blue devils": *Oxford English Dictionary*.

165   *The color that started it all:* M. Oz et al., "Cellular and Molecular Actions of Methylene Blue in the Nervous System," *Medical Research Reviews* 31.1 (2011): 93–117.

165   *whites of their eyes turned blue:* R. H. Schirmer et al., "Lest We Forget You—Methylene Blue . . ." *Neurobiology of Aging* 32.12 (2012): 32.

165   *affinity with nerve cells:* Francisco López-Muñoz and Cecilio Álamo, "Monoaminergic Neurotransmission: The History of the Discovery

of Antidepressants from 1950s Until Today," *Current Pharmaceutical Design* 15 (2009): 1563–86.

165 *"a picture of impressive beauty"*: Quoted in Bernhard Witkop, "Paul Ehrlich: His Ideas and His Legacy," *Science, Technology & Society in the Time of Alfred Nobel: Nobel Symposium 52*, eds. Bernhard Witkop, E. Crawford, and P. Sörbom (Oxford: Pergamon Press, 1983), 149.

165 *Ehrlich set out the hypotheses:* Dilip Jeste et al., "Serendipity in Biological Psychiatry," *Archives of General Psychiatry* 36.11 (1979): 1175.

166 *Pietro Bodoni:* Jette E. Kristiansen et al., "Phenothiazines as a Solution for Multidrug Resistant Tuberculosis," *International Microbiology* 18 (2015): 2; Healy, *The Creation of Psychopharmacology*, 44.

166 *"serendipity":* Thomas Ban, "The Role of Serendipity in Drug Discovery," *Dialogues in Clinical Neuroscience* 8.3 (2006): 335.

166 *By 1950, researchers:* Jeste et al., "Serendipity in Biological Psychiatry," 1175.

166 *sometimes caused by anesthesia:* David Healy, *The Antidepressant Era* (Cambridge: Harvard University Press, 1997), 43.

167 *called chlorpromazine:* Healy, *The Antidepressant Era*, 43–48; David Healy, "Roland Kuhn." Obituary. *History of Psychiatry* 17.2: 253.

167 *At Sainte-Anne hospital:* Healy, *The Antidepressant Era*, 45.

167 *"One has the impression":* H. E. Lehmann and G. E. Hanrahan, "Chlorpromazine: A New Inhibiting Agent for Psychomotor Excitement and Manic States," *AMA Archives of Neurology and Psychiatry* 71.2 (1954): 232.

167 *richer by seventy-five million dollars:* Healy, *The Creation of Psychopharmacology*, 225.

167 *Geigy Company had also been seeking:* Healy, *Antidepressant Era*, 49.

167 *a dye from 1898 called summer blue:* Healy, "Roland Kuhn," 253; López-Muñoz and Álamo, "Monoaminergic Neurotransmission," 1568. The dye is called summer blue by some and sky blue by others.

168 *chosen compound G22355:* Healy *The Antidepressant Era*, 51–55. I have drawn mainly on Healy (48–59) for this story of Kuhn and imipramine. Many other writers offer versions, including Edward Shorter, *Before Prozac* (Oxford, 2009), 59–64; Gary Greenberg, *Manufacturing Depression* (Simon & Schuster, 2010), 181–84; Elliot S. Valenstein, *Blaming the Brain* (Free Press, 1998), 38–40.

168 *One of these doctors was Roland Kuhn:* Healy, *The Antidepressant Era*, 51. See also Healy's interview with Alan Broadhurst, who worked with Kuhn in this collaboration with Geigy, in E. M. Tansey, D. A. Christie, L. A. Reynolds, eds., *Wellcome Witnesses to Twentieth Century Medicine*, vol. 2 (London: Wellcome Trust, 1998), 141.

169 Her "facial expression, her behavior": Quoted in Edward Shorter, A His-
     torical Dictionary of Psychiatry (Oxford University Press, 2005), 141.

169 "We mean by this a general retardation": Roland Kuhn, "The Treatment
     of Depressive States with G22355 (imipramine hydrochloride)," Amer-
     ican Journal of Psychiatry 115.5 (1958): 459.

169 "frequent depressive delusions and suicidal urges": Kuhn, "The Treatment
     of Depressive States," 461.

170 "we were hearing the first announcement": Shorter, Before Prozac, 61.

170 "completely unknown": Kuhn, "The Treatment of Depressive States,"
     459.

170 Geigy was slow to follow through: Healy, The Antidepressant Era, 58–59.

171 "apparently purely reactive depression": Kuhn, "The Treatment of Depres-
     sive States," 463.

171 ad for Tofranil: The image can be seen at http://www.thisisdisplay.org
     /collection/tofranil_geigy.

172 leading global cause of disability: World Federation for Mental Health:
     "Depression: A Global Crisis" (10 Oct. 2012).

172 far fewer people were hospitalized for depression: Healy, The Antidepres-
     sant Era, 58.

173 According to the diathesis-stress model: Anisa Goforth et al., "Diathesis-
     stress Model," in Sam Goldstein and Jack Naglieri, eds., Encyclopedia
     of Child Behavior and Development (Springer, 2011), 502–503.

175 Scientists studying the genetics: Jonathan Flint and Kenneth S. Kendler,
     "The Genetics of Major Depression," Neuron 81 (2014): 484–503.

175 major depression is less strongly heritable: Samuel H. Barondes, Mood
     Genes: Hunting for the Origins of Mania and Depression (Oxford Univer-
     sity Press, 1998), 178–79.

177 emotional distancing: Tom Inglis, Moral Monopoly: The Catholic Church
     in Modern Irish Society (Dublin: Gill & Macmillan, 1987), 210–14.

178 "Shouldn't her tranquilizer?": Meprospan advertisement, AMA: The
     Journal of the American Medical Association 199.2 (1967): 226–28.
     A collection of print ads for psychoactive drugs, including those I
     describe here, can be found online at www.bonkersinstitute.org.

178 "interest in life and living": Dexedrine advertisement, Journal of the
     American Medical Association 160.10 (1956): 79.

178 "the problem that has no name": Betty Friedan, The Feminine Mystique
     (W. W. Norton, 1963), 26.

182 "Stations of the Cross for Children": A Religious of the Cenacle, Stations
     of the Cross for Children [1920] (Paramus, N.J.: Paulist Press, 1936).

184 it all dovetailed perfectly: Character traits can correlate with depressive

illness, as in Peter Kramer's discussion of a depressed female patient whose exhaustion and lethargy are "compounded by perfectionism and low self-regard. She feels guilt all too readily. She focuses on the painful aspects of any situation. She requires solitude. She feels an outsider in social groups. . . . These tendencies are symptoms. The standard definition of depression refers to feelings of worthlessness, excessive guilt, and indecision . . . more complete accounts, in textbooks, refer to social withdrawal and paralyzing ruminations. . . . Betty is, moreover, morally scrupulous. (We have not adopted this criterion in the US, but certain German psychiatrists consider scrupulosity—excessive conscientiousness—to be the core feature of depression, the one that gives rise to every other symptom.)" *Against Depression* (Penguin, 2005), 72.

186 *developing neural pathways:* Dennis K. Kinney et al., "Prenatal Stress and Risk for Autism," *Neuroscience and Biobehavioral Reviews* 32.8 (2008): 1519–32. Also Jonathan R. Seckl and Michael J. Meaney, "Glucocorticoid 'Programming' and PTSD Risk," *Annals of the New York Academy of Sciences* 1071 (2006): 351–78. Also Dustin Scheinost et al., "Does Prenatal Stress Affect the Connectome?" *Pediatric Research* 81.1 (2017): 213–26.

186 *greater vulnerability:* M. Weinstock, "Does Prenatal Stress Impair Coping and Regulation of Hypothalamic-Pituitary-Adrenal Axis?" *Neuroscience and Biobehavioral Reviews* 21.1 (1997): 1–10.

187 *children who expressed excessive guilt:* Jim Dryden, "Depression, Overwhelming Guilt in Preschool Years Linked to Brain Changes," *The Source,* 12 Nov. 2014, and Andy C. Belden et al., "Anterior Insula Volume and Guilt: Neurobehavioral Markers of Recurrence after Early Childhood Major Depressive Disorder," *JAMA Psychiatry* 72.1 (2015): 40–48.

191 *"Each of these career moments":* David A. Karp, *Speaking of Sadness* (Oxford University Press, 1996), 57.

Chapter 7: The Promise of Prozac

195 *"common cold of mental illness":* Gary Greenberg attributes this ubiquitous expression to the World Health Organization. See *Manufacturing Depression* (Bloomsbury, 2010), 10. David Healy calls depression "the common cold of psychiatry" in *The Antidepressant Era,* 58.

196 *"Kraepelin, not Freud":* Shorter, *A History of Psychiatry,* 100.

197 *notecards, over the years:* Shorter, *A History of Psychiatry,* 105–6.

197 *two different manifestations of a single disease:* Horwitz and Wakefield, *The Loss of Sadness,* 77.

197 *biological underpinnings appear to be closely related:* National Institutes of Health, "Same Genes Suspected in Both Depression and Bipolar Illness." *Science Update,* 28 Jan. 2010; Amy K. Kuellar et al., "Distinctions between Bipolar and Unipolar Depression," *Clinical Psychological Review* 25.3 (2005): 307–39.

198 *"disturbances in the* physical foundations *of mental life":* Emil Kraepelin, "Lecture 1: Melancholia," in *Lectures on Clinical Psychiatry* (William Wood & Co., 1904), 1.

198 *no basis in science:* Hannah Decker, "Kraepelin to DSM-III," *History of Psychiatry* 18(3): 340.

198 *presence of organic brain dysfunction:* Shadia Kawa and James Giordano, "A Brief Historicity of the *Diagnostic and Statistical Manual of Mental Disorders,"* *Philosophy, Ethics, and Humanities in Medicine* 7:2 (2012): 2.

198 *Psychiatrists increasingly turned:* John Gach, "Biological Psychiatry in the Nineteenth and Twentieth Centuries," in E. R. Wallace and J. Gach, eds., *History of Psychiatry and Medical Psychology* (Boston: Springer, 2008), 390.

198 *In America, this shift:* Decker, "Kraepelin to DSM-III," 342.

199 *"life problems":* Adolf Meyer, Address (1921), in *A Psychiatric Milestone: Bloomingdale Hospital Centenary 1821–1921.* The Society of New York Hospital.

199 *"more Freudian than Freud":* Karl Menninger Obituary, *New York Times,* 19 July 1990.

199 *"we propose to think of all forms":* Quoted in Mitchell Wilson, "DSM-III and the Transformation of American Psychiatry: A History," *American Journal of Psychiatry* 150:3 (1993): 400.

200 *The APA also recommended:* Shorter, *History of Psychiatry,* 173.

200 *psychoanalytic training institutes:* Jeffrey A. Lieberman, *Shrinks: The Untold Story of Psychiatry* (Little, Brown, 2015), 74–83.

200 *"Show me the pathology":* Peter Kramer, *Against Depression* (Penguin, 2006), 50.

201 *Stanford professor David Rosenhan:* David Rosenhan, "On Being Sane in Insane Places," *Science* 179 (1973): 250–58.

201 *"terrible sense of shame":* Quoted in Wilson, "DSM-III," 405.

201 *"defense of the medical model":* Quoted in Wilson, "DSM-III," 405.

201 *As Spitzer recalled:* R. Bayer and R. L. Spitzer, "Neurosis, Psychody-

namics, and DSM-III: A History of the Controversy," *Archives of General Psychiatry* 42.2 (1985): 187–96.

202 *threshold for the diagnosis:* American Psychiatric Association, *Diagnostic and Statistical Manual of Mental Disorders,* 3rd ed. (Arlington, VA: American Psychiatric Association, 1980), 213; Allan V. Horwitz, Jerome C. Wakefield, and Lorenzo Lorenzo-Luaces, "History of Depression" in *The Oxford Handbook of Mood Disorders,* eds. Robert J. DeRubeis and Daniel R. Strunk. Online Publication Date: April 2016. 15.

203 *Or perhaps not:* Daniel Goldberg, "The Heterogeneity of "Major Depression," *World Psychiatry* 10.3 (2011): 226–28; Jenny Chen, "Why Depression Needs a New Definition," *Atlantic,* 4 Aug. 2015.

203 *"high prevalence":* Jeffrey Mattes, Letters to the Editor, *Archives of General Psychiatry* 38 (Sept. 1981), 1068.

203 *"all of the heterogeneous categories":* Horwitz and Wakefield, *The Loss of Sadness.*

204 *Depression Awareness, Recognition, and Treatment (DART):* Darrel A. Regier et al., "The NIMH Depression Awareness, Recognition, and Treatment Program: Structure, Aims, and Scientific Basis," *American Journal of Psychiatry* 145:11 (1988): 1351–57; Horwitz and Wakefield, *The Loss of Sadness,* 150–52.

205 *"Unique . . . Specific":* Ad reproduced in Cristina Hanganu-Bresch, *Faces of Depression: A Study of Antidepressant Advertisements in the American and British Journals of Psychiatry 1960–2004,* PhD diss., University of Minnesota, May 2008. 272.

205 *imipramine blocked:* Barondes, *Mood Genes,* 38.

205 *Schildkraut published a paper:* Joseph Schildkraut, "The Catecholamine Hypothesis of Affective Disorders: A Review of the Supporting Evidence," *American Journal of Psychiatry* 122.5 (1965): 509–22.

206 *an additional hypothesis:* López-Muñoz and Álamo, "Monoaminergic Neurotransmission," 1575–77.

206 *Carlsson and his team:* Information on Carlsson and zimelidine comes from Shorter, *Before Prozac,* 170–74.

206 *it wasn't until 1985:* Healy, *The Antidepressant Era,* 168; David T. Wong et al., "The Discovery of Fluoxetine Hydrochloride (Prozac)," *Nature Reviews Drug Discovery* 4 (2005): 764–74.

207 *"We created the name Prozac":* Interbrand Health, "How Prozac Brought Depression out of the Dark," Oct. 2017.

207 *"Promise of Prozac":* Geoffrey Cowley et al., "The Promise of Prozac," *Newsweek,* 26 Mar. 1990, 38–41.

207 *"ever designed"*: Natalie Angier, "New Antidepressant Is Acclaimed but Not Perfect," *New York Times,* 29 Mar. 1990; Robert Whitaker, *Anatomy of an Epidemic* (Broadway, 2010), 288–91.

207 *"cosmetic psychopharmacology"*: Peter Kramer, *Listening to Prozac* (Viking, 1993), xv–xvi, 15.

207 *news article reported*: Richard Restak, quoted in Fran Schumer, "Bye Blues," *New York,* 18 Dec. 1989.

207 *Decade of the Brain*: Project on the Decade of the Brain, Presidential Proclamation 6158, Library of Congress/ National Institute of Mental Health.

208 *"their not inconsiderable side effects"*: Quoted in Shorter, *Before Prozac,* 176.

208 *effects on the central nervous system*: Shorter, *Before Prozac,* 177.

208 *"For many patients"*: "What Are the Real Risks of Antidepressants?" *Harvard Health Publications,* Mar. 2014.

209 *little incentive to advertise*: David Herzberg, *Happy Pills in America* (Baltimore: Johns Hopkins University Press, 2009), 178.

209 *Compared to the tricyclics, Prozac was safer*: See J. Guy Edwards, "Suicide and Antidepressants," BMJ 310:205 (1995). However, the families of a number of people who killed themselves in the first weeks on Prozac brought lawsuits arguing that the drug caused the behavior, as reported in detail by David Healy in *Let Them Eat Prozac: The Unhealthy Relationship between the Pharmaceutical Industry and Depression* (New York University Press, 2004).

209 *triumph of drug advertising*: "Turn the Volume Down on Drug Ads," editorial, *New York Times,* 27 Nov. 2015.

210 *three of the ten best-selling drugs*: Shorter, *How Everyone Became Depressed* (Oxford University Press, 2013), 98.

210 *twenty-one billion dollars*: Bethany McLean, "A Bitter Pill," *Fortune,* 13 Aug. 2001.

210 *Metzl writes*: Jonathan Metzl, *Prozac on the Couch: Prescribing Gender in the Era of Wonder Drugs* (Durham, NC: Duke University Press, 2003), 31.

210 *sad, sighing blob*: Zoloft Commercial, 2001, YouTube. Also Kate Arthur, "Little Blob, Don't Be Sad (or Anxious or Phobic)," *New York Times,* 2 Jan. 2005.

210 *"complex biological state"*: Schildkraut, "The Catecholamine Hypothesis"; Alice G. Walton, "Metabolic Problems in the Brain May Help Explain Treatment-Resistant Depression," *Forbes,* 14 Aug. 2016; Oksana Kaidanovich-Beilin et al., "Metabolism and the Brain," *The Scientist,* Dec. 2012.

211 *Daniel Carlat describes his conversation*: Carlat, *Unhinged,* 12–13.

211   *"Your illness is biological":* Carlat, *Unhinged,* 75.

211   *diabetes analogy:* Alix Spiegel, "When It Comes to Depression, Sero-
      tonin Isn't the Whole Story," *Morning Edition,* National Public Radio,
      23 Jan. 2012.

215   *sexual lives were compromised:* R. C. Rosen, R. M. Lane, and M. Menza,
      "Effects of SSRIs on Sexual Function: A Critical Review," *Journal of
      Clinical Psychopharmacology* 19.1 (1999): 67–85.

220   *"The Bad Thing":* David Wallace, "The Planet Trillaphon as It Stands
      in Relation to The Bad Thing," *The Amherst Review* 12 (1984).

220   *This person should be your psychiatrist:* I'm aware that the prescriber of
      medication and the psychotherapist may not be the same person. In
      that case, someone in the condition I'm describing should be in close
      touch with both.

221   *Exercise became a necessary daily stress reliever:* Since then, researchers
      have established that exercise contributes to the health of the brain's
      neural networks. See Gretchen Reynolds, "For Your Brain's Sake,
      Keep Moving," *New York Times,* 4 Oct. 2017.

222   *"Life for both sexes":* Virginia Woolf, *A Room of One's Own* (Harcourt,
      1989), 34–35.

222   *depressive people lack the self-inflating illusion:* Lauren Alloy and Lyn
      Yvonne Abramson, "Depressive Realism: Four Theoretical Perspec-
      tives," in *Cognitive Processes in Depression,* ed. L. B. Alloy (Guilford
      Press, 1989), 223–65. For a more recent discussion see Maria Kon-
      nikova, "Don't Worry, Be Happy," *New Yorker,* 18 June 2014.

224   *Patenting the mirror-molecule:* Eiji Kirino, "Escitalopram for the Man-
      agement of Major Depressive Disorder," *Patient Preference and Adher-
      ence* 6 (2012): 853–61.

224   *"most selective":* H. Zhong, N. Haddjeri, and C. Sánchez: "Escitalopram,
      An Antidepressant with an Allosteric Effect at the Serotonin Trans-
      porter . . . Current Understanding of Its Mechanism of Action," *Psy-
      chopharmacology* (Berl) 219.1 (2012): 1–13. All three authors of this study
      list affiliations with Lundbeck, the maker of Lexapro, but researchers
      without ties to Lundbeck have arrived at a similar conclusion.

225   *the loss of BDNF:* Bun-Hee Lee and Yong-Hu Kim, "The Roles of
      BDNF in the Pathophysiology of Major Depression and in Antide-
      pressant Treatment," *Psychiatry Investigation* 7.4 (2010): 231–35.

226   *"at the upper end":* Laura Blue, "Antidepressants Hardly Help," *Time,*
      26 Feb. 2008.

226   *Angell's article:* Angell, "The Epidemic of Mental Illness: Why?" *The
      New York Review of Books,* 23 June 2011.

227 *"substantial and long-lasting alterations"*: Steven Hyman et al., "Initiation and Adaptation: A Paradigm for Understanding Psychotropic Drug Action," *American Journal of Psychiatry* 153.2 (1996): 151–62; Whitaker, *Anatomy of an Epidemic,* 164–69.

227 *"Oppositional tolerance"*: Giovanni Fava and E. Offidani, "The Mechanisms of Tolerance in Antidepressant Action," *Progress in Neuro-Psychopharmacology & Biological Psychiatry* 35.7 (2011): 1593–602.

228 *For people like me:* See Peter Kramer, *Ordinarily Well* (Farrar, Straus & Giroux, 2016), and *Against Depression* (Penguin, 2006).

228 *"neuroprotection" against the physiological processes:* The neuroplasticity hypothesis holds that depression is a disorder of neural connectivity in the brain, and that antidepressants protect against and reverse at least some of its causative processes. Chittaranjan Andrade and N. Sanjay Kumar Rao, "How Antidepressant Drugs Act: A Primer on Neuroplasticity as the Eventual Mediator of Antidepressant Efficacy," *Indian Journal of Psychiatry* 52 (2010): 378–86; Gianluca Serafini, "Neuroplasticity and Major Depression: The Role of Modern Antidepressant Drugs," *World Journal of Psychiatry* 2.3 (2012): 49–57.

229 *"hypothetical risk"*: Richard Friedman, "Ask Well: Long-Term Risk of Antidepressants," *New York Times,* 3 May 2013.

229 *"and hold them steady"*: Kramer, *Ordinarily Well,* 222.

230 *just what depression produces:* Jonathan Price et al., "Emotional Side-effects of Selective Serotonin Reuptake Inhibitors: Qualitative Study," *British Journal of Psychiatry* 195.3 (2009): 211–17. Also Randy Sansone and Lori A. Sansone, "SSRI-Induced Indifference," *Psychiatry* (Edgmont) 7.10 (2010): 14–18.

231 *longer than ten years:* Friedman, "Ask Well: Long-Term Risk of Antidepressants."

231 *so-called "pipeline"*: Richard A. Friedman, "A Dry Pipeline for Psychiatric Drugs," *New York Times,* 19 Aug. 2013; Mary O'Hara and Pamela Duncan, "Why 'Big Pharma' Stopped Searching for the Next Prozac," *Guardian,* 27 Jan. 2016.

Chapter 8: No Feeling Is Final

233 *"monstrously arrogant act"*: Phillip Lopate, *To Show and to Tell* (Free Press, 2013), 86.

234 *"For those who have dwelt"*: William Styron, *Darkness Visible* (Vintage, 1992), 84.

234 *"where hope never comes"*: John Milton, *Paradise Lost,* 1:63–67.

235 *"myself am Hell"*: Milton, *Paradise Lost,* 4:75.

240   *At its dedication:* Sara Cedar Miller, *Central Park: An American Master-piece* (Abrams, 2003), 63–67.

240   *a healing angel:* John 5:2–4, King James Bible.

244   *"No feeling is final":* Rainer Maria Rilke, *The Book of Hours* 1:59, in *A Year with Rilke,* ed. and trans. Anita Barrows and Joanna Macy (HarperOne, 2009).

245   *following message: Selected Letters of William Styron,* ed. Rose Styron with R. Blakeslee Gilpin (Random House, 2012), 640.

245   *"he had misled people":* Quoted in Tim Teeman, "Rose Styron, The Truth about Life with Her Husband, Literary Legend William Styron," *Daily Beast,* 3 Apr. 2016.

246   *World Health Organization figures:* World Health Organization, "Depression Fact Sheet," February 2017.